"A perceptive and penetrating view o.   ...υμι υιιυαι.

ALVIN L. RING
President
Phoenix Data Systems, Inc.

"There is gold in what David Silver has to say about the entrepreneur. For fifteen years he has been coming in contact with a steady stream of entrepreneurs. In the process, he has developed a real feel for the entrepreneur. He gets a gut feeling of the situation that others do not; that is an element hard to measure.

"David shows you what to watch out for in the entrepreneur and why. He demonstrates the motivations of the entrepreneur. He shows you the metamorphosis that the entrepreneur goes through and the role of the partner and the entrepreneur. He also shows you the ten qualities of the entrepreneur and you can have fun measuring yourself as an entrepreneur."

SOMERS H. WHITE
President
Somers H. White Company

"I can truthfully say that the book is a must read for anyone who has ever considered going into their own business. The book is a valuable contribution to an area of business which has been neglected far too long."

LANCE S. NELSON
Securities Vice President
Central Life

"This book does for the entrepreneurial crisis what *Passages* did for the midlife crisis. It tells you that you are not alone, that others have gone through the same difficulty and have come out happy and successful at the end."

GEORGE C. McQUILKEN
President
Spartacus Computers, Inc.

THE ENTREPRENEURIAL
LIFE

Wiley Series on Small Business Management
Rick Stephan Hayes, Editor

THE ENTREPRENEURIAL LIFE

How To Go for It and Get It

A. David Silver

A Ronald Press Publication

JOHN WILEY & SONS

New York   Chichester   Brisbane   Toronto   Singapore

Library of Congress Cataloging in Publication Data:

Silver, A. David (Aaron David), 1941–
    The entrepreneurial life.

    (Wiley series on small business management)
    "A Ronald Press publication."
    Includes index.
    1. Small business—Management.   2. Entrepreneur.
I. Title.   II. Series.

HD62.7.S53   1983   658.4′2   82-24828
ISBN 0-471-87382-9

Printed in the United States of America

10   9   8   7   6   5   4   3   2   1

To Sylvia Werner Silver

PREFACE

This is a book about heart. There exists in our society a group of people, primarily young men, but increasingly women, who are loving, caring and sensitive, and who have one goal: to do some one thing extremely well. Their hearts focus their knowledge, determine how they use it, and drive them toward whatever goals they choose. These people do not childishly strive for wealth or power or to overcome the fear of failure. They have grown out of experiences in their homes, schools, and corporations where these strivings were once important. No longer. Power, wealth, and the fear of failure are not valid reasons for work. They are myths, blown out of proportion by corporate America. These people do not have a value system based on what is *out there*. They did at one time, but they have since rejected it. What is important now is what is *in here*, in the heart.

The people who detach the head from the heart work in large corporations where they apply their intellect toward the success of the organization and their movement vertically within the organization. They had hearts once, but the big corporations had them carefully removed. They become frustrated because their work requires them occasionally to do the wrong thing, to keep silent when they should speak up, to knife a co-worker in the back. The people with heart do not have these frustrations, although they did at one time. They no longer "eat their hearts out."

The people with heart work in the valleys, frequently within a short drive or long walk from their homes. They wear whatever they like to work. They select co-workers who have similar values. They accept *all* of the responsibility for their decisions and never write memorandums to others to protect themselves from failure. They do not fear failure, because the thing they are building is constantly changing and neither failure nor success is quantifiable with so many unknowns. They are free to choose their own destiny; and, although failure would be losing that freedom, they are moving too rapidly to think about failure.

Envy is not a consideration, because these people are creating something new, unique, and of their making. There is nothing comparable in the market for them to envy. Greed is not a factor, because what they are building takes a team effort, and ownership and rewards must be shared with everyone who works. These people are not workaholics. They work hard because it is pleasureful. But what is important is how they work: they work smart.

The people with heart create innovation and change in the society. The people without heart look down from the top of the hill and see the people with heart scurrying around in the valley carrying things from cottage to cottage. The people without heart ignore the companies that the people with heart create to market their innovation and change. "Crumbs from our table," said the heartless people at the telephone company when the people with heart began to sell better and cheaper telephones. "A fly speck in black pepper," said the airfreight companies when the young man started his small package airline. "There is no need to replace mimeograph," said the photographic equipment companies to the developer of xerography. Where are they now? The telephone company is being dismantled to allow it to compete. The people who ran the airfreight companies have been fired. The photographic equipment companies have tried to catch up with xerography.

The people with heart always beat the people without heart. The reason is quite simple. The people with heart know what drives the people without heart, but the people without heart do not know how the people with heart play the game. So the people with heart build their unique products and pluck from the large corporations the most intelligent people to join their teams. The new recruits, called achievers, get their hearts back along with some ownership in what they are doing, and they work smart, attacking the weak points of the big corporations they know so well.

The people with heart are called entrepreneurs. They are an interesting group and growing in size. Entrepreneurs will change America in the next few years. What they are doing is beginning to be noticed; how they do it is beginning to be studied. People are beginning to ask: Should I become an entrepreneur? Have I got what it takes to leave this corporation and go into business for myself?

This book will help you answer these three questions:

1. Do you have the heart to become an entrepreneur?
2. How do you become an entrepreneur?
3. How does an entrepreneur assure himself of success?

Can you do it? How do you do it? How do you do it well?

This book attempts to define the characteristics of successful entrepreneurs. It does not attempt to explain why certain people choose to become entrepreneurs. The book also explains the entrepreneurial process, the six-step process followed by entrepreneurs in launching their new companies. The research that I have relied on is essentially my own, and it is based on hundreds of interviews with entrepreneurs, managers of entrepreneurial companies, and venture capitalists. Further, I have worked closely with and been an investor in over 100 entrepreneurial companies since 1966, and I have formed some opinions about entrepreneurs and the entrepreneurial process. Because it appeared that I possessed many of the drives, pains, and guilts of entrepreneurs, I have launched a few companies of my own. I suppose, therefore, that I am as qualified as anyone to describe the characteristics of successful entrepreneurs and the entrepreneurial process. I certainly trust that some of my observations will stimulate others to explain why certain people choose the entrepreneurial path in life.

A. David Silver

Santa Fe, New Mexico
February 1983

≡ ACKNOWLEDGMENTS ≡

I have had the inestimable joy of spending my professional life in the presence of entrepreneurs, helping them package their dreams into readable business plans that venture capitalists might find fit to invest in. I owe them many thanks, particularly Frank J. Lautenberg, the late Charles Tandy, William Y. Tauscher, Thomas Kelly, Andre Blay, Robert M. Feldman, Jeffrey Norton, and Robert F. Sikorka, for trusting me with their dreams. All of my entrepreneurs over the last 15 years have shared valuable insights with me some of which are repeated in this book. In addition, several fellow entrepreneur-watchers have provided me with interesting opinions about the characteristics of successful entrepreneurs, including Don A. Christensen, William T. Comfort, Jr., Tommy J. Davis and John L. Hines, as well as my mentors at Kuhn, Loeb & Co., particularly John S. Guest, Harvey M. Krueger and J. Emerson Thors.

Others who have been sources of invaluable assistance to me in thinking, sharpening the focus, or critiquing the style include Helen Kelly, Dr. Robert J. B. Osnos, Dr. William B. Head, Michael J. Hamilton, my editor, and Katherine C. Werner, and at the keyboard, the indefatigable Elizabeth A. Meyers, whose speed and accuracy are humbling sights.

If an entrepreneur remains married, it is because of the spouse's forebearance more than any other single factor. But an entrepreneur who makes his living solving problems for entrepreneurs and then goes to the trouble of writing about these experiences must have an angel for a wife. That is my fortunate circumstance.

A.D.S.

CONTENTS

THE ENTREPRENEURIAL
LIFE

INTRODUCTION

Entrepreneurs are responsible for a significant amount of the change in our society, much of the economic growth, practically all of the sustained growth in employment, plus the new technologies that make our life easier and more enjoyable and the new drugs and medical instruments that keep us healthy and cure us when we are sick. The new companies launched by entrepreneurs solve social and industrial problems and are driven forward, rather than held back, by the problems of society. There has been an increase in the amount of private venture capital available to support the entrepreneurial process, and as a result there are more entrepreneurs writing business plans and launching companies than ever before. The *entrepreneurial process* is being investigated by business schools. Corporations are beginning to think in terms of work modules that employee groups can bid on as *performance contracts*; this is one of many business techniques entrepreneurs are teaching us.

The personal computer industry, which will be as large within seven years as the automobile industry is today, is dominated by entrepreneurial companies. The biotechnology industry, which is expected to locate cures for terminal diseases, eliminate the need for chemicals in agriculture, and discover cheap means of reclaiming oil, is dominated by the entrepreneurial process. The telecommunications industry, which is filling the gap that the transportation industry failed to fill is dominated by entrepreneurial companies. Mail and overnight package delivery, movies, consumer electronics, fashion, and restaurants are other industries dominated by entrepreneurs.

The age of multinational corporations, large government, and unionization is dead. The large corporation was an outgrowth of the

1

first stages of the Industrial Revolution; a logical form of organizing people to mass-produce products.

In the early nineteenth century, according to a paper presented by Maccoby and Terzi, "some 80 percent of all Americans were self-employed. By 1950, only 18 percent of all employed persons were self-employed, and this figure shrank to 14 percent in 1960 and 9 percent in 1970."*

The Age of Entrepreneurship, which we entered as a response to Sputnik in 1957, is a period of individualism, a return to simpler organizational forms. The entrepreneur is not interested in power, prestige, high visibility, or wealth in and of themselves. Thus, work is performed in cottages, delivered to the entrepreneurial company for inspection, and shipped to the customer. Or work is performed on the customer's site, as in performance contracts. Or the customer provides the capital equipment and energy (car and gas) and comes to the entrepreneurial company to have the service performed. Entrepreneurial companies are smaller, more profitable, and quicker to respond to change. When they grow too large to be "fun," the entrepreneur sells them to a larger corporation.

There are approximately 10 million entrepreneurs and twice that many potential entrepreneurs in the country today. Their common goal is *to start a company to do some one thing extremely well.* They have become aware of, or are about to become aware of, a problem that lends itself to a new solution. They are developing, producing, and marketing the solution, attracting skilled people to assist them and venture capital to pay for the start-up costs. The economy is sprouting an incredible number of exciting new companies every day.

Yet we do not know very much about the entrepreneur. Where does this person come from? What makes him or her take fanatical financial risks? What are the characteristics of entrepreneurs? There are not much more than abstractions and one-liners in the form of answers. Potential entrepreneurs pay hundreds of dollars to attend seminars that deal with "wealth creation" and suggestions on busi-

---

*Michael Maccoby and Katherine A. Terzi, "Character and Work in America," in Philip Brenner and others, eds., *Exploring Contradictions: Political Economy in the Corporate State* (New York: David McKay, 1974).

ness plan preparation from venture capitalists most of whom have never met a payroll, a quota or an important crisis head on. The entrepreneurial process is not well understood. Economists have simply ignored the entrepreneurial process, because their models do not include an equation for uncertainty, risk, and change. Social scientists are busy studying other types of people, for the most part. Behavorial scientists have skipped over the entrepreneur as well.

My qualifications for writing this book are two-fold: I have been a venture capitalist for 15 years and an entrepreneur for 10. My entrepreneurial company is an investment banking firm that assists entrepreneurs in raising capital in a multitude of different ways. In addition, it acts as a principal in launching new companies. My firm has worked with hundreds of entrepreneurs over the last 15 years, and I have launched some interesting businesses as well, with mixed financial results. Through it all, I have made a serious attempt to find and back the most competent entrepreneurs. My entrepreneur clients know that I do not believe bachelors make good entrepreneurs, that I believe entrepreneurs who are married have outstanding wives, that I believe entrepreneurs carry a heavy load of guilt and that they suffered from some form of deprivation as an adolescent. Although I have not consistently backed winners, I have improved my ability to select competent entrepreneurs over the years. This book is a summary of my research and observations.

OUTLINE

Some guideposts will be useful to you before proceeding. Chapter 1 positions the entrepreneur historically. The second chapter defines the entrepreneur. A profile is presented socially, emotionally, psychologically, and experientially. You will know after reading Chapter 2 if you have what it takes to become an entrepreneur.

Entrepreneurs are born to certain kinds of parents, and are generally raised in middle-class families. Entrepreneurs rarely come from introverted parents who look within themselves to find direction and values. Rather, in their cocoon stage entrepreneurs are encouraged by their parents to succeed, to obtain recognition, to make their parents proud, to gain leading roles in their communities and success as measured by society's value system. Entrepreneurs rarely come from the lowest economic class, and when they do, they are frequently too full of bitterness and resentment to make a long-running success of their business. Children from families with internally derived values such as entrepreneurs, statesmen, and scientists rarely become entrepreneurs either. But then, John Adams, a political entrepreneur, predicted this two centuries ago when he said, "I work hard so that my children may study politics and their children may study art."

Entrepreneurs leave their homes, get jobs, marry, and start families, and grow through a maturation process in which the carefully learned values of their childhood are suddenly and violently rejected. At this juncture, the entrepreneur adopts a new set of "drivers." He finds a new set of values deep within that force him to start a company to do some one thing extremely well; to let nothing stand in the way of that accomplishment. The entrepreneur develops uncommon courage—"Shoot at me, but I'm going to succeed in any event"—to face over-sized competitors and creditors. The entrepreneur finds enormous self-confidence within—"Come and join me. We're going to topple IBM." He or she brings to the task an uncanny will to win—in this feature the athlete and the entrepreneur share. The former fast-track corporate team player is transformed quite suddenly into an impassioned, expressive, individualistic, egotistical, diverse, complex, driven human being. Quite literally, the entrepreneur is a fanatic.

The violence and suddenness of the the transformation frequently rocks the marriage—if there is one—to its foundation. The house is all too often second-mortgaged to finance the dream. James L. Ling sold his house in 1946 for $3,000 to start the forerunner of LTV Corp. The savings account is depleted. The entrepreneur finds discussing the new venture with his or her spouse difficult. There are hundreds of thoughts competing for air time, and that makes conversation difficult as well. But always the dream, the goal: to do it well, to do it better than it has ever been done before. That is the driver.

Chapter 2 finishes with an explanation of the 10 significant characteristics that most successful entrepreneurs possess. They include the following:

Ten Significant Characteristics of Entrepreneurs
1. Outer-directed background
2. Absent father/dynamic mother
3. Optimal childhood deprivation
4. Guilt
5. Ability to focus intensively
6. Courage; no fear of failure
7. Creativity
8. Insight
9. Happiness
10. Communications Skills

At this point, the entrepreneurial process begins. Chapter 3 takes you by the hand through the six-step process of launching a new company, which steps are:

Six-Step Entrepreneurial Process
1. Identification of the opportunity; problem formulation
2. Creation of the solution
3. Planning the business
4. Selecting the entrepreneurial team
5. Producing and test-marketing the product
6. Raising venture capital

The first three steps in the entrepreneurial process are largely mental, involving realization, creativity, and reasoning. This is a period of intense concentration, which is frustrating to spouses and subordinates. Of one passionately driven entrepreneur, an employee said, "When you work for Bill Lear, you work for 50 cents a day and all you can take." The second three steps are more action-oriented: seeking partners and employees, producing, communicating, persuading, and negotiating. Through the entire launch process, the entrepreneur relies on judgment, sometimes known as common sense, the wisdom of others, sometimes known as mentors, who have taken similar paths, and, if he or she is fortunate, constructively helpful financial backers, sometimes known as godfathers.

Having covered who the entrepreneur is and what it is that he does, in Chapter 4 we begin to put obstacles in his path and show how he knocks them down. Although the entrepreneurial process is systematic in principle, in fact it is a series of random collisions. It is the competent entrepreneur who can bounce off these obstacles with confidence intact because failure is never considered a real possibility. The Polaroid Corp. was formed in 1937 to develop polarizing filters that would reduce the glare of car headlights. Detroit refused to purchase the product in 1945, at which point Polaroid's founder, Edwin Land, undaunted, began developing the instant photography process which, of course, has made Polaroid one of the most successful growth companies since there have been scorekeepers in this area.

"Failure" to an entrepreneur means that a bunch of people lost some money on him, and they think he's a jerk for awhile. But then they take the write-off and he's only half a jerk.

A carefully drawn business plan, although as vital to the entrepreneurial process as headlights are to a car, will be knocked cockeyed by the randomness of the marketplace. Trouble comes from day one. The entrepreneur will hear 50 nos a day for awhile. Tommy J. Davis, whose successful venture capital investments include Atari, Tandem, and Teledyne, looks for the entrepreneur who can spot trouble and deal with it quickly. Says Davis: "Some people have built-in filters that filter out the boos and amplify the hurrahs. That's not the guy who will know when he's in trouble."*Successful entrepreneurs plan for the customer's order, the lender's approval and the supplier's patience; but they have several plans that will go into effect immediately upon the occurrence of the opposite results. This is called downside planning. It is the quick deployment of the alternative plan. Ask your Federal Express driver about the time Fred Smith, its founder, had all the employees pawn their watches to raise capital under a contingency plan.

In Chapter 5, we deal with another hard reality: Some people

*Merwin, John, "Have You Got What it Takes?," *Forbes*, August 3, 1981.

who would otherwise make excellent entrepreneurs are insuffi-
ciently creative to develop a new product or service. Many of these
people make the transformation from outer- to inner-directed, adopt
the new set of drivers, and desperately want to do some one thing
well. But they cannot conceive of a solution to a problem that holds
their interest. Or, conversely, too many ideas have rushed into their
head. Chapter 5 provides solutions and ideas for passing the creativity stage in the entrepreneurial process without sacrificing the excitement of the launch. For one thing, the entrepreneur can team up
with a more inventive person. For another, he or she can buy existing
companies and shape them to his or her personality. Several ideas
are put forth of problems in search of entrepreneurial solutions.

The goal of the sixth chapter is to provide useful tools for the
entrepreneur. Among these are the use of leverage, a handy tool for
all stripes of entrepreneur. Financial leverage, borrowing on one's
assets, is merely one form of leverage. There are other assets that can
be leveraged, off-balance-sheet, such as customer lists, boards of
directors, highly visible names, and so forth. Another tool is convincing people to do what they had no intention of doing. Successful
entrepreneurs are highly communicative. They are able to control
meetings, convince bankers to loan them money, convince suppliers
to take a stretched payout, convince customers to pay in advance for
a product demonstration, and convince employees to tough it out.

Another tool is the multiplier or cookie cutter theory of marketing.
Frequently, there is a low end product that can be produced cheaply
in cookie cutter fashion and sold over and over again. Its cash flow
can support development of higher margin customized products. A
final tool is offered for the entrepreneur's bag: a new way of looking
at new markets. It is called the pyramid method, and it is a guide to
starting a company without capital. Entrepreneurial fortunes are made
quickly, but the size of the fortune is directly proportional to the
length of time a monopoly position is maintained.

The seventh chapter offers some final thoughts. I ask if becoming
an entrepreneur is worth the effort. Are entrepreneurs closer to their
spouses and children? Are they better lovers, better parents, more
fulfilled? I also predict that the role of the entrepreneur will become
easier and less costly over the near term as more people learn the
process.

What entrepreneur book would be complete without a fresh supply of entrepreneur stories? I have scattered dozens throughout the book with the intent of profiling the leveraged buy-out entrepreneur, the creative genius, and the entrepreneur who has positioned himself in front of a tidal wave. Finally, there is the entrepreneur who cannot rest until he has toppled IBM.

Like all prototypical entrepreneurs, I come up with many ideas, most of which I fervently believe should be implemented immediately. I have another troublesome characteristic that is indigenous to entrepreneurs. I think my ideas are the best. These two personality flaws are unwittingly carried over into this book, as indeed they are part of me. Thus, the hypotheses expressed herein are mine, the examples are taken from my personal experiences as an entrepreneur-watcher and the conclusions are mine. Where I have used someone else's thoughts and ideas, I have cited the source. There is no evidence to support many of the conclusions herein except my interviews with entrepreneurs; but a scientific pursuit was not the intent of this book at all. In fact, it is not clear that entrepreneurship is a discipline capable of scientific study. The entrepreneur's actions can be described, but can they be explained? Consider the book a baton, of the kind used in track events, that I pass to you in order for you to win your race. As you read the book, it helps to keep asking the questions:

1. Do I have the heart to become an entrepreneur?
2. How do I become an entrepreneur?
3. How do I assure myself of success?

You should find the answers within.

INVESTIGATIVE METHODS

In 1978, I asked two friends who happen to be psychiatrists to help me design a questionnaire for an investigation of the behavioral characteristics of successful entrepreneurs. The objective was to find some recurring themes that I could then apply to potential entrepreneurs, discarding those who lacked the proper bag of characteristics and accepting as clients those that came psychologically equipped. The questionnaire appears in Appendix I.

I selected 100 entrepreneurs who had achieved personal wealth of at least $20 million through the entrepreneurial process. Only those who had taken their companies public qualified, because market values are not discernible for private companies. Respondents were promised anonymity, but most of the questionnaires were returned in corporate envelopes, which made the research more entertaining. Of the 100 questionnaires mailed out, 54 were answered and returned. The results of the investigation, scattered throughout the book, are suggestive rather than definitive. I am not qualified to interpret the results of the questionnaires, but I can follow the paths down which they lead. Most of the respondents were deprived as children, are guilty that they have let down someone important to them, had strong mothers and absent fathers, and attribute their success to the creative solution of a large problem.

The answers suggest further questions about childhood, locating the "pain" and what is meant by creative. I have followed up the questionnaire by asking hundreds of entrepreneurs thousands of sensitive questions. The answers form the substance of the book.

I wrote the book because the cost of being an entrepreneur is too great. The sacrifices are staggering — long absences from home, divorce, loss of friends. The capital risks are unrealistic. Some entrepreneurs lose their houses to the federal government; others lose their companies to venture capitalists. New business failures on a large scale are not necessary. If would-be entrepreneurs could be screened before signing up, those without heart could avoid the losses. If the entrepreneurial process were better understood, there would be fewer business failures.

Further, not everyone should or can become a successful entrepreneur. The costs are extraordinary, and a solid marriage, a comfortable home, a gaggle of friends, a well-rounded lifestyle, and financial security are frequently of greater importance to people than launching a new company that will deliver a problem-solving product to a large number of people. Yet there is a need for a middle ground, where partially hooked potential entrepreneurs can maintain their corporate ties while delivering an entrepreneurial solution and participating in the personal growth that entrepreneurship brings.

Large corporations are beginning to seek out more entrepreneurial employees in order to implement new, labor-saving technologies and to increase productivity. This is what the current entrepreneurial revolution is all about: various kinds of people, not all of them entrepreneurs, learning and using the entrepreneurial process to bring about change, growth, and personal satisfaction. With this point of view in mind, the book takes on an expanded meaning.

THE SEARCH FOR ENTREPRENEURS

There is suddenly a great deal of interest in and curiosity about American entrepreneurs. Who and what are they? Do American entrepreneurs spring from the lower classes with an unswerving drive to overcome poverty? Or are they more a product of the middle classes, from an engineering or technical background? Can anyone become an entrepreneur, start one's own business, and, armed with some fundamental training in management and accounting, expect to succeed? Is it possible to receive training in entrepreneurship? Where does one receive help? Is entrepreneurship for everyone?

HISTORICAL PERSPECTIVE

The word *entrepreneur* appeared originally in the French language in the early sixteenth century to refer to men engaged in leading military expeditions. In the early eighteenth century, the French began moving the word around to apply to other adventurers, such as bridge builders, road contractors, and architects. The function of the entrepreneur was first defined in an economic sense by a French writer, Richard Cantillon, in 1755,* as the process of bearing uncer-

*Richard Cantillon (1755), *Essai sur la nature du commerce en general* (Paris: Institut National d' Etudes Demographiques, 1952.)

tainty: that is, virtually everyone engaged in economic activity save landowners and salaried workers was an entrepreneur. The term was given other definitions throughout the eighteenth century by other French economists, the differences arising largely from the characteristics of the sector of the economy that chiefly attracted their attention. Those economists interested in government saw the entrepreneur as a contractor, the specialists on agriculture as a farmer, and the proponents of industry as a risk-taking capitalist.* The "classic" definition of the entrepreneur, which was to survive until the twentieth century, was written by Jean Baptiste Say, an aristocratic industrialist. In his *Catechism of Political Economy* (1815), Say's entrepreneur " ... unites all means of production and ... finds in the value of the products ... the re-establishment of the entire capital he employs, and the value of the wages, the interest, and the rent which he pays, as well as the profits belonging to himself."

In Say's *A Treatise on Political Economy*, written in 1803 but not translated into English until 1827, the entrepreneur must have "judgment, perseverance, and a knowledge of the world as well as business. He must possess the art of superintendence and administration." However, because he ignored the critical entrepreneurial functions of innovation and capital formation, Say's entrepreneur failed to become a ponderable factor in general economic theory.

As economic theory became more carefully formulated in the late eighteenth and early nineteenth centuries in Western Europe, no role was found for the entrepreneur. There was no attempt made by either of England's two great economists, Adam Smith and Alfred Marshall, or any other classical theorist to include entrepreneurship in the economic board game. This was because English economic theory was based upon a normal state of equilibrium established by the multiple reactions of businesspeople, consumers, investors, and workers to the prices of goods and services. Innovation, risk-taking, and capital formation were not addressed. Individual variations in behavior were seen as either cancelled out in the aggregate or suppressed by competition. Unknown and unmeasurable social or cultural factors such as entrepreneurship had no place in a system

---

*Bert F. Hoselitz, "The Early History of Entrepreneurial Theory," *Explorations in Entrepreneurial History*, Vol. 3, pp. 193–220, 1951.

where every factor and relation is theoretically measurable. To say that risk taking, or profiting from uncertainty, existed within this system was to deny the proper theoretical explanation of the system.

The American economists of the early twentieth century were the first to recognize risk taking and capital formation as the distinguishing traits of entrepreneurship. Entrepreneurs were considered "engineers of industrial progress" and "the chief agents of production." An "entrepreneurial profit," it was believed, resulted from " . . . successful introduction into the economic process of technological, commercial or organizational improvements."*

In 1934, the entrepreneur acquired a prominent spokesman in the person of Joseph A. Schumpeter who emigrated from Germany to the United States, to accept a chair at Harvard. His theory placed the entrepreneur more in the center of the economic system. Profit arose from change, wrote Schumpeter, and change was the work of innovative businessmen. Change stimulated further change which produced long upswings in business activity and profits.

For Schumpeter, innovation was the criterion of entrepreneurship: " . . . the defining characteristic is simply the doing of things that are already being done in a new way (innovation)."* The "new way" was a "creative response" to a situation that had at least three characteristics:

> First . . . it can practically never be understood ex ante. . . . Secondly, creative response shapes the whole course of subsequent events and their 'long-run' outcome. . . . Thirdly, creative response . . . has . . . something to do (a) with the quality of personnel available in the society, (b) . . . with quality available to a particular field of activity, and (c) with individual decisions, actions and patterns of behavior. Accordingly, a study of creative response in business becomes coterminous with a study of entrepreneurship.†

Although Schumpeter was the first economist to give importance to the role of innovation and creative response in an economic system,

---

*Joseph A. Schumpeter, *The Theory of Economic Development* (Cambridge, Massachusetts: Harvard University Press, 1934). (First published in German in 1912.)
*Joseph A. Schumpeter, "The Creative Response in Economic History," *Journal of Economic History*, Vol. 7, 1947, pp. 149–159.
†Ibid.

he does not support his hypothesis with facts, but, rather, suggests that further study of "creative response in business" must involve a "study of entrepreneurship." This book, in part, takes the baton from Schumpeter and runs the next leg.

There is considerably more to entrepreneurship than creative response to change; indeed, corporate executives are capable of innovation without significant risk taking or capital formation. In fact, it will be seen very shortly that entrepreneurs and corporate managers are radically different socially, emotionally, culturally, and psychologically. The risks of becoming an entrepreneur have never been seriously examined in the history of Western economic thought. Although Schumpeter and his colleagues defined the role of the entrepreneur within an economic system, there still existed — and it is as true today as it was 40 years ago — the theoretical problem of finding a place for socially influenced forces in mathematically oriented theories. The difficulty for economists in dealing with entrepreneurs is that although entrepreneurial profits can be accounted for, few economists are willing to tackle the problem of measuring the theoretical cost of entrepreneurship. In a contemporary summary of historical economic thought regarding entrepreneurs, Thomas C. Cochran writes:

> Students of entrepreneurship generally have come to agree that while it is a definable function, entrepreneur is a term denoting an ideal type rather than a term continuously applicable to a real person. Any businessman or other official may exercise entrepreneurship, but a classification cannot be devised that would empirically separate entrepreneurs and non-entrepreneurs.*

Unable to fit the entrepreneur into their rather closed loop models, economists tossed the entrepreneur over to the social scientists, saying in a paraphrase of Cochran, "We can't tell the difference between entrepreneurs and non-entrepreneurs in an economic sense except

---

*Thomas C. Cochran, "Entrepreneurship," *Encyclopedia of Social Sciences*, pp. 87–90, 1969.

that when a businessman innovates, he is acting entrepreneurially." As we shall soon discover, social scientists have studied the entrepreneur far less than have economists.

WHY STUDY ENTREPRENEURS?

Entrepreneurs have been discovered recently by three important groups: (1) journalists; (2) investors; and (3) people seeking to control their own destinies. Three publishing entrepreneurs discovered in 1977 that no single publication was servicing the needs of entrepreneurs. If such a magazine were created, advertisers would flock to pitch office equipment, financial services and consumer products to subscribers. Bernard Goldhirsh started *Inc.*, and he aimed it at the small business owner, up to $20 million in sales. Judith Daniels started *Savvy*, and she staked a claim on the female segment. Joseph Giarraputo launched *Venture*, whose readers are primarily early-stage entrepreneurs.

There are other media and service organizations proclaiming the joys and wonders of entrepreneurship. Public Television has recently discovered the entrepreneur, although he or she has yet to be seen fit for the networks. Additionally, at least three seminar and workshop groups are profiting from the uncertainty of taking the step into entrepreneurship: The Center for Entrepreneurial Management, The School for Entrepreneurs in Tarrytown, New York, and Venture Founders. Over 200 graduate schools of business have rushed out courses in entrepreneurship, despite the fact that it has not been determined whether entrepreneurship is a discipline. Harvard has upgraded its importance by naming a chair in the field, endowed by several overachieving alumni who, perhaps misguidedly, attribute their entrepreneurial fortunes to the "B-School." Fledgling entrepreneurs may also buy tapes, books, and a wide range of services from business plan preparation to technical evaluation.

There are an estimated 10 million entrepreneurs in America, of whom less than 1 million subscribe to the new magazines dedicated to servicing them. This says either that the magazines are poorly marketed or that entrepreneurs are not active readers. William Lear, the inveterate entrepreneur (Lear Jet, Lear Siegler, 100 patents) said: "If a man has time to read, he isn't working." Nonetheless, the media have found the entrepreneur and he is excellent copy.

Sophisticated investors have found the entrepreneur as well. Since 1978, approximately $6 billion has been invested by hundreds of conservative financial institutions and corporations in venture capital partnerships whose business is finding entrepreneurs with interesting companies to invest in and help launch. According to the *Venture Capital Journal:*

> Record commitments to the venture capital industry in 1981 swelled the capital resource pool to $5.8 billion by year end, providing for the continued expansion of business development investment—a record $1.4 billion estimated disbursements to portfolio companies during the year. An atmosphere of euphoria generated by back-to-back years of record capital commitments, an improved climate for venture capital, increased investment opportunities, and the recent demonstrated success of venture capital investment should not obscure the fact that it is a long-term—five to ten year—process.*

There are approximately 200 venture capital partnerships in the country, most of which have 10-year lives and a strong desire to turn their capital between the sixth and tenth years. Thus, $6 billion must be put to work in the first five years, which means $100 million per month is trying to find competent entrepreneurs. On top of this are the approximately 400 SBA–sponsored Small Business Investment Companies with perhaps $1 billion to invest, the Small Business Administration with $3 billion per annum to loan to small businesses, the new issue public market that from time to time has shown its ability to come up with $1 to $2 billion per annum for new companies, and the unknown but estimated $3 billion of tax shelter dollars seeking start-up companies and research and development projects to invest in. From time to time the federal government comes up with a billion or two for entrepreneurs such as the

---

Venture Capital Journal, June 1982, p. 7.

Economic Development Administration's $1.5-billion-per-annum, inner-city-oriented loan guarantee program. Then there are grants, customer financing, supplier financing, the occasional unsecured bank loan, and family money. All told, entrepreneurs are enjoying the luxury of nearly $10 billion per annum to use for dream fulfillment. Just 10 years ago, the number was more like $3 billion. Ten billion dollars will attract the attention of a lot of corporate climbers who have toyed with the notion of starting their own business.

The third group to discover entrepreneurs are the candidates for entrepreneurship. Increasingly, men and women are deciding that starting and building a business is more fun than working for someone else. Although they cannot relate to legends such as Henry Ford or Isaac Singer, they can relate to the 26-year-olds who founded Apple Computer or the occasionally foot-in-mouth Ray Kroc of McDonald's fame who seem downright neighborly. As friends and co-workers become entrepreneurs, the ones who stay behind become less of a majority. In some regions of the country, such as Silicon Valley, just south of San Francisco, and Route 128, just west of Boston, entrepreneurship is the normal pattern of behavior. The fact has been lost on no one that entrepreneurs appear to make more valid contributions to society than corporate managers, that their work is done with a greater sense of purpose, and that they seem to be more interesting people than corporate managers and institutional bureaucrats. After all, the media are not hyping the White Collar Man, nor have billfolds opened in Hartford to help him shoot the moon. Entrepreneurs seem to be smiling, do not need to jog every day to avoid stress, and have more interesting days to tell their friends about. People who have considered an entrepreneurial role for themselves are beginning to explore the question in far greater detail.

Large corporations are beginning to recognize that entrepreneurial companies effect greater change than many of them do. Although many large corporations were founded by entrepreneurs, they tend to resist change once hierarchies of management are established to tell underlings how to use their imaginations and hands. As one after another large corporation thrashes about looking for a survival plan (e.g. the auto and steel makers, entertainment companies, retailers, and transportation companies), they see that inevitably entrepreneurs have caused them their biggest headaches. The result is that the large corporations have begun to assist certain of their employees in establishing part-risk relationships for the purpose of introducing greater productivity in certain divisions. The other thing that large corporations are doing is investing in venture capital funds in order that they can see through "windows into innovation and new technology." Pitney-Bowes has an investment in Hambrecht & Quist's venture capital fund for the purpose of viewing changes in the office of the future. Surely Pitney-Bowes would like advance notice if their ubiquitous postage meter will not be part of future offices. Beatrice Foods has an investment in Centennial Management Co., a Denver-based venture capital fund whose management has unique skills in cable television. Perhaps Beatrice Foods thinks that consumer goods might be sold through the mechanism of cable television in the future. Nabisco, Gillette, 3M, General Mills, GT&E, Honeywell, and Xerox have investments in venture capital funds. Several corporations operate their own venture capital funds, but that has historically proven unrewarding as the corporate venture capitalists leave to start their own funds and gain an equity interest in their investments. Nonetheless, large corporations in many cases have seen the entrepreneur, studied his movements, and begun to emulate him.

DO YOU HAVE WHAT IT TAKES?

Alas, we know very little about entrepreneurs and the entrepreneurial process. One would think that some of the $10 billion of risk capital would be put toward studying the thoughts and actions since birth of America's 100 most successful entrepreneurs in order to attempt to clone Kemmons Wilson's (Holiday Inns) and Henry Singleton's (Teledyne) in the future. But our keenest entrepreneur-watchers, the venture capitalists, are fairly busy managing the aforementioned $6 billion; and it would not make economic sense for them to go public with an entrepreneur-cloning system should they develop one. What has been stated in the way of defining the characteristics of entrepreneurs amounts to a collection of one-liners. Among the more interesting are the following:

On Single-Mindedness of Purpose

These people have an unusual ability to focus for long periods of time on one or two important things, excluding the rest.

BURTON J. MCMURTRY
VENTURE CAPITALIST
AS QUOTED IN *FORBES*

(On Howard Hughes) I never saw a man who could concentrate that hard or for that long.

JEAN HARLOW
MOVIE STAR

I find it very important to work intensively for long hours when I am beginning to see solutions to a problem. At such times atavistic competences seem to come welling up. You are handling so many variables at a barely conscious level that you can't afford to be interrupted. If you are, it may take a year to cover the same ground you could cover otherwise in sixty hours.

DR. EDWIN H. LAND
SUCCESSFUL ENTREPRENEUR

Entrepreneurs make a total sacrifice. Family life comes second. The object is success, and that means being evangelical about it.

GEORGE QUIST
VENTURE CAPITALIST
AS QUOTED IN *FORBES*

Entrepreneurs have a drive to do something well. They also have the intellectual honesty to face facts rigorously when they are wrong.

PATRICK LILES
VENTURE CAPITALIST
AS QUOTED IN *FORBES*

On Risk-Taking

Entrepreneurs are opportunity hunting mechanisms. They are like Marines landing on the beach and firing in all directions. If something falls down they move in that direction.

DAVID J. PADWA
SUCCESSFUL ENTREPRENEUR

So after six months I took my heart and my noodle in my hands and marched into Wyckoff one day and said I was no office boy, I wanted to be a broker.

JOSEPH H. HIRSHHORN
SUCCESSFUL ENTREPRENEUR

[On the founders of the longest lived business success, The Hudson's Bay Company, Messrs. Radisson and Groseilliers] A more daring pair of international promoters cannot be found in the history of commerce. Glib, plausible, ambitious, supported by unquestionable physical courage, they were completely equipped fortune hunters.

A SINCE FORGOTTEN HISTORIAN

On Where Entrepreneurs Come From

Just before the Civil War, the small and now forgotten Bettlebeck & Co., dry goods store in Newark, New Jersey, employed three clerks. They were Benjamin Altman, Abraham Abraham and Lyman Gustave Bloomingdale. Within a few years, each founded great stores, the first B. Altman & Co. in New York, the second Abraham & Straus in Brooklyn and the last Bloomingdale Bros., Inc.

JOHN THOMAS MAHONEY
AUTHOR, *THE GREAT MERCHANTS*

The [entrepreneur's] childhood is likely to have been rough.

DR. ALFRED E. MESSER
EMORY UNIVERSITY PROFESSOR

[From a 1960 Small Business Administration research paper in which 110 entrepreneurs were interviewed] There was found to be a high incidence of parental death or divorce . . . Which creates massive insecurity . . . and makes . . . the person more self-reliant.

DAVID MOORE, ET AL
CORNELL UNIVERSITY

L. L. Bean was born in 1872 on a farm at Greenwood, Maine, the fourth of six children. . . . When he was eleven . . . his father gave him the choice of going to a fair . . . or using the money to buy five muskrat traps the boy had been wanting. Young Bean settled for the traps.

When he was thirteen both parents died. . . . His first big business deal was transacted at sixteen. . . . In 1912, after many jobs and ventures, L. L. became a partner of his brother Guy in a small clothing store.

JOHN THOMAS MAHONEY
THE GREAT MERCHANTS

Eight scientists and engineers have left Shockley Semiconductor Laboratory in nearby Mountain View [California] to set up their own firm, Fairchild Semiconductor Corp. here . . . [to make] high speed computer transistors . . .[including] . . .H. E. Hale, Dr. Robert N. Noyce, Gordon E. Moore, Julius Blank, J. W. English, Philip Haas, Richard Hodgson and Eugene Kleiner.

ELECTRONIC NEWS
October 20, 1957

Four members of Fairchild Semiconductor, Mountain View, California, have resigned their posts to form an electronics company [named Signetics] to be located here in the Bay Area . . .[to] concentrate on the microcircuitry field . . .Dr. B. David James said financing had been arranged by Lehman Brothers.

ELECTRONIC NEWS
March 1961

Signetics was barely underway when two members of the Fairchild inner circle, left on 'very friendly terms', according to Noyce) to launch one of the initial companies in an aggregation then shaping up as Teledyne, headed by Dr. Henry Singleton.

ELECTRONIC NEWS
March 1965

Noyce, weary of a job that had become increasingly administrative, resigned [Fairchild] in June, 1968. His R&D chief, Gordon Moore, followed right behind . . . . Noyce and Moore, joined by another member of the Fairchild technical staff, Andrew Grove, put their heads together with Arthur Rock, a San Francisco financier, and came up with Integrated Electronics, later shortened to Intel . . . to chip away at a massive core memory market ripe for penetration by MOS technology.

ELECTRONIC NEWS
January 25, 1982

Note the progression of Robert Noyce. He leaves Shockley in 1957 with seven other scientists to form a new company that will develop transistors with financing provided by Fairchild Camera & Instrument Corp. on the East Coast. Over the next 11 years, team members leave Fairchild to start a myriad of new electronics companies in the San Francisco Bay area. Fairchild's talent pool is nearly depleted; so the parent takes control via an exchange of shares. Noyce and the other executives become wealthy, but the corporate world becomes "increasingly administrative" and Noyce is beginning to experiment with placing many transistors on tiny chips of silicon. He has to leave Fairchild in order to carry out his dreams.

There are many bits of wisdom and history about entrepreneurs, such as those recorded above, that act like bait to a social scientist. Yet there is no scientific study of the social, emotional, and cultural forces that cause one person to become an entrepreneur and another to drive in the slow lane. Into the breach this book is hurled.

2

WHO IS THE ENTREPRENEUR?

My business is to help entrepreneurs find seed money. Early in the game I learned that success depends as much on the person commandeering the product or service as on the product or service itself. The nos come so early, so fast, so often, and for so long, that the entrepreneur must be able to remain confident and happy throughout and inspire some technicians and managers to stick it out through what are almost always very lean times.

Since I can spot a likely success, many people—especially venture capitalists who want to make informed decisions, or entrepreneurs who want some clues and caveats—have asked me to describe the successful entrepreneur. Every time I tried, I'd come up with words like "sixth sense," "intuition," "insight"—which didn't help the questioners and didn't satisfy me. So I decided to try for a systematic approach to asking and answering the question.

To begin to get a handle on how to answer, I sent a questionnaire to 100 entrepreneurs whose business had generated for them personal capital gains of at least $20 million. (Interestingly, the return on questionnaires was one out of two: 54% of my target audience returned theirs.)

The questions were designed to provide me with personality characteristics, personal and professional life histories, and the entrepreneurs' own descriptions of their motivations to succeed.

I do now have a composite of the successful entrepreneur, drawn from my observations, talks with dozens of venture capitalists, and responses to the questionnaire, and in this chapter I shall draw as detailed a replica of that picture as I can.

But please note: I *describe* the personality of the classic entrepreneur, common background threads, motives they themselves name. I *do not* make any attempt to *explain* what I observe, nor do I propose any theory of my own about how a particular combination of environment and internal forces shapes the archetypal entrepreneur.

Such explanations could, no doubt, be formulated—though to my knowledge none exists. And since the analysis is yet unwritten, I offer my observations with an invitation to social and behavioral scientists to take a look and see if they can help us understand why some enter into such a risky existence to follow this particular form of a dream.

To the portrait, then.

Ken Laskas, not his real name, is the eldest son of a Greek couple who came to America as children in 1936, fell in love on the streets of a large midwestern city, and married. Ken was born in 1944, when the young couple felt that their flower shop could support them and a child. They lived behind the store, but with a baby they would need more room, an apartment.

Little Ken soon had a baby sister, and the two were raised by Ken's aunt because both parents worked in the store. Ken's father got sick from delivering the flowers in the snow one winter, lingered in a hospital with pneumonia, and lingered at home and eventually died in his sleep when Ken was seven years old. The safety net was removed. Ken realized then and there that nobody was going to be around to pick him up when he fell down.

Surprisingly, Ken's mother introduced some new services at the flower shop that increased its revenue. This permitted her to hire a manager and thus spend breakfast and the evenings with her children. They got their mother back, and she gave Ken and his sister lots of love and stroking and, of course, guilt. "Ken," she would say, "I want you to study math and science to be an engineer. Running a shop is not for you." But, of course, Ken liked to help his mother in the store on Saturdays and after school. He had few friends, because he was little for his age and terrible in sports. He could make tips by delivering flowers and being extra nice to the customers. Some of the customers called him "that little Greek kid," which burned into his soul.

Ken went to college and studied engineering and physics and graduated with a B.S. degree in electrical engineering in 1965. He joined a large electronics firm in his home town, married his high school sweetheart, and was at peace with the world.

Ken began to rise through the ranks at the corporation, but he needed to make more money to support the three children that he and his wife quickly produced. So he changed jobs for more money, but the commute was longer. The 30-minute drive was a bore, until Ken began using it to *notice*. He noticed that along the route home from work there were no fried chicken restaurants, only hamburger joints. Thousands of workers passed this way in the evening, and many of them would pick up a chicken dinner for the family if such a fast-food restaurant existed.

Ken began exploring the possibility of obtaining a Kentucky Fried Chicken or Church's franchise and found they were taken. He began reading about the fast-food business, and he got a subscription to *Restaurant Business*. He attended conferences and asked lots of questions of fast-food managers in town. Ken then found a site for lease and decided to open a fast-food restaurant featuring fried chicken and a Greek salad, with the intent of selling franchises nationally in a year or so.

Ken sprang the news on his wife and mother one evening, and his mother wept openly. Her professional was becoming a merchant. How could he do this to her? It was a terrible scene. His wife was supportive but nervous. She prepared for the worst.

Ken refinanced the house, emptied their $12,000 savings account, and borrowed $100,000 from everyone he knew. The capital was inadequate, so he got 10 charge cards in names similar to his and borrowed $20,000 on them. His mother, aunt, and sister even loaned him money. He opened his first store, but forgot outside lighting. The sign could not be seen and dinner was a flop. Ken went to an uncle and the next-door gas station manager for a $10,000 loan. Finally, with some proper lighting, signage, advertising, and promotion, the restaurant got the dinner business that Ken knew it would. It became profitable in the fifth month. One of the employees had been stealing from the cash register, and Ken's prices were too low. Adjustments were continually made until by the tenth month, the store was earning $8000 per month after all expenses.

Ken then entered a new world: franchising. He poured himself into it day and night, traveling all over the country, selling, training, hiring, firing, and building a chain. Within a year, 12 franchised stores were open and operating. But Ken's wife and children had left him. He didn't mind the absence at first. It gave him more time to focus on the business. He had only one date in the first six months after the separation, and that one was a mere one-night stand with a stewardess in Denver where he was setting up a franchisee. Ken needed venture capital to grow faster. He had hired sound middle management from the fast-food industry who were attractive to the investors. A venture capital fund in Chicago formed a syndicate which put in $2,000,000 for a 40% interest. Ken and his management team used the money to vault the business from 12 to 140 stores in operation. A quality underwriter took the company public, and Ken made the cover of *Restaurant Business*. He married a 22-year-old and had a child, but the marriage was a convenient means of coupling and not a Rock Hudson-Jennifer Jones situation. He was in love with his business and the challenge of proving to some *bête noire* somewhere that the little Greek flower delivery boy had made something of his life.

WHO IS THE ENTREPRENEUR?

The entrepreneur is someone dissatisfied with his or her career path (though not with his chosen field) who decides to make a mark on the world by developing and selling a product or service that will make life easier for a large number of people.

The entrepreneur is energetic, single-minded, and has a mission and clear vision; he or she intends to create out of this vision a product or service in a field many have determined is important, to improve the lives of millions. Consider the number of successful entrepreneurial ventures undertaken over the last 15 years in the computer, biomedical, and communications industries. Yes, the entrepreneur will probably make a lot of money and knows it; when, who knows and who cares.

What drives this kind of person? Why will he or she forego the conventional career path, ignore all warnings about the likelihood of failure, take on enormous financial burdens, assume responsibilities such as management decisions or marketing plans for which he or she is poorly trained, toss aside the tranquility of home and marriage as if possessed by this single goal?

At what point does the entrepreneur jump into action? What is the personal history behind such determination? And what does he or she say are the driving forces?

Typically, the entrepreneur is between 27 and 34, and is male. This is not to be interpreted as a reflection on the capabilities of women to be entrepreneurial or to become entrepreneurs. In fact, an increasing number of dynamic young women are becoming dissatisfied with their corporate roles and leaving to start more personally rewarding businesses. There is no difference from my point of view between men and women entrepreneurs. But because only men responded to my questionnaires, and because for most of the 15 years I've been working with entrepreneurs, 99% plus have been male, for the remainder of this chapter I would like the reader to allow me to refer to the entrepreneurs as "he."

This archetypal individual represents—to some—a contradiction. Until the time he conceived of his entrepreneurial (ad)venture, he worked fully within the scope of traditional societal values, for a corporation, perhaps, or for a laboratory, a medical school, or research center. He had been hired, he believed, for his creative potential, and was rewarded, he believed, for his creative contributions. He was well satisfied.

Lurking in the wings, however, was a foil. For although initially he trusted that the organization valued him and rewarded him principally for his creative potential and output, and he had joined the organization in part because of its prestige, as he became more energetic and needed increasing latitude and funding for invention, the organization's commitment to creative output and its willingness to invest in his personal research and development efforts emerged as less than he wanted, less than he expected. At first surprised, he became increasingly dissatisfied, though for a time he did nothing, said nothing.

At the same time, as trust in the workplace faded, strong commitment to his own capabilities was unfolding. More and more, he experienced a sense of directedness; an inner voice was asking him questions about personal values, expression of self-worth, self-sufficiency. He was not necessarily asking the abstract philosophical stock-taking questions that observers and analysts of mid-life change report are raised so frequently by people in the mid-30s and 40s, questions like, "What have I accomplished in my life?" "What have I sacrificed?" "What will I do with the rest of my life?" Those questions are as likely to come to the entrepreneur as to anyone else. But at this point in his life, the Big Question for the entrepreneur was: "What will I do with my creativity?"

He was intense, deadly serious about homesteading somewhere and so being able to exercise his confidence in himself. So, before he even knew it had started, the entrepreneurial race was on. For a time, as he continued to do his job for his employer, dissatisfaction increased and the idea for the one product or service he would develop—one that would take the marketplace by storm—was putting down roots in his mind. The first growth might be a primary shoot that withers, but the root system was secure, come sunny weather or violet storm. And, as I will discuss in more detail, he will be protected by enormous potential to replenish psychic energy, by intense pleasure at his activity, and, if he is to be successful, by excellent communication skills and exquisite judgment.

At this point, he comes to me.

I have the enormous pleasure, then, of meeting complex, intense, determined, imaginative people who have faith in themselves, and whose enregy isn't sapped by pervasive anger, bitterness, or disappointment. The workplace has not been satisfying, true, and hasn't rewarded what he most respects in himself; the not-yet-active entrepreneur has put in a lot of time and has tried to contribute his best. He has become dissatisfied and to some extent disillusioned. And he is not politically adept, so pure commitment to human potential irritates rather than inspires management, making it impossible for him to maneuver budgets and other forms of influence the way others can to make the organizational dynamics work for, not against, them.

Nevertheless, though he resents the system, he proceeds in the disillusion and goes on to create his own reality; thus, *the true entrepreneur does not feel victimized*. He doesn't plot and plan retaliation. Rather, he accepts that the organization will not provide a place to do what he wants to do and believes should be done, and he decides to create such an organization on his own.

Acceptance of reality brings determination, not depression, distraction, or diffuse, flailing attempts to get even, to show them. (He has others to "show," as we will see later on.)

It brings dedication to building on his own strengths rather than to demonstrating the weakness of the organization (and thereby deluding himself that it would change anything with respect to his position). He knows he cannot reduce its power, so he decides to establish his own.

And since personal goals and needs have been emerging as the strongest forces, they take over to govern his behavior, and he directs his psychic and creative energy into building on the emotional self-sufficiency that has been slowly, steadily taking hold. He does this with an ease that astounds people who know or hear about him.

The creative intelligence he brought to his employer's business is now directed toward designing a product or service and positioning it for the marketplace. He examines opportunities, perhaps for licensing, sees none he likes, may work for a short time as an independent consultant or for a consulting firm, continues to see the need he himself identified, and finally decides to create his own opportunity.

He is getting ready to break ground, carve out his niche, and build his place in the sun. "Build a place in the sun," I said, not "build an empire"; for empire building is not what he is about. Rather, he is planning for, and is after, self-reliance, a quality-controlled provision for creative output. He talks about building an organization where people will not get lost; where creativity will be rewarded; where salaries and benefits will be just; where participative management (though he doesn't call it by that name) will be the rule, not the exception. And to the amazement of people who are not able to turn anger, energy, disappointment, dissatisfaction into focused personal directedness, he begins to experience intense pleasure. The undercurrent of basic optimism and trust in his professional power, the certainty that has always existed that his expertise in his field is unequalled, govern a clear decision to be on his own and succeed. He has no fear of failure, though he makes careful, detailed plans to avoid it. Statistics of new business and small business failure offered to him by well-meaning friends and family are dismissed as irrelevant. "Sure, lots of people fail, but since I'm going to succeed, why are you telling me these numbers?" he demands. Then he goes on with his phone calls to bankers, brokers, friends of friends, presentations end to end. Failure is simply not a possibility. He has spotted an opportunity and is leaping forward to take advantage of it as rapidly as possible.

With confidence, optimism, courage, focus, and determination, the would-be entrepreneur sets out to look for money. What happens then depends on whether he carries two other attiributes, and seems as well to correlate with several factors in his childhood home life. (Here we must assume that the product or service is, in fact, one for which a market exists.)

Next: second-stage predictions of success. To succeed not only in finding venture capital but also in building a successful business, the would-be entrepreneur must be able to lead his team by exercising good judgment—knowing the right thing to do at the right time. But since he may not have a clue about *how* to do the right things, he will eventually get tangled up in the snare of trying to plan a business. Without knowing word one about functional areas like strategic planning, sales projections, market research, or even simple accounting practices, he will at this point select a manager who does, and one who can at the same time allow the entrepreneur chieftain to maintain leadership.

The higher the entrepreneur reaches for a manager, the more likely is his business to succeed. Entrepreneurs exhibit the keen judgment they are known for when they ask an achiever to join them; someone who has demonstrated first-class management ability in a growth situation.

To tie up the venture capital package, the entrepreneur must be able to make and keep the process simple, and convince others it is so.

What might make others topple into confusion and frantic despair nourishes his spirit and his spirited intellect. Out of the complexity he pulls the necessary interim funding—usually the day the bank loan interest is due—from the most unlikely sources, a first-rate impressive venture group presentation, a corps of dedicated partners or colleagues, determination and confidence enough to refuse equity-hungry venture tempters. Those would-be entrepreneurs who have the product or service and the character prerequisites will become wealthy; those who don't will be wiped out in the marketplace.

You know who some of the well-known young men are, those who have told of transformations overnight, abrupt decisions to do something on their own. Edwin H. Land, while walking in Times Square, New York City, one night and staring at car headlights, decided to leave Harvard in his freshman year. Ted Schad, at 44, left Peat, Marwick, Mitchell & Co. in New York to buy a highly over-leveraged, slow-growth, marginal little company called Lou-Ana Foods, in Opelousas, Louisiana. Tom Kelly founded TIE/communications with a few thousand dollars in the pit of the 1974 recession to try to topple AT&T.

Why these men and the hundreds of others who have been entre-preneurially successful develop this particular line of competence is an open question; as I said above, the "whys" are not my ballgame. The wherefores, though, are easier for me.

The successful entrepreneur brings his well-known brand of emotional baggage to the work. His parents admired and worked toward a place in the status hierarchy. They valued a traditional, socially acceptable, orderly life, a position vis-à-vis others. The future entrepreneur's father either died early or was absent from family life often, due to divorce or business, dissatisfaction with himself, his marriage, his perceived place in the family. So all was held together by a devoted, attentive mother, apparently well-intentioned but very ambitious for her children.

Doing double duty, his mother pushed for achievements, compe-tence, and public recognition of her son's accomplishments. It's no surprise that the successful entrepreneur starts his professional life seeking to work in a well-regarded "establishment" organization; and that when he leaves he has the motivation to succeed at all costs.

Here are some brief entrepreneur case vignettes. Kemmons H.

Wilson put his wife and five children in their station wagon in 1951 for a family vacation in Washington, D.C. The motels there charged the Wilsons' kids $2 a head even though they were sleeping in the same room as their parents. Wilson's Scottish blood boiled and he pledged that when he got back to Memphis he would build a chain of motels that would never charge extra for children. One year later, Wilson opened the first Holiday Inn, named for a Bing Crosby movie of that title. Within 18 months, he had built three more, covering all four main approaches to Memphis. Wilson built his motels with swimming pools, air conditioning, 24-hour telephone service, televisions in every room, ice and soft-drink machines in the halls, and baby-sitters, dentists, and clergymen on call. These features reflected Wilson's preferences.

Wilson was an entrepreneur by the time he was 12 years old. He bought a $50 popcorn machine with nothing down and payments of $1 a week, installed it in a Memphis theater, and took in $30 a week. This was done out of necessity. Wilson's father died when he was nine months old, and he was raised an only child by his mother, Ruby (called "Doll" because she was less than five feet tall). Doll supported the family with a variety of low-paying jobs, but when she got sick, Wilson dropped out of high school and began an early career in the vending equipment business: pinball machines, jukeboxes, and cigarette machines. Wilson once bought 250 cigarette machines with six postdated checks of $10,000 each, and pulled the quarters out of each machine three or four times a day to cover the checks.

To expand Holiday Inns, Wilson teamed up with Wallace Johnson, an experienced builder who had the contacts and the financial expertise to build a franchised network. Holiday Inns changed the lodging industry, crushed the competition, and grew to 1750 establishments, the world's largest lodging chain.

W. Clement Stone's father died when he was very young, and his mother worked as a seamstress in their native Detroit to support the family. She was a deeply religious woman who talked to God as if he were a provider of customers and capital. She invested her savings in an insurance agency. The first day that she owned the agency, she sold no policies. That night she and young Clement, still a teenager, prayed that she would be better the next day. In the morning she marched into a bank and sold policies to bank employees. She came home and told Clement to go to an office building the next day and sell insurance policies to everyone he saw. He sold 12 policies in his first three days.

Stone moved to Chicago three years later and started his own agency at age 20. He was unusually successful, achieving a personal high of 122 sales one day in Joliet, Illinois. Ten years later, with over 1000 employees, Stone sought an insurance company to purchase. He bought Pennsylvania Casualty Co. from Commercial Credit Corp., on a fully leveraged basis, for $1.6 million. It became the foundation of Combined Insurance Co., which had revenues of $869 million in 1981 and earnings of $100 million. As a venture capitalist, Stone has done nearly as well, obtaining one-fourth of the ownership of Alberto-Culver Corp. for a loan guarantee of $450,000 in the mid-1950s.

Joseph H. Hirshhorn, an unusually successful mining entrepreneur in Canada from the 1930s through the 1960s, who in retirement turned over his immense art collection to the Smithsonian Institution, was raised by his mother as well. She worked in a sweatshop pocketbook factory, 72 hours per week for wages of $12 per week.

Daniel K. Ludwig's parents were divorced. Howard Hughes' father died when he was 18. Bernie Cornfield's father died when he was 9 and his mother went to work as a nurse. David Geffen, the wunderkind of the music industry, remembers his mother operating a seamstress business in their living room in Brooklyn. The list of successful entrepreneurs whose fathers were absent due to death or divorce or often away on business seems virtually endless. That in itself is not enough to put a leg on the entrepreneurial stool. It is of equal importance that the mother-son bond be as strong as iron. I call this mother-stroking: making the child self-reliant at an early age.

In *The Lives of William Benton*, Sydney Hyman writes that when Benton left home for college, he wrote his mother every day, trying to justify his actions to her. Benton's father died when he was an early teenager. He subsequently founded the advertising agency of Benton & Bowles, which he sold after six years to launch several other hugely successful enterprises, including Muzak and Encyclopedia Britannica.

Did these men develop early a sense that if they fell down, their fathers would not be there to pick them up? The entrepreneur, it seems, did the high wire act without the net below. Courage and no fear of failure are predictable outcomes.

Erik H. Erikson, keen observer of families and a giant in the field of human development, wrote a scenario that could have been about non-entrepreneurs:

> The grandfather, a powerful and powerfully driven man . . . sought new and challenging engineering tasks in widely separated regions. When the initial challenge was met, he handed the task over to others, and moved on. His wife saw him only for an occasional impregnation. His sons could not keep pace with him and were left as respectable settlers by the wayside; only his daughter was and looked like him. Her very masculine identification, however, did not permit her to take a husband as strong as her powerful father. She married what seemed, in comparison, a weak but safe man and settled down. In many ways, however, she talks like the grandfather. She does not know how she persistently belittles the sedentary father and decries the family's lack of mobility, geographic and social. Thus she establishes in [their son] a conflict between the sedentary habits which she insists on, and the reckless habits she dares him to develop.

> . . . The father . . . does not hide his relative weakness behind a mask of inflated patriarchal claims . . . If the father plays baseball with his son, it is not in order to impress him with the fact that he, the father, comes closer to the perfection of a common idea type . . . but rather that they play together at identifying with that type, and that there is always the chance, hoped for by both, that the boy may more nearly approach the ideal than the father did.

> Fraternal images, boldly or gingerly, thus step into the gaps left by decaying paternalism . . . The father's occupational group, the mother's club, the adolescent's clicque and the children's first friends . . . These interest groups determine the individual's privileges in his family; it is they who judge the family. The sensitive receptor of changing styles in the community and the sensitive arbiter of their clash within the home is, of course, the mother. . . . The adolescent swings of the American youth do not overtly concern the father. . . . The boy has a delinquent streak, as had his grandfather in the days when laws were absent or not enforced. This may express itself in surprising acts of dangerous driving or careless destruction and waste

. . . carelessness [underscores] the fact that there is no boss—and that there need be little thought.

Our boy is anti-intellectual. Anybody who thinks or feels too much seems "queer" to him. This objection stems from an early mistrust of sensuality . . . and is representative of a general tentativeness . . . not to make up his mind until . . . a number of chances may force him to think.

The type of adolescent I am discussing here is not and will never be a true individualist. But then it would be hard to point out any true individualist within the orbit of his experience—unless it be the myth of the mother's father . . . our adolescent is allergic to . . . professional kinds of individualism . . . [it] makes him feel uncomfortable.

This adolescent will make an efficient and decent leader in a circumscribed job, a good manager or professional worker and a good officer, and will most enjoy his recreation with 'the boys' in the organizations to which he belongs. . . . They know how to accept a circumscribed task . . . but on the whole, they respectfully shy away from all bigness, whether it is dollars or loud words.*

Entrepreneurs have precious little time for a weekly poker game, Kiwanis luncheon, or seats on various boards. They receive very little support from clubs and organizations. Lack of time forces them into the easy-to-do sports like tennis and away from those that take more time.

Erikson has not described an anomaly. He is not speaking of a certain kind of adolescent who is "anti-intellectual," who "objects to feeling and thinking," who has "an early mistrust of sensuality," and who grows up to "make a good officer" and to "shy away from all bigness." Indeed, this is Erikson's view of much of post-World War II American society. The grandsons of self-made men, themselves the grandsons of rebels, are not likely to be individualistic. The products of a home where the mother dominated the father are not likely to be individualistic.

Entrepreneurs come from homes where the mother is more like ". . . [Erikson's] American woman in frontier communities" (Erik-

*Erik H. Erikson, *Childhood and Society*, Second Edition (New York: W. W. Norton and Co., Inc., 1963).

son, p. 291). "[She] was the object of intense rivalries on the part of tough . . . men. At the same time, she had to become the cultural censor, the religious conscience, the aesthetic arbiter, and the teacher."

Erikson again, but here he could have been describing the entrepreneur's mother:

> In that early rough economy hewn out of hard nature it was she who contributed the finer graces of living and that spiritually without which the community falls apart. In her children she saw future men and women who would face contrasts of rigid sedentary and shifting migratory life. They must be prepared for any number of extreme opposites in milieu, and always ready to seek new goals and to fight for them in merciless competition. For, after all, worse than a sinner was a sucker.*

One can see Clement Stone's and Kemmons Wilson's proud, gritty mothers in Erikson's paragraph. Are there enough frontiers left to produce frontier mothers? The inner-city has become a frontier. Parts of the Sun Belt, the Midwest, and Alaska are frontiers. The cushy suburbs are the last place venture capitalists will look for entrepreneurs in the future. However, it is not the location of the entrepreneur's adolescence that is important, but the maternal grandfather (one would hope he was not a dragon slayer), the mother (one would trust, a gritty, determined, proud, gracious woman), and the father (absent much of the time, one would expect). Behind every entrepreneur there are likely to be a frontier mother and an absent father.

Like his mother, the son does double duty—in the loneliness arena. Not only must he be a boy on his own longing for a much-absent father. Typically, the future entrepreneur feels lonely among his peers because he has a relatively minor, but in his youth, powerful handicap with regard to society's idealized picture of the American male. Many are of shorter-than-average stature; many were very poor (though the mother's drive denied that the poverty could keep any of her sons down); perhaps excessively poor eyesight or a worst-case acne condition imposed a hurdle to social approval the family—and adolescents—needed so much. So our boy grew up longing to

*Ibid., p. 291.

be more "like other boys," but not being seen, or necessarily seeing himself, so. Early approval from the traditional sources wasn't available, and he carried a deep longing for it into his adult life.

An entrepreneur whose childhood was one of bone-chilling deprivation would be wise to obtain a partner to offer guidance and support so that the options can be expanded in difficult times. Astute venture capitalists are quick to measure the length of the hill that the entrepreneur has climbed. Vertical movement through extraordinary deprivation does not make for successful entrepreneurship. The pain is often borne forever, making the entrepreneur excessively bitter and too much the street-fighter.

On the other hand, those who don't suffer during the formative and adolescent years simply are not likely to become successful entrepreneurs. Entrepreneurs do not come from pampered childhoods, where life has been full and abundant; perhaps there is not the staunch determination, or the need to reverse things, that lead to such extreme transformations.

To satisfy my curiosity about deprivation, I have asked applicants for venture capital over the last 15 years to describe childhood and history and feelings about it. The most successful seem to have endured one or more of these:

Small physical stature

Physical illness that prevented athletic or social participation

Skin conflagration (acne, eczema) that prevented social aggressiveness

Relatively less wealth than peer group

Arrested educational development

Charles Revson, the dynamic founder of Revlon, was less than 5½ feet tall. He was not above walking on top of the conference table during management staff meetings. Gino Paulucci, the founder of Chun King, is slightly over 5 feet tall. He too paced on top of the conference room table during management staff meetings. Tom Kelly of TIE/communications is a bantam weight as well. Among other successful entrepreneurs who are shorter than the average American adult male are:

Meshulam Rilkis	Rapid-American Corp.
Charles Bluhdorn	Gulf & Western Corp.
H. Ross Perot	Electronic Data Systems Corp.
Erroll Beker	Beker Industries Corp.
Bernie Cornfeld	Fund of Funds
Joseph H. Hirshhorn	Rio Tinto Mines
J. Paul Getty	Getty Oil Co.
James L. Ling	LTV Corp.

The great merchant bankers who wheeled and dealed with the rail-roads in the first two decades of the twentieth century—Jacob H. Schiff, J. Pierpont Morgan, Jay Gould—were all short men. One 5-foot-tall entrepreneur once told me: "I'm really 6 feet 2, but wound up real tight."

Other common threads in entrepreneurs' backgrounds are child-hood physical illnesses that prevented active participation in sports or social activities. Francis Copolla was bed-ridden with polio for a year. Among the infirmities most frequently listed are:

Vision impairments

Asthma or hay fever

Skin eruptions, acne

Motor impairments

It bears pointing out that regardless of the physical impairments of youth, adult entrepreneurs are almost never sick. There are two explanations for this: (1) they are having too much fun to miss a day of work; or (2) entrepreneurs do not know how to delegate respon-sibility, and cannot afford to be absent.

The successful entrepreneurs who dropped out of school are too numerous to list. There are substantially more entrepreneurs who never finished college than there are entrepreneurs who graduated from the 10 most highly regarded universities in the country. The better schools turn out professional managers and highly paid bureaucrats.

Possibly the most potent generator for entrepreneurial drive and ultimate success is fixed and pervasive guilt. Now, guilt is a psychiatrist's term as well as one we all use in our day-to-day experience to a greater or lesser degree. And it is a slippery subject with which highly trained professionals wrestle. I don't pretend to know and so am not attempting to offer any explanations about the psychosocial or psychosexual ramifications or manifestations of psychological guilt. I am describing only feelings of guilt that entrepreneurs have reported to me. And all did, which is why I bring it up here.

The entrepreneur reports a continual sense of guilt in merely existing as an entrepreneur. Brought up to meet traditional expectations and gain approval from society (since not from parents, peers, or self), as he strikes out on his own, society tugs at him, pokes fun, queries him endlessly, questions his sanity, patronizes him, reminds him he has not done what was expected of him.

This guilt manifests itself profoundly on a personal level, and to a much lesser extent as a minor recurring annoyance when society tells him he has not done well.

A TYPICAL PICTURE OF PERSONAL ENTREPRENEURIAL GUILT

Picture the room behind a Chinese laundry where the father has been on his feet washing shirts for 12 hours, the mother has been standing just as long over a steam iron and the eldest daughter, a 12-year-old, is teaching the abacus to the eldest son, an 8-year-old. As the son grows older, the parents encourage him to pursue his study of mathematics and pay for the best books, schools, and so forth with the only capital they have: longer hours. Their hard work is not lost on the son, who applies himself diligently in school and is accepted at a major university, where his achievements in mathematics gain for him high marks and a doctorate in record time. The parents attend all of his commencements, so proud are they to have produced a professional, a scientist, a professor. The American dream has been achieved.

One year later, the son leaves academia to start a computer manufacturing company. Thinking they will be pleased, he is thunderstruck by the sorrow his news causes them. He returns to his small office in great sadness. His drives are entrepreneurial, but he has done something very bad to his parents. The guilt that he now carries with him will become an agency of great force and energy to make his parents very proud of him once again.

Society seems either to envy or to be disdainful of the entrepreneur, and he is an easy target because the process, grueling as it is, is a very enjoyable process for the entrepreneur. He is happy virtually all of the time. Until recently, and even now only in certain entrepreneur enclaves such as Silicon Valley, Route 128 west of Boston, the Raleigh-Durham area, and a few others, the entrepreneur has not been viewed kindly. At best, entrepreneurs in postwar America have been considered promoters: either packaging a plan, planning a program, programming a package, planning a pilot, piloting a program or packaging a programmed pilot for a plan. Journalists have approached entrepreneur thrashing with about the same relish and exuberance as they have approached politician bashing. As recently as 1970, one did not admit to being an entrepreneur in the company of gentlemen. Entrepreneurs become bored with being asked, "Yes, but what do you *do*?" or, "Who are your people?" or, "Who are you with?" More recently, entrepreneurs have been hoisted higher by the pulley-and-lever combination of money and publicity. Yet, entrepreneurs are not revered, as are heart surgeons; not trusted, as are bankers; not looked to for wisdom, as are college professors. To the public, they are still opportunity-hunters, somewhat more colorful or more amusing than the average Joe due to their inexhaustible enthusiasm, or their penchant for risk taking, but ultimately they are dismissed as people who could not cut it professionally and took the last resort—going into business for themselves; something akin to being a consultant, I guess.

The entrepreneur sees his role quite differently, of course. It's all a matter of connotation, nuance, inference; perception of self and his place in the world as he views the world. His decision to go on his own was conscious, positive, and affirmative. He was not fired; rather, he became dissatisfied and left with some ideas to test in the marketplace. He sees himself not as an opportunist but as a creator of a solution for one or more of the country's tangled sets of problems. He sees himself not as a promoter but as a builder. He and other entrepreneurs are warmed by the fact that their ideas and energies—

and not smokestack America—create jobs. While the audience places the entrepreneur somewhere between Glenn Turner and P. T. Barnum, the entrepreneur regards himself as excellent dinner company for Albert Schweitzer and Selman Waksman. He is proud, believing himself to be a social good. Furthermore, he would like to be given recognition for the social goods that his company provides—problem solving, job creation, a more efficient product or service—than for any entrepreneurial wealth that he might create. Why must the audience use money as the entrepreneur's scorecard? Scientists are awarded Nobels. Artists' works are hung in museums. Writers are awarded Pulitzers. Entrepreneurs are discussed in a handful of magazines in terms of the wealth they have achieved.

Thus, the irony of the happy entrepreneur's creation of more new jobs in three years with an investment of $100,000 than the entire automobile industry's in the last 10 years, and the circumspect view of him held by family, friends, corporate America, professionals, and the media. Dr. Schweitzer versus Glen Turner.

Practically every entrepreneur with whom I have discussed this subject has three reactions, usually sequenced as follows:

Admits to being guilt-driven
Is delighted to be able to discuss a shared experience
Is able to tell me what he thinks makes the guilt

The stony silence maintained by most entrepreneurs, which in the man's eyes is a survival mechanism, often leads to misunderstandings between the entrepreneur and his wife. His wife wants equal time with the new business, of course, which is an impossibility. Recognizing the unlikelihood of achieving anywhere near equilibrium in the entrepreneur's world, she strives to become an advisor or confidante. In most circumstances, an entrepreneur does not select another entrepreneur for a spouse. Thus, she cannot provide a sounding board for the entrepreneur. If the entrepreneur is alert to having his wife achieve a sense of fulfillment of the kind that he does, he will locate an area of his business where she can contribute meaningfully.

Many entrepreneurs utilize their spouses to interview potential managers. This is done unobtrusively at dinner or the equivalent, and the wife's judgment is taken seriously. Frequently, a spouse can intuit things that the entrepreneur cannot because of extraneous bits of information that truncate a clear and logical reasoning path of information. The entrepreneur who relies on his spouse to contribute in a meaningful way is often rewarded with a tenacious, enthusiastic cheerleader.

Alas, the opposite happens with greater frequency. The spouse is frozen out of the entrepreneur's thoughts, actions, and conversation. He does not seek her advice, does not welcome it when it is given, and, in a moment of business stress, launches a verbal tirade of invectives at her for "butting in." A few of these, several weeks of extensive travel and a lonely bed mixed with brain rot at the sandbox, and the marriage crashes.

But the end of a marriage only strengthens the entrepreneurial drive. Venture capitalists have long known that a post-divorce entrepreneur is a neutron-bomb-carrying missile, exploding with an order of magnitude more energy than when the marriage was intact. So demanding is the entrepreneur's lifestyle that if they remain married it is because the wife possesses equal doses of courage, pride, and drive. She wants to make the marriage work.

The guilt of the divorced entrepreneur is turned inside and energizes the entrepreneur to "show her that I can make it without her." Departing for just a moment from my vow to avoid Freud, I'll share with you the fact that he described guilt as fear of losing love. Without the spouse available when needed for companionship, romance, or producing and rearing children, the divorced entrepreneur lives a lonely existence—too similar to that of his childhood. He may feel he has failed, as he did as a child when (he believed) he caused his father to stay away. To erase the flaw in his otherwise noble character, the entrepreneur plunges more earnestly into his business to show his ex-spouse that *she* made a tragic error in terminating the marriage; it wasn't *his* fault. The energy that divorce releases in an entrepreneur is titanic. It is not always well directed, but so many shots are taken that a few are bound to reach targets.

Note: Venture capitalists are high on divorced entrepreneurs and the "guilty marrieds," but they are loath to back the never-married bachelor.

A married entrepreneur feels guilty because his parents put in for a doctor or other professional but got an entrepreneur, and he also bears the constantly-out-of-town guilt. A divorced entrepreneur carries these two guilts plus the I'll-show-the-wife guilt. But the bachelor, never having committed himself to either a wife or children, has much lighter guilt baggage to carry around. Less guilt transfers into less drive.

The biggest strike against the bachelor is that he has not made and may not be able to make commitments. There may be no meaningful relationships in his life. He may not have even one close personal friend; he may not intend to marry any of the girls he dates; he may never become involved. Bachelors tend to be, or become, narcissistic. They are happy with this existence, but those who work for them and with them and those who loan to them, invest in them, or provide services to them sometimes walk away disgusted and discouraged at the insensitivity of the bachelor entrepreneur.

Although I am certain that there are a handful of committed bachelor entrepreneurs who have succeeded, it would be the exception rather than the rule. This is not a condemnation of bachelors; rather, it is a statement that the condition of bachelorhood does not appear to blend well with the other ingredients in the entrepreneurship recipe.

I want to describe in more detail the positive outcome of developmental distress, entrepreneur style. Part of the pleasure of my work is the pure joy they experience. It is contagious and stimulating, and, since so many people don't see the upside, I'll take some space here to read the recommendations, especially because there is a need for entrepreneurial people who may not strike out into entrepreneurship but could contribute to our work and personal lives.

Entrepreneurs see options. Many of us know brilliant people who have creative solutions to myriad problems, but who are unable to implement them. They are not entrepreneurial. If you have spent any time in or around New York City, you have undoubtedly heard countless solutions to New York City's commutation problems. The problem, in a nutshell, is how to move eight million people in and out of Manhattan twice a day with some semblance of speed, safety, and comfort. It is not insoluble. The roadbeds for high-speed electric trains exist, should someone want to fix them someday. This would permit the trains to run at speeds in excess of 120 miles an hour, as fast as the trains of Tokyo and Osaka, and cut the present commutation time in half. The commuter business would be sold to entrepreneurs. They could raise venture capital to pay for the capital investment in roadbed reconstruction and in new trains. Passenger revenues would increase as more cars were left at home.

An acceptable alternative solution is the hovercraft. Port cities such as Hong Kong and Honolulu ferry their commuters on these high-speed boats that float on top of the water. They have stewardesses who serve coffee, rolls, and the morning newspaper. There was a hovercraft experiment in New York City in the mid-1970s; the acceptance rate was fairly high, but a couple of icy days on the East River stopped service and the project folded.

There are other alternatives, such as time-sharing STOL aircraft and large helicopters, ferryboats operating on the Hudson River, and double-decker buses operating in bus-only lanes, but these projects have not been initiated.

It is possible to flip through the pages of large city newspapers that index the world's problems and discover tough problems in search of solutions. The New York City commutation problem is one of many that seem too difficult to conquer.

Fortunately, that is not the case. This particular problem, and others of long standing, have not been addressed entrepreneurially. It remains in the political arena. Few problems are solved here, but quite a bit of patronage is generated to enlarge and define the problem. In the case of New York City's commutation problem, the politicians address the issue by spending taxpayers' money to tear up and rebuild the roads, usually at rush hour, and nationalizing the railroads to crush workers' incentive.

Why could this problem be solved entrepreneurially? The principal reason is that an entrepreneur stays with a problem from beginning to end. He selects a problem that he *likes*. He does not attack a problem because his seniors assign it to him. Rather, he commits himself to one in a very personal, almost religious way. He becomes strongly identified with its solution. There is not one thought ever given to the possibility of walking away willfully from a problem before it has been solved. He will solve the problem, and the marketplace will reward him.

The greater the problem, the larger the reward. The stock market has said this for years by maintaining extraordinarily high prices on the shares of companies that lose money continually in pursuit of solutions to large problems. The best example in recent years is Genentech Corp., an early-stage biotechnology company that is attempting to develop a cure for cancer among other things. Possessing all the major risks that a company can bear—the research risk (can a product be found?), the manufacturing risk (can a product be produced?), the marketing risk (can a product be sold?) and the management risk (can the company make a profit in this business?)—Genentech's common stock was offered to the public in mid-1981 at a price of $35 in order to raise capital, and the public bid the price up to $88 by the afternoon of the day of the offering. Remember, Genentech had no products, no production facility, no marketing plan, and a management team headed by a scientist and a former venture capitalist. That spells no track record. At a price of $88 per share, Genentech was worth more than either Control Data Corp. or the Chase Manhattan Bank. If the Genentech story is not sufficient proof that problems are worth millions of dollars, Cetus Corp., another biotechnology company, went public on the heels of Genentech and raised $120 million. This offering represents the largest new issue of all time; more than Ford Motor Co., Coors, the New York Times, or any of the large new-issue public offerings of the last 25 years. Cetus Corp. possesses all of the risks that Genentech has, but it too is on the trail of a cancer cure as well as solutions to some other problems involving pesticides and fertilizer.

Although Genentech and Cetus are examples from the biotechnology field, there are companies with targets other than cancer cures with high market values and no product on the market. They abound in the fields of medicine, telecommunications, defense, and urban development, among others. For examples, MCI Telecommunications, an earlier challenger of AT&T, was forced to go public to raise capital to install microwave links long before it had revenues of any meaningful amount. The Rouse Co., rebuilder of downtown Baltimore, Boston (Faneuil Hall), and New York (South Street Seaport), has a price-earnings ratio greater than 10 times that of any other comparably sized real estate development company because it tackles the huge problem of rebuilding America's inner cities, rather than the replacement of farmlands with tract homes.

Thus, if the problem is large enough, the capital will flow to the entrepreneur to spend for developing the solution. Look at the billions of dollars that have flowed into leveraged buyouts to help smokestack America deconglomerate and downsize to more efficient companies. Further, the federal government has become increasingly liberal about solving problems with its money. Research and development tax shelters have become increasingly popular since the Economic Recovery Act of 1981. Entrepreneurs are attracted to areas where capital is easier to obtain. With capital more abundant in areas of greater problems, solutions tend to be addressed entrepreneurially.

The result, then, is that the entrepreneur picks a problem that he likes, likes the problem that he picks, and finds ample funds to spend on its solution. In this situation, the entrepreneur is able to focus intensively for long periods of time until a solution is found. It would be difficult to accomplish this if the problem were not chosen personally or if the resources of time and capital did not permit it. Fortunately, the marketplace produces problems, time, and capital for its entrepreneurs.

Intensity of focus means hours, days, and frequently weeks and months spent on one or two problems to the exclusion of all other things. The entrepreneur's mind envelops the issues at hand, blocks out all others, and wrestles with the issues until they are solved. Returning to the New York commutation problem, the initial problem that an entrepreneur would have to address would be obtaining the rights to operate the trains and all related equipment. This would require negotiating with the Department of Transportation and other branches of the federal government. Although this might take months to accomplish, an entrepreneur who adopted the New York City commutation problem would be prepared to lobby, negotiate, and arm-twist in Washington until he obtained a satisfactory result.

Washington is a tough sell. The Wright Brothers asked the U.S. Department of War for over five years to see a demonstration of their airplane. The British and French were placing orders while Washington was still saying it would not work.

Some industries that were not begun by, or peopled with, entrepreneurs are forever losing ground to politicians, because the members of these industries are not prepared to live in Washington for 90 to 120 days to talk to legislators and regulators. The venture capital industry is certainly a case in point. The Reagan Administration is killing most government guarantee loan programs plus the SBIC program without a concerted opposition. The accounting profession is another. But entrepreneurs understand that if they get into the ring with a problem and stay on their feet for a full 15 rounds, they have a good chance of winning. However, they must never take their eyes off their opponent, and they must keep on sticking him with the jab and countering with the hook.

The entrepreneur's intensity of focus is a trait common to successful scientists. Charles Darwin, for example, in 1837, at the age of 28, was a confirmed evolutionist. "Acquainted by his education and readings with the controversial evolutionary thinking of others, he had been impressed by symptoms of evolution observed during his five-year voyage of geological and biological inquiry on the *Beagle*— symptoms such as the variations in species on islands isolated from the mainland."* He then set out to *prove* that evolution was a reality. It was 15 months later that he discovered the principle to explain evolution. And 20 years after the discovery, on July 1, 1858, when all of his data had been painstakingly gathered, collected, and assembled, Darwin went public with: "On the Origin of Species by Means of Natural Selection, or the Preservation of Favored Races in the Struggle for Life." This quality—the intensity of focus—is shared with scientists by artists and entrepreneurs.

Speaking of Darwin, a precursor of today's entrepreneur was the fifteenth and sixteenth century explorer. The length of time he was able to focus intensively on a problem was frequently measured in years. One of America's favorite explorers, Christopher Columbus, is a perfect case in point. Once Columbus had convinced himself that he could sail to India by going west, he had to raise the capital and obtain the ships necessary to produce the proof. He moved to Spain from Italy and devoted six years to getting an audience with King Ferdinand and Queen Isabella (who were preoccupied with the Inquisition) and then convincing them to invest. Once, when his fortunes were at their lowest, Columbus went to England to try to raise the capital there. When the king and queen of Spain got wind of this they called Columbus in for a meeting. Two years later, he was on his way. Not everyone is prepared to focus on one single issue for six lean years. If you are from the explorer-as-entrepreneur

*D. N. Perkins, *The Mind's Best Work*, (Cambridge, Mass.: Harvard University Press, 1981).

school, note in the "courage" category that Cortez had his men burn their ships after landing in Mexico.

Chester Carlson, the inventor of xerography, spent more than 10 years finding venture capital and an engineering firm to build a prototype of the first Xerox machine. Dr. Edwin H. Land focused on a series of interrelated problems related to the polarizing of light for nearly 20 years. When Jean Harlow noticed that Howard Hughes could "concentrate that hard and for so long," she was listing one of the critical characteristics of successful entrepreneurs.

People who are more comfortable with a nine-to-five workday, a 40-hour week, and weekends free to relax, garden, or play a sport may not be able to stay focused on an entrepreneurial venture. Frequently, the weekends are merely a time to turn the afterburners on a problem, because the office is quieter and there are fewer interruptions. A 90- to 110-hour week is not uncommon for entrepreneurs in the launch phase of their company's history. Not surprisingly, the marketplace rewards the problem-attackers and the problem-solvers with capital. It understands that an intensively focused entrepreneurial team has considerable value.

Entrepreneurs take risks, choose to be vulnerable, are courageous in the face of overwhelming odds against their success—not only with respect to their particular venture, but in general about life's exigencies. Late one night, about five years ago, an entrepreneur was sitting in a bar with one of his investors having a couple of beers and discussing the problems besetting him and his company. He had recently been removed from the presidency by the board of directors because of a felony indictment brought by a disgruntled early investor. Violations in the sale of securities are felonies, and when a discouraged stockholder wants to get his money out, he normally screams, "Securities fraud!" at the top of his lungs and doesn't let up until he gets a check in his hands. The charge is serious, and there is normally more gray than black or white.

Further, this particular entrepreneur did not have the money to return to the investor and did not want to return it in any event. A fighter, he; he decided to let the court resolve the matter.

The second problem was that the company was desperately short of capital and could meet only a few more payrolls before it would be down the shooter. Many payrolls had been met by the skin of his teeth in the past, but he had been the chief executive officer then;

now he had to work through the board and various people. Time was of the essence to raise a third round of equity from the investors.

Third, the principal suppliers of raw material to the company had just announced a large price increase that would eradicate the company's gross profit margin. It had to go along with the price rise, for which more capital would be needed urgently. Further, it would need marketing dollars to pour into advertisements in order to blunt the negative effect of its price increases passed through to customers. The other usual problems—banks, personnel, accounts receivable, production delays—were there, just to add frosting to the cake.

The investor offered solace. He said he would try to raise interest for the entrepreneur in a third round, but there were problems. If the felony indictment stuck, the company would remain leaderless and probably sink. The supplier's price rise made the original business plan appear faulty and unattractive. The need for working capital for the umpteenth time caused serious doubts about the entrepreneur's management team.

The entrepreneur urged the investor to try very hard. They got up from the table and left the bar, got into separate cars, and drove off. The entrepreneur did not see a man wander into the highway in front of him, could not swerve out of the way in time, and ran over him, killing him instantly. The charge: murder two and driving while intoxicated. To all of his problems, this new one was added.

The story ends on a happy note, not because of good luck. The entrepreneur had the courage to stay in the ring with each opponent and resolve each matter one by one. The man he ran over was drunk, not he. Thus, the charge was reduced to manslaughter. The felony indictment: case dismissed, not guilty. The capital was raised for the third time, and one year later, another working capital shortage was solved with a successful public offering. Entering the 1980s, the company was one of the fastest-growing firms in the country and the entrepreneur was on everyone's pedestal, including that of the stockholder who once cried, "Stock fraud!"

Entrepreneur-watchers tend to have their favorite stories of courageous entrepreneurs. These stories become amplified and expanded over time until eventually they become Bunyanesque. In fact, the courage possessed by entrepreneurs is a quality not unique to them.

Courage is the inability to permit failure. You hear it in interviews with certain spectacular athletes such as Jack Nicklaus, in his prime,

John McEnroe, and Pete Rose. You can see it in the way Alberto Salazar tortures his body in order to win marathon races. Watch the last three rounds of the Frazier-Ali "Thrilla in Manila" and you will see the adrenalin pumping. Muhammad Ali simply would not let himself lose that fight.

Successful entrepreneurs cannot conceive of failure. Obstacles may have to be jumped, danced around, or crawled through—or maybe they'll find new paths. But obstacles will not stop them. In the worlds of David J. Padwa, founder of Agrigenetics Corp., the entrepreneur's attitude toward his obstacles is: "Shoot me. It doesn't matter. I'm going to do it anyway."

Although the obstacles may deter the entrepreneur and may knock him off his path and cause a variation in the business plan, they will not kill the company. New businesses die for a variety of reasons; but if the entrepreneur possesses most of the characteristics listed here, he will succeed. If the entrepreneur possesses only half of these characteristics, but is long on courage, the company will thrive as well.

One entrepreneur expressed well how many entrepreneurs respond to doom-and-gloom messages. We were driving to a difficult meeting with a very distressed banker, and the entrepreneur said, "What can the bank do to me if I don't pay them? They can't harm me physically. They can't hold my children for ransom. They can't kill me. I am worth more to them alive and operating my company than dead with no company. So, they have got to work with me. That's why I am smiling today even though my loan is in default. I will convince the bank that they must put down their guns and get out their pens and write me a new loan."

Tom Kelly, founder and President of TIE/communications, tells about his summer jobs during college. It seems that Kelly took a job as a truck driver for a soft drink bottler to help pay for college, and the other drivers thought that life was too sweet for young Tom. So they tried to run him over with a truck. If you are going to climb into the ring with AT&T in 1974, you don't back down from a bunch of 200-pound truck drivers in 1958. So Kelly grabbed a bottle, broke off the bottom until the piece that he held was jagged, and told his co-workers that if he got hurt they would have scars to show for it. By that afternoon, Kelly could have been elected their union representative. It takes moxie—or, as they say in Yiddish, chutzpah—to be an entrepreneur.

Courage is entirely consistent with the entrepreneur's penchant for making the complex simple. No matter how many people scream no, the entrepreneur keeps saying yes. No matter what obstacles are placed in the entrepreneur's path, he will find a way to get around them. If the job needs doing, he will do it. When an entrepreneur proposes marriage and is rejected, he says, "ok, I can deal with that. Now let's talk about the wedding."

Entrepreneurs become extraordinarily self-reliant. This was functional a half century ago when the new industries were somewhat simpler; that is, housing, transportation, broadcasting. Today, when many entrepreneurial solutions are technological, most entrepreneurs need partners to cover the areas at which they are weak.

Courage is visible. People can sense leadership and courage in others and they flock to those persons. One of the reasons leveraged buy-out entrepreneurs are able to turn around tired old companies is that the employees are happier working for a charismatic leader and perform well for him. They grew tired of the "woe-is-me" president and did not produce well for him.

Entrepreneurs are very much aware of the fact that they are set apart from the rest of society because of this unique quality. It is another thing that cannot be discussed openly with others, or even defended. Thus, entrepreneurs are even further misunderstood. Considered by many to have the ethics of a used shoestring salesman, the entrepreneur regards himself as walking stride for stride with Churchill. When the entrepreneur selects a book to read for pleasure, a rare occurrence at best, it is usually a biography of a great historical figure; someone with whom the entrepreneur can draw comparisons and be strengthened. It is for him like drinking a cup of courage.

Courage is the counterbalance for fear. The successful entrepreneur is not blind to the possibility of failure. On the contrary, he knows well about the forces that could lead to the collapse of the company he is building. As Tommy Davis, a successful venture capitalist, says, he "tunes in" the signals of doom and destruction and sets up contingency plans that will provide a soft landing. For example, when a customer's important check is "in the mail," the entrepreneur knows it is still in the checkbook. He flies to the customer's office, pretending to make a service call, and picks up the check. He picks up another order along the way. By leaving town suddenly to get the check, the entrepreneur may have aborted an important staff meeting, stood up a supplier at lunch, missed his son's Little League game. But he got the cash necessary to keep the company floating. The time-tested war cry, "Get the cash before they crash!" must have been coined by an entrepreneur.

Robert Davidoff, a veteran venture capitalist, places a lot of stock in what he calls "downside reasoning." In his investigation of an investment opportunity, Davidoff keeps boring in after the entrepreneur's contingency plans. To each answer, Davidoff fires back, "Okay, but if things don't work out that neatly, then what?" The entrepreneur who does not have multiple contingency plans to protect the company's downside does not get Davidoff's investment.

Successful entrepreneurs treat failure as the adversary. They acknowledge it more intently than any other businessman and set up contingency plans to help avoid it if the original plans lead them too close to the edge. Their courage, neither blind nor foolish, is part of a sound, and usually successful, plan for survival.

Entrepreneurs can identify problems, or potential problems, and also solve problems creatively. The creative person is fortunate in being able to avoid displeasure and gain personal satisfaction by the mere act of creating. He has a special gift that sets him apart, for he can lift himself out of the muck and mire of everyday frustrations.

Entrepreneurs are rarely sick. They are rarely overweight because excess weight slows them down and leads to sickness.

Typically, entrepreneurs don't distort the world—not many are alcoholics—and they don't participate actively in ordinary rituals, passive escapes from reality, socially acceptable outlets for hostility and aggression. That is, the typical entrepreneur does not drink, garden, go to church or synagogue regularly, play competitive sports, read fiction. He tries to recreate the world in only one way—by first focusing on reality and then improving a small portion of it through the creation of a new product or service that gives positive benefits to a large number of people. Can one ask more of a life than to be creative? The entrepreneur is indeed twice blessed.

THE NONCREATIVE ENTREPRENEUR

Many entrepreneurs are not creative, which by my operational definition means they are unable to identify a problem and then the
solution. Yet they possess most of the other characteristics common
to successful entrepreneurs. Do they become successful entrepreneurs?

Typically, these people become experts in buying businesses or
developing real estate. I refer to them as leveraged buy-out and real
estate entrepreneurs.

The Leveraged Buy-Out Entrepreneurs

When an entrepreneur possesses all of the characteristics of the trade
except the problem-finder's kind of creativity, he frequently begins
buying companies. This is not to imply that conglomerateurs such
as Charles Bluhdorn or Henry Singleton lack imagination. Rather,
they and others like them desperately want to build a business, but
they lack an idea of a problem that requires a solution. So they buy
a company and then another, and another and still others, and mold
and shape the companies they buy.

Leveraged buy-out entrepreneurs have a wonderful time putting
deals together, making all the pieces fit, trying to wring more profits
out of old companies, selling off the losers, and spinning off winners
to the public. Royal D. Little, the founder of Textron Corp., and
subsequently a successful venture capitalist with Narragansett Capital Corp., put together some marvelous companies under the same
roof, including Bell (helicopters), Speidel (watchbands), Talon (zippers),
Scheaffer (pens), Gorham (silverware), Homelite (chain saws), Jacob-
sen (mowers), and Bostitch (fasteners). The purpose of the acquisitions was to smooth the cycle of textile equipment sales picked up
in Textron's first round of acquisitions.

Charles Bluhdorn seemed to acquire for Gulf + Western companies that had entertainment possibilities. These included Paramount
Pictures Corp. and South Puerto Rico Sugar Corp. The latter owned
a large corner of the Dominican Republic on which Bluhdorn had
built a unique resort.

James J. Ling built LTV Corp, through a series of acquisitions that began with Ling Electric Contractors, which he launched in 1946 by selling his house for $3000 and then selling stock from a booth at the Texas State Fair. Ling went at the deal-making business with an unusual zeal as well as a sense of humor. After acquiring Wilson, he split it into three separate corporations: sporting goods, pharmaceuticals, and dairy products. Then he sold 20% of each of these corporations to the public. The brokerage community detected the humor as well and nicknamed these companies "Golfball, Goofball, and Meatball." They even began a rumor that Ling was going to acquire AT&T:

Broker One: Yeah, and then he's going to split it into three separate corporations and sell 20% of each one to the public.

Broker Two: What is he going to call them?

Broker One: Ding-a-Ling, Ding-a-Ling-a-Ling and Ding-a-Ling-a-Ling-a-Ling.

A leveraged buy-out is the purchase of a company by borrowing on its assets and repaying the loan in the future out of its cash flow. It is relatively simple for an entrepreneur to locate, investigate, negotiate for and acquire a $20 million (sales) company without investing more than $20,000 in legal, accounting, travel, and lodging costs. Most leveraged buy-out entrepreneurs become so adept at investigating, negotiating, and buying companies that they keep doing it. In this way they build conglomerates, potpourris of different companies. If there are several industry groupings among the companies they acquire, the brokers may later attempt to put a label on the company other than conglomerate. But the company is the result of one man's lust to do some one thing very well, and absent a solution to a problem he had first identified, he set about buying companies. As the venture capitalist Herman Goodman says of these men, they have "whims of iron."

The Real Estate Developer Entrepreneur

Another variety of entrepreneur is the man who changes the topography of the countryside rather than the shape of industries. These are real estate entrepreneurs who are expert at spotting undervalued properties, buying them, and developing them into valuable properties. They do not develop unique solutions to difficult social or industrial problems. Rather, their skills lie in deal making, in financing and managing a large construction project. As they begin building a portfolio of properties, the cash flow from the rental income of the first properties supports new borrowings. If the properties increase in value, they can refinance them with more debt and plow that into new deals. Inflation and low interest rates help the real estate developer entrepreneurs, but so great is their desire to keep building that new forms of financing are created when debt money is too dear.

Real estate developer entrepreneurs ply their trade in full view of the public and are somewhat more open to criticism if their taste runs afoul of the public. Condominium converters, for example, have been criticized for forcing the elderly out of relatively inexpensive apartments when the developers bought the building and resold the apartments to the highest bidders. The argument is that the apartments were worth more. Tongues wag when strip centers replace lovely landscapes, but the critics could have formed landmarks committees to maintain the beauty of a Cooperstown, New York or Santa Fe, New Mexico had they wished. In the real estate developer's eyes, there is social utility and his process is purely entrepreneurial.

What can a person do who is not sufficiently qualified to become an entrepreneur, but desperately wants his own business? A cold shower will not work in this case. The drive is too great, but the characteristics necessary for success are not there.

For the creative person, or the inventor, the answer is licensing the idea or the product to someone else. The licensor does not have a company to build and run, but there are some aspects to licensing that are extremely businesslike, among them negotiating the terms of licensing agreements, investigating the licensee to determine its ability to meet the sales targets that you agree to, supervising the production of the licensed product, and assisting in developing the marketing plan. Certain industries are particularly difficult to break into entrepreneurially. For instance, the medical and laboratory equipment and instrumentation industries have a high cost of entry. Hospitals, clinics, and laboratories are rarely eager to order equipment from a start-up company. The Federal Drug Administration has a say in the manufacture of those products that go on or in the body. This adds time and increases the need for venture capital, which in turn reduces the entrepreneur's ownership. Facing the costs and difficulties of a medical equipment start-up, a person who lacks most of the characteristics of the successful entrepreneur would be well advised to license his product to an existing company.

INSIGHT

Entrepreneurs have exquisite judgment, a kind of peripheral vision that allows them to see the opportunities in the marketplace which most of us miss. It's something like those pictures for children with objects "hidden" in them—if you look carefully and have an imaginative eye, you'll find them. Some refer to this perceptiveness and imagination as judgment. They do the right things to launch a company at the right time. Felda Hardymon of Bessemer Venture Partners places a great deal of value on what he calls the "lift-off entrepreneur." Although he may not be the right man to run the company above $10 million in sales, "Without the lift-off man," Hardymon says, "there would be no company." In the burgeoning field of personal computers, many are the lift-off men who turned the reins over to others once their company became full of people and departments. Steve Edelman launched Ithaca Intersystems, Ithaca, New York, but James D. ("Hank") Watson runs the company. They were 26 and 25 respectively when the company began in 1978, with Edelman selling pc boards via direct mail. Watson, who knew very little about computers, was drafted to play the role of housekeeper, and it looked as if another entrepreneurial team was being formed. As sales grew and different functions had to be filled by experienced people, Edelman's intense, highly focused entrepreneurial style became less effective. Watson, with a more diplomatic, open, communicative operating style, grew into a leadership role. He has been Ithaca's chief executive officer since 1981. However, there would not have been a company without Edelman.

These clean lines of judgment are not something one learns in school. Such judgment distinguishes a leader. A leader is willing to make a decision based on careful analysis and then design and implement an action plan. (One is comfortable sticking one's nose out if it was an adolescent survival technique.) If he stopped pointing the direction for the group, he would be a follower and get lost in the pack. To avoid anonymity, he leads and, over time, becomes better at it and increasingly comfortable with the role.

Rod Coleman, 30, one of three founders of Sage Computer Technology Corp., tells the story of how the company's plant burned down just after the first prototype was completed. The three partners were called at night by the fire department, and they rushed to the scene of the fire. One of Coleman's partners sat on the street and wept, and another was clearly very upset. Coleman was in a pay telephone calling the insurance company.

The company's drawings and source code were in another location and did not go up in flames. That was Coleman's judgment. Thus, the prototype could be rebuilt. The capital would come from the insurance company, but they can drag their feet if the urgency of the situation is not made to seem paramount. By acting quickly and systematically, Coleman had generated a $35,000 advance from the insurance company within a week.

Whether in a start-up or a crisis operating mode, the entrepreneur's judgment is apparent and continually on call. He seems to know unfailingly which invoices get paid first, to what extent he can play the float, and how far a good customer can be pushed before he takes his business somewhere else. Many people, assembly-line workers, for instance, do not exercise judgment during the course of a day. Others make one or two independent decisions during the course of a day, but nothing that affects too many lives or too many dollars. The entrepreneur makes important judgments all day long that affect all of the employees and the integrity of the business.

In his description of the start-up period at Xerox Corp., John H. Dessauer said the following:

Recently in an interview, I was waiting for the interviewer to complete his particular variation of questioning about the philosophy which guided our research and development of the xerographic technology. Instead of the usual answer, what came to mind was the Latin quotation *mihi res, non me rebus*. It is a Latin proverb that means literally, "things to me, not me to things." An idiomatic translation would be, "I shall control my destiny, my destiny will not control me." I consider this quotation to be the main explanation for our success at Xerox.*

Entrepreneurs are asked time and again to pinpoint the critical steps along the road to their success. Whether they say it in Latin or in English, they rarely say it clearly. But if you listen to them carefully, you can hear "judgment and instinct," "sixth sense," "hunch," and "lucky call."

Alan F. Shugart, founder of Seagate Technology Corp., speaking before an American Electronics Association council dinner in May 1982, said, "Cash is more important than your mother." He was only partly joking. Sandra L. Kurtzig, founder of ASK Computer Systems, Inc., speaking at the same dinner, advised entrepreneurs as follows: "... (1) believe in yourself, (2) expect to sacrifice and (3) surround yourself with people more qualified than you are in critical areas."

Making judgment calls all day long is a way of life for the entrepreneur. It is not a recommended daily affair, warns William T. Comfort, chairman of Citicorp Venture Capital, for those "who get stomach palpitations at breakfast reading that the stock market is off so-and-so many points."

One of the things that professional venture capitalists such as Bill Comfort do best is to force discipline on the entrepreneur. They have witnessed many failures; thus, through these experiences they know when decisions should be made.

It's not pressure on [the entrepreneur]. It's a question of getting him to realize what he needs for survival. Remember [entrepreneurs] are doing the impossible to start with. You're not talking about ordinary performances. But still, some companies don't finance early enough. Or they don't hire a marketing man early enough. They may be able to generate one growth base but not another. Maybe management ought to be changed. Proper financials, accounting—a lot of little companies don't have them. If someone doesn't put discipline in there to make them have it, then you'll get into problems.†

*John H. Dessauer, "Xerography—A Single Idea Transforms a Company," *IEEE Transactions on Engineering Management*, Vol. EM–15, No. 2, June 1968.
†*Forbes*, November 12, 1979.

Frequently forgotten is that J. Paul Getty was a self-made man. Although his wealth came quickly, as it does for many successful entrepreneurs, Getty's $500 investment in 1916 was worth hundreds of thousands of dollars one year later. Call it luck. The story has a lot to do with judgment.

In January 1916, Getty decided that he wanted to bid on a one-half interest in an oil lease in Muskogee County, Oklahoma. Embarrassed to bid against wealthy oil men, the young man asked a banker to bid for him. The oil men thought that the presence of the banker meant that a major was in the bidding, and they dropped out. Getty was able to buy the half interest for the sum of $500. He sold off interests to raise capital for drilling, but held on to 15%. Shortly thereafter the well came in at 720,000 barrels per day. Even at pre-OPEC prices, Getty's small interest was extremely valuable. It gave him a war chest with which to launch the Getty Oil Corp.

Entrepreneurs always say and mean, "I had a great day." Entrepreneurs are happy people, probably because their involvement in everything they do is intense, complete, and built around confidence. Even though their days are filled with people saying "no" and "you can't do that," entrepreneurs keep smiling. They do not become exhausted by anxiety; rather they get tired from working hard at what they love. And they derive pleasure from their own mental life, often to the exclusion of traditional social activities. For example, entrepreneurs are not joiners. They are not sitters, chatters, or gossipers, and their hobbies and vacations are frequently suspended until their new companies are on surer footings. Entrepreneurs don't tell "Polish jokes," or knee-slappers that denigrate minority groups. They don't choose, and often refuse, community service organizations, spicy conversation, hobbies, vacations, even a good book or movie, and they are very happy people.

If an entrepreneur does decide to do something, his involvement is total; he steamrollers no matter what it is, and enjoys his involvement thoroughly. He even enjoys business travel. The entrepreneur does not go about business travel in a casual, indirect manner through a travel agent; rather, he is likely to have an official airline guide in his briefcase in order to check available flights and arrival and departure times prior to calling a travel agent. First-time entrepreneurs are loath to delegate responsibility. Entrepreneurs are not put off easily by airline personnel who will not bend on a policy, even when it would be easy to do so. Ask an entrepreneur to tell you his favorite airline story. It will undoubtedly involve talking an attendant into bringing the plane back from the top of the runway for him or reopening the closed doors. Entrepreneurs are frequent airline passengers, and many of them have learned how to make airline travel more pleasant. Thus, while others may gripe and moan at a flight delay, the entrepreneur has checked alternative flights in his Official Airline Guide and he is on a dead run to another gate.

If you understand how entrepreneurs make airline travel work for them, several things come into sharper focus. Speed means time, time means money in a thinly staffed, start-up organization. Their ability to communicate gets stiff-necked airline personnel to agree to bend rules for them. Their willingness to delegate a function as small as buying tickets only after they have studied all available flights indicates that they are, at all times, thoroughly prepared and leaders.

The way entrepreneurs handle baggage is revealing, too. Entrepreneurs will do anything to avoid checking bags. There is too much time lost waiting for bags and too great a risk of lost baggage. The fellow who gets on the airplane with a variety of carry-on gear, who crushes your garment bag and throws his briefcase on your jacket in the overhead compartment, is an entrepreneur.

The fellow who works during a least three-fourths of the flight, with his papers and files spreading over into your seat, is an entrepreneur. This is a further annoyance since entrepreneurs usually occupy aisle seats, the quicker to disembark from.

Airport car rental desks are another place to spot entrepreneurs. They are generally first in line because they carried their baggage on and sat in aisle seats. They generally use the car rental company whose lot is nearest the airport. For example, at O'Hare airport in Chicago, Budget is practically adjacent to the terminal, whereas the other car rental companies involve much longer bus rides. Entrepreneurs, as well as other travelers in a hurry, line up for Budget while the other car rental companies are less busy. Preferred airports are those where no bus ride is required in order to rent a car. These include San Jose, Phoenix, and Albuquerque. Up until 1982, United Airlines' terminal was a short walk from Hertz Rent-a-Car at the Los

Angeles airport; this was reason enough to fly United into that busy airport.

Entrepreneurs are also noticeable when returning car rentals. Frequently, they have cut their time too short and approach the airport about 10 minutes prior to the time of departure. The entrepreneur is likely to pull up in front of the terminal, lock the car, and throw the keys to the car rental attendant with a big smile and the suggestion: "I figured one of you would be getting off soon and would need a ride back to the lot." Sometimes they do need a ride back, and the entrepreneur has solved that problem. Further, what can the car rental company do about it? By the time they call for a tow truck and go through those peregrinations, someone could have driven it back and they might rent it again.

Entrepreneurs keep score against the system, and small victories over bureaucracies such as airlines, airports, and car rental companies are pleasing.

Entrepreneurs tend to prefer sports that are open-ended and rely on the performance of the individual, rather than the team. They do not as a rule prefer fixed-time-limit, team sports such as football and hockey. More popular are baseball, the racquet sports, and golf. Entrepreneurs do not usually jog, or if they do, rarely alone. Jogging is not sufficiently intense or competitive. It is a lonely activity, and entrepreneurs tend to avoid that which is lonely. It is not easy to be happy and alone; sharing pleasure makes it more pleasureful.

The entrepreneurship period of one's life, it is worth reiterating, is only a stage in a maturation process. It is intensely inner-directed, challenge-seeking, vigorous, and experimental. But above all, it is brimful of pleasure. Some of the happiest moments in a person's life are spent in this entrepreneurial stage. As one entrepreneur friend said, "It's the most fun you can have with your clothes on." Yung Wong, a venture capitalist with Menlo Ventures and an early backer of Nolan Bushnell of Atari, said, "I enjoy working with entrepreneurs so much, I probably would do it without the equity incentive."

Entrepreneurs can "kiss" it better than anyone around. They make it simple, plain, and tell anyone they need to about it in a most convincing way. For the most part, they are excellent talkers. Among the best of the communicators is Fred Smith, founder and chief executive officer of Federal Express Corp. Smith has talked people into doing things they never intended to do. For example, he asked Federal Express' employees to pawn their watches one day in order to raise capital. He asked the Federal Aviation Administration to permit Federal Express to fly larger aircraft without going through the costly and time-consuming certification requirements necessary for people carriers. Prior to flying to Washington to meet with FAA officials, Smith addressed the Venture Capital Club of New York on the subject of communications. His message was simple: "Bureaucrats are only people. They can say yes or no. If it's no, I will ask why and keep working on changing the problem rather than finding an impossible solution." Smith was successful within the year.

Entrepreneurs like Smith understand that in order to convince people to change their minds and do something they had no intention of doing, *they* (the entrepreneurs) must control the questions. In any situation in which an entrepreneur is speaking, he is the seller and the other person is the buyer. Bankers, investors, customers, and suppliers are always the buyers and the entrepreneur is trying to obtain money, an order, or extended payment terms. It is impossible to pull a yes out of a buyer who is trained in problem finding if the buyer controls the questions. If the seller asks the questions, he opens up the buyer, relaxes him, and wins his approval.

Picture if you will a conversation between the general manager of a start-up retail computer store and the credit manager of an established personal computer manufacturer.

Scenario One

Credit manager: Our terms are three computers with the first order, $10,000 COD. Take it or leave it.

Store manager: But can't you make an exception for me?

Credit Manager: Who are you? There are plenty of you, but there is only one of me. You need me, I don't need you.

The conversation is ended. The credit manager will ship COD or not at all. The manufacturer passes up an order and the store manager has three fewer computers that he could be selling. An entrepreneurial store manager would go about the situation much differently. He would control the conversation with questions in order to determine whether he should work on changing the problem or on finding a solution. More than likely, the credit manager has a small amount of discretion and leeway, but in refusing to ship unless the minimum order is $10,000 and the terms are COD, he is carrying out a policy. Thus, the entrepreneur can determine through communications that he should work on the solution, not the problem. The alternative solution might go something like this.

Scenario Two

Store manager: Would you drop ship to a customer if they paid you COD?

Credit manager: Yes, if UPS picked up a total of $10,000.

Store manager: Well, the wholesale cost for each computer is $3,300 and the retail is likely to be $5,000. So, if I sell two computers you will have your $10,000 and I will have the third computer for my store, right?

Credit manager: If we get $10,000 you get three computers, and I don't care where we deliver them as long as it is to your market.

Store manager: But I can't sell two computers unless I have a model on the floor for my salesmen to demonstrate. Can you ship one on 30-day net terms and let me demonstrate our skill at selling?

Credit manager: No way.

Store manager: Well, can you tell me if your district sales manager could demo the computers in sales meetings that I set up?

Credit manager: You'll have to ask him.

Store manager: We are good salesmen. Does that count for anything, or is good credit more important?

Credit manager: I prefer cash above both of the others.

Store manager: But the district manager might prefer hitting his targets, right?

Credit manager: Could be.

Store manager: May I tell him that you approved delivering three computers if he and I can go out and sell two of them?

Credit manager: If UPS picks up $10,000, I don't care what deal you work with him.

With this much of a change in the rules, the store manager can go to work on the district sales manager to wangle a demo unit and to get him involved in order to make the two required sales. If the store manager is successful, he will have (1) demonstrated his sales ability, (2) bought inventory with the customer's money, and (3) established credit with the supplier.

Entrepreneurs enter into conversations with people in order to learn things as well. They talk to street vendors while they munch a hot dog in between meetings, they talk to taxi drivers to learn about cities, they talk to fellow travelers to learn whatever they have to say, and they talk to just about anybody else, from children to geriatrics. Talking is a form of entertainment, a means of relaxation, that eases the strain of being an entrepreneur. "As long as I keep talking to the IRS," said one entrepreneur who had not paid his company's with-holding taxes for 18 months, "they aren't shooting."

Raising money is talking—an axiom frequently stated by entre-preneur-watchers. An entrepreneur long on communications skills will persuade investors that he could sell used shoelaces and in the process, persuade them to invest. It should be noted though that in this area, many entrepreneurs fall short because of boundless enthu-siasm unstructured and not yet organized. It is not often the case that a complex, inner-directed, intense, creative, guilty, formerly deprived engineer who takes the sudden leap into entrepreneurship will also be blessed with the gift of gab. Therefore, the need for the achiever partner who is an excellent communicator; the former corporate manager who is persuasive and convincing. A company is more likely to be built by William Hewlett (engineer) and David Packard (marketing), a Mr. Inside and Mr. Outside, than by Fred Smith, a Mr. Inside-Outside. Complete, self-contained, all-in-one entrepreneurs such as Fred Smith are rare.

EFFECTIVE COMMUNICATION

A lot of what has been written in the field of communications is useful, particularly to entrepreneurs who have sung from the corporate choir book for many years and have lost their personal voice. I recommend books, tapes, and seminars on public speaking, negotiating, and effective communication. The most useful tools in becoming an effective communicator are the following three:

1. Understand the buyer/seller formula.
2. Control the conversation with questions.
3. Understand the other person's gut values.

Understand the Buyer/Seller Formula

In any conversation involving two people, one is the seller and the other is the buyer. The seller is a problem-solver and the buyer is a problem-finder. What is being offered generally is a solution, and it is up to the buyer to accept or reject it. Doctors, lawyers, teachers, and other professionals, merchants, and entrepreneurs are sellers. Patients, clients, students, customers, and other problem-finders are buyers. The coming together of a buyer and a seller is a market.

Now in a market, the buyer is protected if he makes the wrong decision. The seller, however, is killed by an incorrect decision. Incompetence, as Laurence J. Peter instructed us, is rewarded in a hierarchical organization. But in an entrepreneurial organization, incompetence kills. Thus, if a buyer says no to a seller, the seller will be out the time and the cash and the buyer will be doing what the corporation pays him to do: Listen politely, but say no. Change is worse than the problem.

If you have a better mousetrap, the world will not beat a path to your door. Inventors and entrepreneurs spent years taking energy-saving devices to Detroit in a thoroughly wasted effort. It is critical that the entrepreneur understand that no matter how effective is the solution he has created, buyers are not likely to purchase it unless they are sold. The company will require a marketing plan and people to implement it. Marketing is communicating.

Control the Conversation with Questions

Using a pencil Somers H. White, a communications consultant and uniquely gifted speaker and trainer of speakers, explains the methodology of convincing people to do things for you that they had no intention of doing. White asks to borrow a pen. The willing victim hands White a pen. He says thank you, then breaks it in half and throws the pieces away.

Before the person can speak, White hands him or her a pencil and says, "Here's a ten-cent pencil to replace your eighty-nine-cent pen. Are we even?" he asks.

The willing victim replies, "No."

White continues, "But have you thought about how much more useful a pencil is than a pen? Why, a pencil can do many more things than a pen. I bet you can name 15 things that you can do with a pencil that you can't do with a pen." The willing victim thinks for a second. He begins naming the things—erase, write upside down, shade—and then gets into the game with gusto. By the time he crosses 10 on his way to 15, he has forgotten that the smiling questioner broke his pen.

If you can control the meeting with questions, White says, you can convince people to do things for you. Translating this to a meeting to raise venture capital, the entrepreneur should ask questions continually. For example, he should find out the names, industries, and stage of development of the venture capitalists' other investments. This gives him a feeling for the level of technical sophistication of his audience. He can pace himself once he knows that and the amount of time they have to spend with him at the meeting.

The entrepreneur should insert questions throughout his presentation, on the order of:

How many shipments should we have made by now, in your opinion?

Do you think we could be charging more, or pricing it differently?

What is your experience with that corporation as a customer?

Would you have done it that way?

Venture capitalists, bankers, and other buyers are star-struck by the energy, creativity, and courage of entrepreneurs. When they are asked questions by an entrepreneur who is an effective communicator, it has the effect of flattery. It draws them into the entrepreneur's world and enables them to identify more closely with the entrepreneur. They draw energy from the conversation and become convinced that they would like to sit on this man's board for the next five years. Persuasion is not hard selling; rather, it is asking questions, learning about the buyer, and then involving him in the entrepreneurial life.

Understand the Other Person's Gut Values

Nothing appears simpler on the surface, but is least remembered in practice, than to be aware of the buyer's gut values. This is done primarily visually, when the entrepreneur first sees the buyer. The first things we notice about someone else are sex and age. Most buyer/seller encounters are male-on-male, but the "gut values" rule applies no matter what the sex(es). Assume that the entrepreneur is at the median age of 27 and that the buyer is 53 years of age. As the entrepreneur enters the buyer's room, he logs in the following data: "Male, born about 1930, raised in the Depression, probably served in Korea, delayed in getting a degree, probably did not get into the job stream until his mid-20s." The entrepreneur sizes the buyer up as born and raised poor and unwilling to take chances with an overweening, spoon-fed, draft-dodging, child-of-the-sixties-hence-pothead 27-year-old.

They exchange pleasantries and do the sit-down, coffee, lovely-office dance. But early in the conversation, the 27-year-old must find an opening and let the 53-year-old know that his suffering and personal drive to overcome Depression roots and a GI bill college degree have not gone unnoticed. It's tricky, but necessary. The 27-year-old can blow it by appearing to be a "wise-ass," or he can do it just right and gain a supporter.

"Tell me what was it really like growing up during the Depression?" simply will not work.

A much more plausible statement would be, "You remind me somewhat of [a thirties or forties man-of-the-people hero like Gene Sarazen or Red Grange]. You wouldn't happen to be from Illinois, would you?" If he thinks the entrepreneur is sincere (and entrepreneurs are, if not sincere, at least intense), the buyer will leap at the opportunity to talk about himself. The buyer will say a number of things about his origins or family or background that will provide hooks to hang on later in the conversation. The important things for the entrepreneur to listen for are gut values.

It is likely that the 53-year-old buyer has positive feelings for things traditional, conventional; he is cautious, likes stability, doesn't want to be upset. The entrepreneur could adjust his presentation to be responsive to those values. He could say things like, "We've developed a cautious attitude at our shop," "We avoid risk and uncertainty in our manufacturing operations; quality control procedures are out of an old engineering textbook", or "it's the tried and true for us; we don't run a plant that looks like Fibber McGee's closet."

With a younger buyer, perhaps in his middle 40s, the gut values were formed in the early 1950s. Since this was the era of the "Silent Generation," not many things touched his life that were of national moment. He will have to be drawn out more to determine whether he was early fifties—Doris Day, Guy Mitchell—or rock 'n roll and Elvis. In any event, it is critical to take an accurate reading of the buyer's gut values before proceeding with the presentation. All could be lost by using a painful word or phrase when a friendlier one would have worked miracles.

No one understands these communications techniques better than the entrepreneur. It is a matter of winning or losing with him and an area in which he invests the time needed to be skillful at it. In many instances, the communications skills were developed in childhood and expanded as the child matured. Some entrepreneurs have an inbred sensitivity to the listener. With other entrepreneurs, perhaps those whose careers began in the sciences, communications skills have to be learned and practiced.

FINDING A MANAGER

An entrepreneurial venture is sprung by someone who can see opportunity where no one has shown him it exists, someone who can see pieces of his jigsaw puzzle flying about among pieces of dozens of other puzzles and pull them from the air, someone who cannot conceive of lightning striking *his* house, someone who knows the right things to do but not how to do them. In other words, he has certain unique gifts, but practicality is not necessarily one of them.

Therefore, the entrepreneur often finds that when he must prepare his presentation of himself in the everyday world of business, he needs someone who can do business-related tasks accurately, practically, and efficiently. It is his way to safeguard against disaster or failure, so he looks for a partner. Let's call that partner a manager.

Although it is the initial dissatisfaction, followed by entrepreneurial insight and energy, that brings about radical innovations, very few entrepreneurs succeed without a strong partner to *manage* the companies they launch. For the most part, the partners are selected from among managers—people who are leaders in business and government, professionals who take pride in bottom line achievements, love comfort and affluence, and know how to organize and manage business.

Some entrepreneur-manager pairs who have been successful are these:

Edwin Land	Julius Silver, attorney
Chester Carlson	John Dessauer, Xerox executive
Malcolm McLean	Disque Dean, investment banker
Kemmons Wilson	Walter Johnson, hotel executive
Steve Jobs (Apple Computer)	A. C. Markulla, marketing executive at Intel
David Packard	William Hewlett

In fact, successful entrepreneurs spend a great deal of their time with achievement-oriented managers because this team can continually convince managers in other areas to support them, supply them with venture capital, credit, and legal and accounting advice, ship them product on terms, and take a seat on their board of directors.

Note some of the differences between the entrepreneur and the manager. The entrepreneur is energetic, creating piles of work for the manager to sort through, implement, or dispose of. Where the entrepreneur is extraordinarily energetic, the manager is extraordinarily thorough. The median age of the manager is 16 years greater than that of the entrepreneur. The manager is more likely to be married, live in the suburbs, drive a luxury American car, and vote Republican. The entrepreneur is as likely to be married as single, lives in the city, drives a European import, and votes Independent. The entrepreneur believes that his greatest achievements lie ahead of him; the manager is optimistic about the future, but pleased with his accomplishments to date. The manager is likely to have accumulated some assets whereas the entrepreneur has nothing to lose.

Occasionally, but not with great frequency, there exist entrepreneurs who combine in one person the qualities of both the entrepreneur and the manager. Venture capitalists do handsprings in their offices when they are in the presence of such a person. So few are these Renaissance men that they can be named within a few minutes and most entrepreneur-watchers will nod their heads in agreement. At the top of everyone's list is Dr. Henry E. Singleton, the founder and chief executive officer of Teledyne Corp. Founded in 1961, Teledyne had sales in 1981 of $3.2 billion in aviation equipment, electronic components, and specialty metals, and earned $412.3 million, for a return of over 24% on stockholders' equity. Dr. Singleton's holdings of Teledyne comon stock, 7.8% of the total, exceed $250 million at current market prices.

Dr. Singleton began his career as an engineer at Litton, where he moved up the corporate ladder. In his last important assignment there, he headed the team that developed the inertial-navigation system for guided missiles, a project that required three years of concentrated, uninterrupted effort. "There are so many people who have done extraordinary things who don't have so much intelligence," Singleton told Nation's Business in June 1981. "They just keep plugging away. I have a great deal of patience to continue to work on projects for a long time. To stay with it is what is helpful."*

Among the other mature entrepreneurs on most lists are Jesse I. Aweida, founder of Storage Technology Corp., David J. Padwa, founder of Agrigenetics Corp., An Wang, founder of Wang Laboratories, Inc., the late Charles Tandy, founder of Tandy Corp. and several spin-offs such as Tandycrafts, Frederick W. Smith, founder of Federal Express Corp., Royal M. Little, founder of Textron Corp., Nolan Bushnell, founder of Atari Inc., and Paul M. Cook, founder of Raychem Corp. This list is not complete, nor was it compiled by a consensus of the

---

*Arthur M. Louis, "What Makes Tycoons Tick," Nation's Business, June 1981.

proverbial "19 bishops" of venture capital. But, the names on this list are representative of mature entrepreneurs, capable of managing every aspect of a new business while simultaneously providing the creative spark, drive, and insight.

Before teaming up, to the point where the entrepreneur suddenly bolted out of the organizational hierarchy to do something of greater personal value, the two had similar workplace histories. The shared experiences are grounds for forming partnerships. The key to the entrepreneurial venture capital process is the respect that these two groups maintain and continue to feel for one another, because venture capital firms are usually headed up by managers. Thus, the perfect entrepreneurial team is made up of an entrepreneur and a manager: a dissatisfied, insightful, energetic, intense individual paired with a competent, hard-working, thorough corporate executive who understands how to get things done. John H. Dessauer, the manager who worked most closely with Chester Carlson to bring about the modern-day miracle known as xerography, explained to the Institute of Electronic and Electrical Engineers (IEEE) in 1967 how he and Carlson worked together:

> In 1948, what was then the Haloid Company employed 672 people, had annual sales of $8.6 million, and manufactured photographic papers, photocopy papers, and photocopy cameras. . . .

> [In 1937], Chester Carlson . . . employed by the Patent Department of P. R. Mallory . . . observed the constant need for faithful reproductions of documents and drawings . . . Carlson deliberately set out to invent a new copying process . . . After many unsuccessful efforts, he achieved the first xerographic image on October 22, 1938 in Brooklyn, New York.

> Every known aspect of Carlson's invention stemmed from scientifically unexplored phenomenon. . . . in spite of these shortcomings, Haloid decided to gamble everything . . . because we thought the potential was very great . . . Although the decision had some logic to it, basically it was faith.

> We had to solve some very unusual scientific problems. . . . We had to recruit solid-state physicists. . . . We had to control humidity. . . . to convince technical people that electrostatics would work in human conditions.

Despite our own trepidations about any possible eventual success, we had to keep convincing our business management to continue to make available the money, equipment and personnel necessary to complete the research.

Perhaps the greatest struggle of all was the effort to convince our management and business people that the world could use a large machine like the 914, provided it was reliable, serviceable, easy to operate, and inexpensive.

The importance of the entrepreneurial team is made all the more clear when one considers the things that are most likely to go wrong in small companies. It is rare that the business plan is faulty and equally rare that the product fails to perform. These two problem areas are soluble by the entrepreneur rather than the manager-partner. The biggest problems are in areas that lend themselves to management solutions.

In a December 1981 special report prepared by the National Science Foundation, entitled *Problems of Small, High-Technology Firms*, 1,232 responding firms ranked their biggest problems as listed in Exhibit 2.1.

Given the profile of the entrepreneur—intense, complex, driven, energetic—it is unlikely that he would be the best candidate to design and implement key personnel stock incentive plans, develop a cash flow budget or an R&D limited partnership financing to maintain a high level of research and development, negotiate a working capital line of credit with commercial bankers, or make certain that the company is in compliance with government regulations. These tasks are pleasureful for the manager because they require attention to detail, thoroughness, communications skills, and the many tools that he learned to handle quite skillfully in his previous corporate occupation.

PULLING THE PIECES TOGETHER

Young and old, pathfinders and traditional thinkers, energetic and thorough—many people become frustrated in their work and dream of having their own business. Venture capitalists tirelessly search for

EXHIBIT 2.1. Problem Areas of Major Concern to Small Firms.

Problem Area	Percentage of Firms Considering It a Major Problem
1. The ability to provide competitive salaries and benefits to key personnel	69.0%
2. The ability to maintain an adequate level of R&D activity	68.0%
3. Dealing with government regulations	67.0%
4. Obtaining venture and working capital	66.0%
5. Attracting and keeping personnel	63.0%
6. Dealing with government procurement regulations	62.0%
7. Ability to obtain capital equipment as needed	62.0%
8. Marketing a product once it has been successfully developed	60.0%
9. Undertaking high-risk R&D projections	60.0%
10. Obtaining information in federal publications	57.0%
11. Patenting and licensing	29.0%

Source: National Science Foundation, *Problems of Small, High-Technology Firms,* December 1981.

successful entrepreneurs to put their chips on. Both groups, entrepreneurs and their backers, want to know in advance: Do they have what it takes?

No magic formula exists to help us determine who should start a business and who should not. But I believe that successful entrepreneurs have a majority of the characteristics and the personal history details I described, and those may be the best of the clues and caveats available.

Since it was not my intent to offer a final word, potential entrepreneurs can use the information and the summary descriptions as a baton. For the reader who sees too few similarities between the lists and himself or herself, leave the conducting to someone else. If the characteristics match up, take the stick and run with it!

3

THE ENTREPRENEURIAL PROCESS

THE ENTREPRENEURIAL REVOLUTION

The combination of available capital and publicity is pulling people out of their corporations to become entrepreneurs. People who once dreamed of launching their own business but hesitated and let the dream pass now throw caution to the winds and take their shot. The models of success are there to emulate in practically every American city of any size. Entrepreneurs are succeeding more frequently too, because they are quicker to join forces with managers, counsellors, and seasoned veterans, and there are more support systems in place to help them. Success breeds success.

Yet it is not for everyone. Relatively few people have got what it takes—the background of guilt, deprivation, and mother-stroking, the insight, energy, creativity, and courage, and the ability to focus intensely on a single problem for a sustained period of time. This odd assortment of baggage, when carried by a person who has become dissatisfied with his or her role in a large corporation and who has the insight to formulate a problem in search of a solution and the energy to solve it, will doubtless produce an entrepreneur.

Yet the costs of entrepreneurship are very high. Although the entrepreneur is quickly becoming a folk hero, with capital and counsellors extending support and assistance, entrepreneurship still takes its toll. The entrepreneur must "sign up," in the sense of giving up friends, sports, social activities, and frequent contact with the outside world. His or her family suffers—if he or she still has one. The entrepreneur's savings are depleted. He or she goes deeply into debt, borrowing from anyone who can be persuaded to extend a loan and leveraging practically every asset that he or she thinks has collateral value.

Clearly, this is fanatical behavior. Only certain kinds of people from certain kinds of backgrounds are going to behave in this manner. It is a form of behavior that, although increasingly common, cannot be emulated by merely anyone, nor should it be. Entrepreneurs behave in special ways. They are born, not made.

The entrepreneurial process, on the other hand, is a series of defined steps that an entrepreneur takes in order to become successful. The process is a discipline that successful entrepreneurs have taught us, and it can be taught to others. The objective of teaching the entrepreneurial process is to give ordinary people more scope for becoming their own masters. Non-entrepreneurs can learn the entrepreneurial process in order to create mini-revolutions in their organizations. Not since the Industrial Revolution have the United States and Western Europe witnessed such a large-scale demand for the dismemberment of large corporations and governments and a return to individual skills exchanged among cottage-sized companies. There are not enough entrepreneurs to cause a revolution, but if enough individuals learn the entrepreneurial process, the return to individualism can come about quickly. Therefore, it is important for non-entrepreneurs to learn the entrepreneurial process in order to participate in the Western world's current revolution without going through the entrepreneurial stage of growth and development.

What form is the entrepreneurial revolution taking? We can see the most obvious change in the end of the era of big business corporations. Virtually everything big is perceived as "bad" by an enlightened populace—morally as well as socially nonuseful. People today have no use for large governments, corporations, newspapers. The telephone company is being dismembered in order to compete. Entrepreneurs will eventually force a major overhaul of the U.S. postal system as overnight air courier and mini-post office companies offer superior service at competitive prices. Unemployment in the industrial Northeast in the 1980–1982 recession will be a mere fraction of what it will be when robots and factory automation are hired and unionized labor is laid off. The change in the way people think about large corporations as providers of stable, secure jobs will be cataclysmic.

The principal catalyst of the demise of bureaucratic methods of production is technology. Every major decision in a large corporation must now factor in a technological option. For example, the decision to send someone to a customer to handle a complaint must now weigh the option of sending a floppy disk with maintenance instructions to the customer overnight via Federal Express, or having the customer transmit the printout via modem and data lines to the manufacturer's computer for readout and repair. The cost of sending a person, perhaps $1,000 including room and board, is replaced by $50 of telephone time or courier charges. This is one of thousands of examples. Managers must continually ask themselves when faced with any decision: "What labor-saving technology should I use to accomplish this task?" The end is in sight for large organizations that block or stifle that question.

Large corporations and institutions, so effective in organizing the means of production over the last 80 years, are organized from the top down. Senior executives sit in offices trying to arrange what the workers in offices below do with their time and minds while the lower-echelon office workers try to arrange what the factory workers do with their time and hands. The fundamental difficulty with this process is that a better educated, younger white-collar worker does not want to be organized, and the factory worker must metamorphose from a hand worker to a brain worker as automation and robotics makes his or her job obsolete.

It is also apparent that the concept of freedom includes being able to select not only one's lifestyle at home, but also one's atmosphere at work. Molecular biologists, electrical engineers, and computer scientists, the three most important workers in the last years of the twentieth century, have been telling us for several years now that they prefer to work among their peer groups (i.e., major research activities going on nearby) with excellent recreational facilities within an easy drive (i.e., skiing, water sports, hiking). Thus Brooklyn offers a major technical university, but lacks the other amenities. Burlington, Vermont offers skiing but is low on neighborhood think tanks. The new Silicon Valleys appear to be areas around Boulder, Colorado, Albuquerque, New Mexico, and Portland, Oregon. When Cetus Corp., the Berkeley, California biotechnology company offered Dr. Winston Brill, a molecular biologist at the University of Wisconsin, the moon and seven stars to join Cetus as head of its agricultural genetics laboratory, Dr. Brill agreed, but on the following terms: Cetus must put the lab in Madison, Wisconsin, and Dr. Brill must be allowed to maintain his position with the university while working for Cetus.

One may consider Chicago a gruesome place to live because of its frigid winters, but it has numerous major research institutions and a wide variety of outdoor recreational facilities, including Lake Michigan with its miles of beaches and nearby skiing in the winter. However, if a science-based worker enjoys Chicago's type of water recreation, but abhors its winters, he would naturally seek out California, where he can improve the weather without suffering a decline in the intellectual level of his peer group. This kind of movement among the most sought-after workers is commonplace. It is a constant exercising of one's right to choose his own lifestyle.

I foresee a new market forming to service this need. Small, entrepreneurial companies will offer contracts to large corporations to attempt to fit workers' needs into job specifications. The small companies will write software for microcomputers which will interrogate workers about their lifestyle desires, work habits, skill areas. The workers will be happier because they are being permitted a large degree of individual freedom. There will be far less need for trade unions. The questionnaires will turn up other interesting results as well. They will uncover a surplus of would-be, part-time, part-risk entrepreneurs. These are the kinds of people who will take advantage of quick-changing, cost-saving technology.

The entrepreneurial revolution will be most evident in the manner in which large corporations relate to part-time, part-risk entrepreneurial employees. Among other things, the large corporations will subcontract with groups of employees, certain production and distribution operations.

A workable mechanism would be for management of large corporations to define the modules of work that it wants done and then to invite "bids" from parts of the staff who think they can accomplish the module more efficiently and happily than under the existing corporate hegemony. Sometimes the bids will be made individually, sometimes by groups of friends within the company, and occasionally by a group made up of people within and without the company.

The bidder will establish with the corporation how much of its existing services (production, marketing, etc.) he or she would wish to use. The bidder would also agree with the corporation that his or her share of the capital gain might be if the venture is sold off or incorporated and taken public in the future. The corporation could act as a lender to the bidder, or an investor. The bidder, if not relatively risk-averse, could agree to pay the corporation back if the project fails. In more risk-averse bidder groups, the bidders would want to be paid by the corporation with the consequence of owning far less of their project.

Some attempts have been made in the direction of rearranging work into modules. The pressure to do so is high turnover, with attendant training and retraining costs and declining productivity. Robert Ford, an AT&T executive, stated in a *Harvard Business Review* article in 1973 that the production of telephone directories for the state of Indiana required 33 minimum-wage employees to accomplish 21 tasks, many of them repetitive verification steps. It took 28 new hirings in one year to keep the group at 33.

The reform initiated at AT&T was to allow certain employees to "own" their telephone books or to "own" certain letters of the alphabet and to be responsible for them. Employee turnover fell and errors were reduced as well because the workers knew they were responsible. The system was introduced to the New Orleans Yellow Pages sales department where more than $100,000 in extra advertisements was sold. Mr. Ford argues for introducing employee responsibility for modules of work, but does not create the reward system. He says they ". . . ought to be paid more."

Ten years after the Ford article, it is possible to develop an innovative reward system. An entrepreneurial contract can be entered into for the compilation of the directory (or a letter of the alphabet in a big city directory) and responsibility vested over the period of a performance contract in the individual or small group responsible for that letter. Once the group delivers a satisfactory job and makes a profit, it will probably want to bid again the next year, and it may want to bid on other directories of other telephone companies or directory producers. The group may even seek to spin off from the telephone company and seek complete independence. A public offering and capital gains could be the eventual goal.

Where we will see performance contracts first is in computer assisted manufacturing (CAM). The microcomputer is so fast, inexpensive, and easy to learn that young people will be entering the workforce fairly computer-fluent. They will be assigned to production tasks, and it will rather quickly occur to them that these tasks could be best done by desktop computers. They will recommend that innovation, in all likelihood, be rebuffed; then they will "bet their job" by offering a peformance contract. H. Ross Perot was the pioneer in performance contracts when in 1964 he launched Electronic Data Systems Corp. (EDS) to operate the data processing departments for large corporations with their people and their equipment, which he purchased, and at their budgets. The large corporations were delighted to receive solutions for the price they were then paying for problems. As EDS added more and more clients, it would sell off some of their equipment and not accept all of their employees. In that way, EDS' profitability expanded geometrically to approximately 50% of revenues. When it went public in 1969, the market pushed EDS' valuation to more than $1 billion. The market speaks loud and clear: Solve production problems for U.S industry, Mr. or Ms. Entrepreneur, and we will make you rich.

Another change that will be evident in the entrepreneurial revolution is that large corporations will rent out time on their underused computers and assembly lines to people with entrepreneurial ideas about how to introduce cost-saving or revenue-producing processes to the corporations. The employee will indicate to his or her employer that if he or she were able to modify certain things in the production process, the quality of the products shipped would increase, and the number of returns and rejects would drop sharply. The employer will accept the recommendation, knowing that if he or she does not, the worker can take the ideas to a competitor.

The employer and worker will then negotiate a contract. The

worker can resign, start an entrepreneurial company, and sell the service back to the employer. Or the worker can enter into a performance contract at a price equal to that division's current dollar value of losses due to product returns and rejects, with the worker guaranteeing to save the company that exact amount by implementing his or her idea. A third alternative could be a new company jointly owned by the worker and the company, funded by the company, which would implement the worker's quality assurance idea and then sell it to other manufacturers. Other alternatives might include variations on these three forms or partial entrepreneuring within a large corporation.

There is an inadequate amount of venture capital and too few brave yet fanatical entrepreneurs willing to risk everything they own to cause the entrepreneurial revolution to happen. Workers in large companies will be the prime movers, and that is why it is important that the entrepreneurial process be learned. The most successful large corporations of the future will be confederations of entrepreneurs. Whereas corporations at one time bragged about how many workers they employed, in the future they will boast of how many subcontracts they let to quasi-employee groups. I can foresee the market research department of a large corporation saying to the vice president of marketing one day: "Several of us have developed an interactive system that operates on ordinary cable TV to test a product quickly before we put it into production. Viewers will be able to see it, test it, and respond within 48 hours, and we will not need to hire any interviewers. The entire market research job can be done via telecommunications. You may not want to risk your job on this new system, nor do we want to risk ours. So we are willing to do the job on our newest product ideas for you as a subcontractor. If we are right, we would be willing to sell the service to you on a one-year exclusive basis before offering it to the market. If our idea is wrong, we will put it back on the shelf—no harm done, because we will run the traditional market research method in tandem. If you refuse us the chance to do it here, we will resign and offer it to the competition."

Do not think for a moment that corporate life is not moving inexorably in that direction and at this very moment. The microcomputer, inexpensive means of transmitting data rapidly, and intelligent software packages that approach artificial intelligence make the once unthinkable not just thinkable but doable.

Nabisco, Gillette, General Mills, 3M, Beatrice, and other consumer goods producers are investing heavily in venture capital funds in order to see how entrepreneurs are changing the way consumer products will be sold in the future. The answers are not in yet, but the conventional department store can be replaced today by a catalog TV show on cable television and order processing via a home computer, touch-tone telephone, or conventional mail. People like direct mail purchasing because they receive more information about the products than the clerk in the store can generally give them. The entrepreneurial revolution will enable us to order goods and services at home, thus freeing up time for more recreation.

THE ENTREPRENEURIAL PROCESS

If you accept the premise that we are returning to an era of individualism and the subcontracting by large bureauracies to entrepreneurs of their production and distribution operations, where will all of the entrepreneurs come from? Everyone cannot be an entrepreneur, because the planet could not support that much combustible force. However, an increasing number of people can learn the entrepreneurial process. Fortunately, more than 200 business schools and several seminar companies are teaching it. What I have seen of the instruction thus far is not particularly effective. Accumulating wealth, raising capital, and strengthening communications skills seem to be stressed. The step-by-step process is not addressed. I think it needs to be described and discussed, and although thoughts are not supported by pedagogy, they are the result of hands-on and first-hand experience.

There are six steps in the entrepreneurial process, and they are as follows:

1. Identifying the opportunity
2. Creating the solution
3. Planning the business

4. Selecting the entrepreneurial team
5. Producing and test-marketing the product
6. Raising venture capital

Identifying the Problem

Successful entrepreneurs have in common a unique ability to formulate problems. In economic terms, this means identifying a market or a problem in search of a solution. One of the compliments managers pay to entrepreneurs whom they join usually goes something like this: "She has the ability to see the whole market, from those customers who are ready to buy to those who need years of education."

Gloria Steinem, the co-founder of *Ms.* magazine, is an extremely successful entrepreneur. She problem-formulated brilliantly in the wispy, smoky arena known as "women's liberation." This problem area runs the gamut from women not receiving equal pay for equal work to sexual harassment on the job to abortion to the political arena. Ms. Steinem absorbed it all, and realized that the cacophony of women's liberation problems needed to be indexed. What better way to sell an index to a market eager to learn more about the women's liberation problems than through a magazine? Broadly read magazines attract advertisers, and so the index should pay for itself.

But Ms. Steinem perceived that corporations would pay her to help them solve large problems dealing with women as customers. Truck drivers were increasingly becoming husband-and-wife teams in the 1970s, and the truck manufacturers wanted to learn more about designing a cab suitable for women. What better place to go for help than to the women's liberators? A $250,000 consulting contract from a major truck manufacturer has more profit than the sale of $250,000 of advertisements in the magazine.

Let us assume that the women's liberation market was not problem-formulated in detail, but, rather, that an entrepreneur opened up shop to begin selling services to truck manufacturers to help them redesign cabs for a newly created female driver market. The entrepreneur in this instance creates the solution before properly identifying the market. The truck manufacturers would rebuff the entrepreneur in one of the following ways:

"I was not aware that we had the problem that you are describing."

"We would like some assistance in solving that problem, but how do we know you have the solution?"

"We have the problem, you have a solution, but what endorsements do you have in this field?"

Many new business failures are the result of inadequate problem formulation. Entrepreneurs make the mistake less frequently than small businesspersons and large corporations. It is the plight of small businesspeople, primarily merchants, to open stores whose products interest them and in convenient or available locations; unfortunately, the market is not interested. Large corporations rush solutions to the market, then try to brute force them onto and then off the shelves with millions of dollars of advertising, only to pull the product a few years later after years of red ink. Feminine deodorant spray is a case in point. "Real" cigarettes produced a $45 million loss for R. J. Reynolds. Topps brought us chocolate bubble gum in 1980. Watching McDonald's Corp. grope for new customers in an attenuating market with such obvious gestures toward the black market as McRib Sandwiches makes one realize how quickly a meteorically successful company can lose its entrepreneurial zest. Even the mighty Xerox Corp. is blowing it in the personal computer market by selling dumb hardware instead of solutions-oriented software. One reason that franchised stores do so well—according to the International Franchise Association, 95% of all franchised stores succeed for at least three years—is that their franchisor problem-formulates for them and writes out the solution delivery method in long, detailed training and operations manuals.

Entrepreneurs and artists have many things in common. Both are problem solvers. The artist tries to solve many of life's problems by expressing solutions on canvas. The entrepreneur focuses intensively on one problem, formulating and reformulating it until he or she is ready to pull out one huge canvas and begin painting. Both species, the artist and the entrepreneur, are individualists, unconventional, sensitive, imaginative, intense, complex, driven, and creative. Although one could argue the differences, the similarities are greater in number. Therefore, the study of creativity among artists by

Jacob Getzels and Mihaly Csikszentmihalyi* has a bearing on our investigation of the entrepreneurial process.

The participants in the study were young male art students. Each participant first completed a still life for the researchers based on an arrangement he made from a collection of objects provided. Afterwards, the artists answered several questions.

One question was: "Could any of the elements in your drawing be eliminated or altered without destroying its character?" The objective of the investigators was to determine whether a student considered his work fixed or flexible.

The answers to this question enabled Getzels and Csikszentmihalyi to draw a correlation between ability and recognition of the possibility of change. A panel of judges rated each artist's drawing. Those who received the highest ratings overall were the ones who said their work might be changed. A follow-up study seven years later by the same investigators indicated that more success had come to the artists who earlier had seen the possibility for change.

Certainly the committed artist is a perfectionist. Why then would there be a correlation between willingness to change a finished piece and artistic success? Quite simply, perfection is too costly to achieve. Rather than spend the time and effort to be perfect, a successful artist will spend less time and be satisfied. Satisfaction is the goal in problem finding, not perfection. The potential entrepreneur should free his or her mind of any notions of finding the perfect problem and supplying that demand curve with a perfect solution.

Getzels and Csikszentmihalyi learned something about the work methods of the artists and their professional success. The most effective artists worked as follows. In arranging the objects that they were preparing to paint, they manipulated them more, moved them about and then rearranged them more, handled the objects more, explored them more closely, touched them more, moved the mechanical parts more, and chose more unusual objects. They tended not to have a predetermined theme in mind prior to beginning to paint, but discovered arrangements through handling the objects.

As they began drawing, they more often rearranged or substituted

---

*Jacob Getzels and Mihaly Csikszentmihalyi, *The Creative Vision: A Longitudinal Study of Problem Finding in Art* (New York: John Wiley & Sons, Inc., 1976).

objects, changed paper, switched media, and transformed the scene and subject of the drawing. The final structure of the drawing tended to emerge later rather than earlier. These artists reported that they tried to develop the drawing beyond the physical objects. In addition, after completing the drawing, they admitted that it could be altered without destroying its character.

The researchers regarded the artists' problem finding as a measure of creativity. The more creative artists, who indeed became the more successful seven years later, devoted more time to problem formulation. The actual drawing, or problem-solving activity, remained open to further changes in matters such as the arrangement of the objects which seemed to have been settled during the problem-finding stage. That is, the more creative artists often found new problem formulations even while working from the original one.

The late George Quist, a venture capitalist since the early 1960s who has provided seed capital to some of the most successful entrepreneurs in the country, said essentially the same thing: "The road to success isn't always going to be straight. The smart guy will realize there will be a lot of turns—changes in the market, for instance. The honest entrepreneur can face up to that."*

David J. Padwa, an entrepreneur with two successful launches (Basic Systems, Inc., a knowledge industry company which he built in the 1960s and sold to Xerox Corp., and Agrigenetics Corp., a biotechnology company which he launched in 1977 and has built to more than $120 million (sales) by 1982), says: "Entrepreneurship is a series of random collisions. Sure you start with a plan and you follow it systematically. But even though you start out in the alternative energy business, you are just as likely to end up in real estate development."†

William Benton sold his interest in Benton & Bowles in 1935 and, in his words, "began making money by mistakes." Soon thereafter, Robert M. Hutchins hired Benton to do public relations for the University of Chicago. Benton knew that Sears wanted to sell Encyclopedia Britannica, because it needed to be updated. He convinced Sears to donate it to the university, but he was unable to convince

---

*"Do You Have What it Takes?" *Forbes*, August 3, 1981.
†Speech to the Venture Capital Club of New Mexico, February 1982.

the university's trustees to pay to have the encyclopedia revised. Benton agreed to invest $100,000, to have it updated, for which he got two-thirds of the stock and the university one-third. The encyclopedia has become a cash cow. Benton expanded the company by enfolding the Merriam-Webster Co. in the mid-1950s.

The message seems loud and clear—find an interesting problem and carefully observe every aspect, because once it becomes the raison d'etre of your business, the various components of the problem will collide with one another and with other variables and force you to rearrange the business plan. Finding problems is a relatively simple procedure. Merely look at five or ten processes currently being managed by a large corporation or bureaucratic organization and you will find that 80% of them are being managed inefficiently or suboptimally. If your preference is to buy rather than start a business, virtually every conglomerate or multinational company has dozens of subsidiaries for sale.

The newspaper is the best source of lift-off opportunities in the country. I have mentioned that the large city newspapers index the world's problems and serve to potential entrepreneurs a banquet of opportunities. The funny paper has several places for the problem-finder as well.

In the height of the fast-food restaurant boom in the mid-1970s, I tested the old saw, "Scratch a large corporation and you'll find several new businesses." It occurred to me that Batman and Robin were as widely known to children as Charlie Brown and Snoopy, but that Charles Schulz, the creator of the latter, was building an interesting licensing business while Batman and Robin were languishing.

I scratched out a plan for a theme restaurant chain called the Batcave. Families would walk into the Batcave for dinner. The children would slide down to the batcave where waiters and waitresses dressed like Batman comic book characters would serve them. The parents would remain upstairs, eating while watching old Batman and Robin movies on the back wall.

I visited Warner Communications, owner of DC Comics, creator of the Superheroes. Forty-five minutes into the conversation, the vice president in charge of the DC Comics division offered me the rights to Batman and Robin plus $350,000 to open the first restaurant.

"Look before you leap" defeated "He who hesitates is lost," and I let the idea die on the drawing board. But the point remains that numerous well-known comic book heroes are available for licensing or joint venture. Why, for instance, spend millions of dollars promoting the name "ABC Computers" when the name "Green Hornet" is available?

Where else might you find interesting problems? Have you been to your post office lately? There is no need to state the obvious. You can set up a private post office next door to the public post office and charge a premium for stamps and box rental. Your unique services would be speed and courtesy. You need only promise that the line of customers would never exceed two. If more than two people are waiting in line, another service person would come to the counter.

Scott Adler, a 34-year-old electrical engineer, has opened several storefront "post offices" in the Los Angeles area. He accepts packages for shipment four ways: United Parcel Service, Federal Express, Trans-box, and U.S. mail. All the services receive their normal fees. Several times a day Adler's "post offices" turn their mail over to the appropriate carriers. His handling fee is $1 to $5 per item, frequently greater than the postage cost. Adler's solution—offer speed, convenience, and courtesy—is simple. His problem formulation is complex and unique.

The "post offices" are in malls and near banks, places that people visit once a day. The U.S. post office is located out of the way in a cluster of government buildings noted for traffic snarls and inadequate parking. United Parcel Service and Federal Express require that the sender or receiver is home when they arrive; thus, people frequently prefer to take those kinds of packages to the courier. Adler's "post office" centralizes that function. His fee represents a savings in gasoline, driving time, and parking hassles. His "post office" idea can be replicated (should be franchised for speed of multimarket penetration), and when it is, the U.S. Postal Service will be whittled down to an efficient, manageable size.

Another entrepreneurial success story that underscores the value of problem formulation is a mail order business known as the Horchow Collection. Roger Horchow publishes a catalog chock-full of beautiful personal items, very expensive and very chic. Others also publish handsome catalogs, but Horchow does better. The problem that he identified goes by many names, but has to do with simple vanity. People love themselves and every once in a while like to strut their stuff. So Roger Horchow has prepared a catalog for gift-givers and he encourages the customer to put the initials of the recipient on the gift. He knows that people are so vain that they will never return gifts with their initials on them.

How does one problem-formulate? Like the successful artists, you adopt a problem, index its many features and parts, and begin arranging and rearranging the parts until you identify areas that appear to be receptive to solutions.

When I first learned that I could solve problems for entrepreneurs, only one aspect of the problem appeared to me: raising venture capital for them. I subsequently learned that the universe of entrepreneurs was quite broad, and some segments of it needed entirely different kinds of solutions than other segments. For example, I estimated that approximately one million people in the U.S. annually considered the possibility of becoming an entrepreneur. I based this on readership of entrepreneur-oriented magazines and attendees at conferences of franchises, small businesses, and new technologies. These people were probably at the dissatisfaction and energy peaks of their personal development curves, but lacked insight as to what to do about it. A possible solution was to steal a page from Ms. Steinem: Index the problems of becoming an entrepreneur. The perfect product is a book.

A smaller group of would-be entrepreneurs, perhaps 100,000 per annum, have a different set of problems. They want to share their problem with others, discuss specific areas such as attracting a manager, packaging a product, dealing with suppliers. This group of entrepreneurs would prefer to come together in a conference room environment. They are best served by seminars. And in the rear of the seminar hall, on the ubiquitous table, books, tapes, cassettes, newsletters, and related paraphernalia are offered for sale.

A yet smaller group of entrepreneurs has put it all together and is ready to write a business plan and begin to raise venture capital. I estimate approximately 10,000 entrepreneurs go through this rite of passage each year.

And finally, approximately, 1,000 entrepreneurs will seek the assistance of an investment banker each year to help them raise venture capital.

Thus, when I problem-formulate the market for my services, I see four tiers, each interested in a separate and distinct product having its own price, payment terms, and means of conveyance. Exhibit 3.1 tells the story better.

EXHIBIT 3.1.   The Market of New Entrepreneurs

By addressing only one segment of the market, for example, investment banking, I would have been ignoring much larger aspects of the market which not only feed into one another but also can easily be serviced profitably by the overall entity. The pyramid method of problem-formulating seems to be applicable in a number of service industries. Further examples of the pyramid approach to launching a new company appear in Chapter 6.

Creating the Solution

Most students of creativity have generally assumed that the crucial cognitive process is the one that starts to tackle a problem already defined. Practically every successful creative person would disagree. Creativity involves the formulation and the reformulation of the problem. What Einstein said about the creative process in science holds true of the entrepreneurial process: "The formulation of a problem is often more essential than its solution, which may be merely a matter of mathematical or experimental skill. To raise new questions, new problems, to regard old problems from a new angle, requires creative imagination and marks real advance in science."*

If the process of entrepreneurial creativity is to be understood fully, the study of what the entrepreneur does cannot be restricted to the visible solution, the finished product. It must include the earlier, crucial step: formulation of the problem to which the solution is a response. In addition, the formulation of the problem is not a constant, but rather, a cumulative process of discovery which begins when the potential entrepreneur enters the period of dissatisfaction, extends through the development of insight into the problem, and often does not end even after the entrepreneur appears at the corner of Wall and Broad Streets for the listing ceremony on the New York Stock Exchange of his or her company's common stock.

Thinking, we know, is equated with rational, methodical, unadventurous problem solving; the unfolding of symbolic links from given premises to known conclusions. Creative thinking does not follow the known path. Rather than accepting the premises of a structured problem, creativity fashions a new problematic configuration. Instead of striving to reach a known solution, the cognitive efforts of a creative person are frequently targeted at goals that had been previously considered inconceivable or not achievable. If behavioral scientists, skilled in structuring measurement systems, would observe entrepreneurs at work, query them continually, and qualify and correlate the results against standards, we would learn more about the creative process that entrepreneurship involves than we would from my or any other lay observations.

One method of measurement would be to put 20 significant problems on pieces of paper, have the entrepreneurs select the one that they would like to build a business to solve, and then formulate the business plan. The launch itself would require capital aplenty, not a long commodity at universities these days; thus, measuring the competence of an entrepreneur—success of the business—against his or her creative process will probably have to be postponed until there is funding for the full study. Still, behavioral science is suffi-

*A. Einstein and L. Infeld, *The Evolution of Physics* (New York: Simon & Schuster, 1938).

ciently developed to measure the creativity in the entrepreneurial process.

The study of creativity by Jacob W. Getzels and Mihaly Csikszentimihalyi mentioned earlier in this chapter also investigates the social, emotional, and experiential "baggage" of artists and their social typologies, not dissimilar from our discussion as it applies to entrepreneurs and managers.

The social typology of artists and that of entrepreneurs have more similarities than we might at first imagine. But the media play a nasty game with entrepreneurs, reminding us that their scorecard is wealth and not the chase, whereas artists are supposed to love the chase and abhor the comforts of life. Artists and entrepreneurs have quite a bit in common, not the least of which is the desire to do some one thing extremely well.

I want to provide you with some of these comparisons but one observation made in *The Creative Vision* is worth spending a moment on. It has to do with male chauvinism.

The fine arts are dominated by males. Very few women artists hang in the important galleries. There are relatively few female entrepreneurial successes as well. If you can name the females who have created personal wealth of $20 million or more through the entrepreneurial process, then they are few. I can name them. I am not so knowledgeable in fine arts, but my wife informs me that she can name the women artists hanging in the Whitney, the Met, and other important museums. They too are few.

Getzels and Csikszentmihalyi trace the reason to art school. Faculty members systematically reward male students for emotional rather than cognitive or perceptual factors. The researchers continue:

> Teachers encourage and reward men who hold values and personality traits that are adaptive to problem finding. Women, on the other hand . . . are evaluated more in relation to skills that are useful to problem solving . . . [the] difference may reflect a biased reward structure on the part of faculty members who reward only male fine artists for the temperamental qualities conducive to discovery. . . . male fine art students are reinforced for displaying personality characteristics consistent with the . . . cognitive process of problem finding.

If the female art student does not score high marks in perceptual ability, she will be systematically discouraged by the faculty from pursuing the fine arts as a career. Getzels and Csikszentmihalyi continue: "Art teachers seem to appraise a male student on the basis of long-range possibilities suggested by his personality, rather than on his perceptual abilities; they seem to appraise a female student on the basis of the perceptual skills she actually displays."

To put it bluntly, if female art students cannot draw, they will be discouraged early from pursuing art as a career. If this kind of exclusionary process goes on in other fields, there is certainly a growing army of *dissatisfied* females. It is only a small leap in reasoning to hypothesize that we will see more female entrepreneurs in the future.

Another bit of information from the Getzels and Csikszentmihalyi book worth passing along has to do with *power*. The entrepreneur is not interested in power, in the sense of persuading large groups of people to do certain things. At a more mature stage of the entrepreneurial process, the entrepreneur begins to indulge in persuasion, when the company begins to need managers to join it, banks to support it, suppliers to ship to it, and customers to try the product. This does not constitute a new company; rather, it is more a functional necessity to grow a new company.

The art students who scored highest in seeking power as a social value became applied artists and entered the fields of advertising and marketing. Their skills, the tests showed, were more in the area of problem solving than that of problem finding. In advertising, one is paid to motivate people to want certain things—products, political candidates—and to guide people toward certain ends. In the measurements of personality characteristics, advertising students are most similar to the general population, reflecting interest in power and persuasion rather than the inner drives that we have found in entrepreneurs. This raises more questions about the kinds of people who become entrepreneurs. Is an advertising-trained individual who creates a successful shampoo an entrepreneur in our definition, or a promoter? Where does one place John DeLorean, who created a new car in a market where supply clearly exceeded demand? That would make DeLorean a problem-producer rather than a problem-solver, a promoter rather than an entrepreneur. Or would it? His dissatisfaction at General Motors, his divorce and remarriage, and other personality characteristics that we were bombarded with (in *Pathfinders** and *Playboy*, among others) would characterize him as an entrepreneur. What seems to be lacking, however, is the problem-finding characteristic, the formulation, reformulation, and continual examination of the market that one intends to address with a new product. What problem did DeLorean find that he could deliver a solution to? Clearly there was none. Perhaps if we knew more about the entrepreneurial process, we could prevent the waste of capital on products such as DeLorean cars.

Getzels and Csikszentmihalyi observed 31 male fine art students and then followed their careers over 7 years. Of these, 16 were engaged in artistic work and 15 left the field. Eight of the 16 artists had achieved success, as measured by gallery owners and art critics. The backgrounds of the successful artists are shown in Exhibit 3.2.

EXHIBIT 3.2. Backgrounds of Successful Artists.

Father's occupation:	50% executives, merchants or professional; 50% white collar jobs, skilled and unskilled workers.
Mother's occupation:	62% mothers employed outside the home.
Family broken due to death or divorce:	13% disrupted.
Sibling position:	81% first born.
Religious background:	19% Protestant.

Source: Getzels and Csikszentmihalyi, p.164.

The successful artists came from more well-to-do families. "The mother's education and occupation are more related to the son's success than the father's education and occupation. Finally, despite common belief to the contrary, family disruption through divorce, separation, or death of parents was three times more prevalent in the unsuccessful than in the successful group.†

---

*Gail Sheehy, *Pathfinders* (New York: William Morrow & Co., Inc., 1981).
†Getzels and Csikzentmihalyi, p. 165.

There are similarities between successful entrepreneurs and successful artists. As we have seen, the relationship with the mother is a critical variable. In my interviews with hundreds of successful entrepreneurs, approximately 80% said their dominant personality characteristics were derived from the mother. Erikson warns us to be wary of second sons, particularly where the maternal grandfather was a dynamic individual. Thus, sibling position is an important criterion. It forces the issue to find more parallels. Indeed, entrepreneurs carry more pain and other emotional baggage than do artists. They have a hurt that drives them to build a far more complex thing than a work of art. Whereas artists have the privilege of working alone and marching to their inner drumbeats—true, they occasionally surface at their openings and sometimes teach—entrepreneurs must get involved with hundreds of moving variables. Entrepreneurs are more complex and idiosyncratic than artists. But the creative processes in art and those in entrepreneurship are not dissimilar.

The creative process in entrepreneurship has not been investigated thoroughly, and is only now being studied in artists and scientists. However, the studies by D. N. Perkins, Getzels and Csikszentmihalyi, and Anna Roe* provide a large body of ideas from which we can draw to learn more about the creative process as it applies to entrepreneurs. D. N. Perkins provides us with good principles of creativity:†

Try to be original. This is, if you want to be creative you should try to build into any outcomes the property of originality. This sounds almost too silly to mention, but I don't think so and have given some reasons for that. Many supposedly intrinsically creative pursuits like painting can be pursued in very humdrum ways. Major figures in the arts and the sciences often were certainly trying to be original. Creativity is

---

*Anna Roe, in a 1963 paper, concluded that creative physician-scientists were (1) very open to experience, (2) highly observant and prone to see things in unusual ways, (3) extremely curious, (4) accepting of unconventional thoughts, (5) ready to recognize and reconcile apparent opposites, (6) tolerant of ambiguities but liking to resolve disorder into order, (7) appreciative of complexity, (8) highly independent in judgment, thought, and action, (9) self-reliant, and (10) not responsive to group standard and control.

†The Mind's Best Work.

less an ability and more a way of organizing your abilities toward ends that demand invention.

Find the problem. This recalls Getzels' and Csikzentmihalyi's concept of problem finding. Early in an endeavor, explore alternatives freely, only gradually converging on a defined course of action and keeping even that flexibility revisable. The evidence is that creative people do this. The principle makes all the more sense because later on in the process is often too late—too late to build in originality or intensity or other qualities you might want.

Strive for objectivity. Problems of accurately and objectively monitoring progress pervade creative activity. The judgment of the moment would prove different tomorrow, the revisions of today wrong in a week. Makers have adopted many strategies to cope with the caprice of their own impressions, such as setting a product aside for a while. Also, learning to fashion products that have a potent meaning for others as well as for yourself is a complex process. Beginning with the child's first experiences of language and picturing, the problem of reaching others reappears throughout human growth in more subtle guises and plagues even the expert maker. Sometimes, it may be best to ignore such hazards and freewheel for a while. But if you always freewheel, you never really take advantage of your own best judgment.

Search as necessary and prudent. That is, explore alternatives when you have to, because the present option has failed, or when you had better, because taking the obvious course commits substantial resources that might be better spent. Of course, the conventional advice of many works on creativity is to explore many alternatives routinely.

Try, but don't expect, to be right the first time. The research found that people trade quality for quantity. Aiming at fluency, they lower the standards of governing their production of ideas, select imperfectly, and achieve no net gain. This is advice against doing just that. Instead, ask your mind to deliver up the best possible results in the first place. Notice that this does not mean fussing over initial drafts, trying to make them perfect by editing in process. Neither does this say that the results will be right the first time. They likely will need revision, maybe extensive revision and maybe the wastebasket and a new start. This is why you have to adopt a paradoxical attitude: trying, while being perfectly comfortable about falling short. The point is to bias the quick unconscious mechanisms that assemble the words we say, the gestures we make, toward doing as much of the work as possible and leaving as little as possible for deliberate revision. To put it another way: ask yourself for what you really want—you may get it, or at least some of it.

Make use of noticing. The ability to notice patterns relevant to a problem is one of the most powerful gifts we have. This can be put to work deliberately by contemplating things connected to the quest. Suppose, for example, you are designing an innovative house and need ideas. Walk around a conventional house and see what transformations suggest themselves. Or examine a conventional house in the mind's eye with the same objective. The latter can be particularly powerful, and the mind's eye takes a willing traveler to places inconvenient for the body or billfold. Often books on creativity recommend exposure to seemingly unrelated things to stimulate ideas. This certainly sometimes works, as Darwin, Archimedes, and others have taught us. But, in my experience and judgment, sensitive scrutiny of things related to the task at hand usually yields a richer harvest of ideas.

When stuck, change the problem. Early on in the space race, NASA spent much time and effort seeking a metal robot strong enough to withstand the heat of reentry and protect the astronauts. The endeavor failed. At some point, a clever person changed the problem. The real problem was to protect the astronauts, and perhaps this could be done without a material that could withstand reentry. The solution, the ablative heat shield, had characteristics just opposite to those originally sought. Rather than withstanding the heat, it slowly burnt away and carried the heat away from the vehicle. Let me generalize this and similar examples into a heartening principle. Any problem can be solved—if you change the problem into a related one that solves the same real problem. So ask yourself what the real problem is, what constraints have to be met and which ones can be changed or sacrificed. (There may be more than one way of formulating the real problem.)

When confused, employ concrete representations. Darwin's notebooks, Beethoven's sketchbooks, a poet's drafts, an architect's plans all are ways of externalizing thought in process. They pin down ideas to the reality of paper and prevent them from shifting or fading in memory. All of us do this at one time or another. However, despite such habits, we may not realize that making thoughts concrete can help to cure confusion on nearly any occasion. When paths lead this way and that, circle back, and refuse to show the way, make notes, make drawings, make models. Think aloud or form vivid mental images, for such internal concreteness helps some too.

Practice in a context. Most advice on how to be creative urges the learner to apply it everywhere. However, sometimes "everywhere" is so indefinite and daunting a notion that it turns into nowhere. When people want to improve their creativity, my suggestion is for them to choose some likely activity they often undertake and try hard to be more creative in that. Focus breeds progress. No need to hold back in other activities, but be sure of one.

Invent your behavior. That is, people should think about, criticize, revise, and devise the ways they do things important to them. Too often, inventive thinking is limited to the customary objects of invention—poems, theories, essays, advertising campaigns, and what not. But part of the art of invention is to select unusual objects of invention—objects like your own behavior. This isn't just nice; it's needed. Performances do not necessarily improve, even when you do them frequently. Indeed, it's common lore that people often end up practicing and entrenching their mistakes.

There, then are some possible plans up front, another contribution to that young and hopeful technology of thought. These principles and others like them try to define and impart the limited but very real "edge" which is about the best you can hope for from very general principles. Perhaps the plans mentioned are hard to take, at least as advice. Their prescription is too broad, too much in the direction of telling the daydreamer to pay attention or the grind to daydream more. Just what they mean in particular cases and how one persuades oneself to behave accordingly are serious questions. But take them as general principles and take seriously the problem of translating them into practice, and then they make more sense. There's no reason why the right principles (whether these are they or not) have to be as easy as a recipe for boiling water.

Planning the Business

Every venture capitalist has a "most ridiculous business plan story," and mine is about one that I saw 12 years ago. The proposed company, called The Bunny Hutch, began its business plan this way: "Assume that every person in America eats one bunnyburger one day per week. That would generate sales of $120 million per week." The business plan, designed to attract capital to launch a chain of fast food bunnyburger restaurants, plotted several other ancillary businesses based on selling various parts of the rabbit's anatomy—the foot, the skin, the blood—ad nauseam. To this very day, I am convinced that The Bunny Hutch business plan was sent to me by a friend with a peculiar sense of humor.

Most entrepreneurs realize the opportunity in this manner: "Wow, if we could get everybody in America to eat a bunnyburger one night a week . . ." or, "If we could get 200,000 transistors on a chip, we could bring the cost of certain control panels down 50% . . ." But realizing that a problem exists and solving it are two distinctly different functions. Problem finding requires laying out on a drawing board a schematic of every aspect of the problem. This schematic is the business plan.

The design of integrated circuits and the creation of a business plan are rather similar. With the former, all the routes and circuits are neatly drawn (see Exhibit 3.3) in a lengthy process by highly skilled technicians. The logic of the circuits is then verified by expensive computer software programs such as MASKAP* and any errors or short circuits are corrected. Then, the design is transferred to silicon. If there are errors at that point, the cost in dollars and time is enormous; this explains the lengthy and extensive checking and rechecking of the logic of the circuitry. The key to producing a successful chip is checking the logic design and circuitry.

In a business plan, the rationale for each step taken and the logic for each dollar spent and for every asset purchase or action are also carefully thought out, so that when the capital is raised and spent, it will not be wasted. The difference, of course, is that random collisions with unknowns can interfere with a business whereas an integrated circuit is not imperiled in that way. OPEC's four-fold increase in the price of oil nearly killed Federal Express in 1973. Avon, the in-home cosmetics selling company, and growth stock in the 1960s, is in a steep decline because its market is not at home to buy; the housewives are at work. Calling on them at night is dangerous, and Avon's workforce is at work elsewhere. To survive, Avon will

---

*A product of Phoenix Data Systems, Inc.

EXHIBIT 3.3.   Design of an Integrated Circuit.

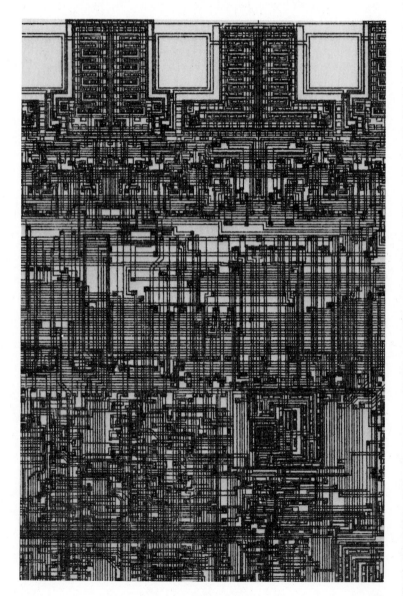

undoubtedly make numerous acquisitions so long as it has the currency.

Tom Perkins, a senior partner in the successful venture capital firm of Kleiner, Perkins, Caulfield & Byers, in San Francisco, has specialized for the last decade in launching state-of-the-art, high-technology start-ups. Perkins spots potentially successful entrepreneurs and brings them into Kleiner, Perkins, Caulfield & Byers to read business plans of other aspirant entrepreneurs, sit in on meetings when they come to make their oral presentations, and critique the entire entrepreneurial process. After several months of this, the entrepreneur goes to his drafting table and begins formulating the business plan. Like Getzels' and Csikzentmihalyi's art students, they handle all the objects, move them around, touch them, change their position, and reformulate, rearrange, and reorganize until they are reasonably satisfied. Then the entrepreneurs present their case to Perkins and his partners. If they convince the partners, the new company is launched. In just this manner did Perkins help to fund James Treybig, the founder of Tandem Computer Corp., and Robert Swanson, the co-founder of Genentech Corp. By most standards, of which market value is only one, Tandem and Genentech are extremely successful new companies.

There are very few creative venture capitalists such as Kleiner, Perkins to spoon-feed entrepreneurs through the business plan preparation process. The number is growing. I would judge there are at least 12 in full operation in the San Francisco and New England science-based entrepreneurial gardens. The careful reader will fix on the name "Kleiner" and remember that he founded Fairchild Semiconductor along with Noyce and Moore. Kleiner, Perkins have carried their start-up methods one step further. They conceive of creative business solutions to problems, pencil in the business plan, and then pull the entrepreneurs and managers from the bellies of the winners in their portfolio. Occasionally, they go too far, as when they launched Seeq Technology by luring people from Noyce's and Moore's Intel which resulted in litigation. But, usually the formula succeeds as with Vitalink, Hybritech, and Imagic, new iterations in satellite communications, genetic engineering, and computer games.

The preparation of business plans is the creation of a schematic that the company will follow once it is launched. It begins with an

exhaustive problem-finding exercise. This perhaps is best understood by example.

In nearly every sentence he speaks, Milton Friedman provides a
problem in search of an entrepreneurial solution. His book, *Capital-
ism and Freedom*, is full of ideas for doing privately what the government bureaucracies have done, but not done well, publicly. The book
was written 25 years ago, but only one of Dr. Friedman's problems
has been attacked. That is the return to private couriers of the postal
system. A major problem that several entrepreneurs have nibbled at,
but none have taken on directly, is that of education, the "why Johnny
can't read" problem that so many administrators have thrown dollars
at.

For the moment, we will don our educator-entrepreneur cap and
begin some earnest problem finding in this enormous market. In the
back of our minds, residing in a floppy disk somewhere, is the
creative idea: a system of private schools run by entrepreneurs where
teachers are rewarded based on ability, and where less desirable
neighborhoods receive government subsidies to enable entrepreneurs in that market to bid for teachers with equal dollars. Schools
charge the parents whatever price is necessary to deliver a quality
education and return a profit to the investors. An entrepreneur bent
on tackling this problem would begin to formulate the characteristics
of the problem somewhat as follows.

Of all the markets to which an education industry could address
itself, the largest by far is the parent market. This market includes all
families with children, and its size is defined by the funds these
families are now spending for what they consider their children's
future. In addition to being large, this market is biologically basic,
like the food market. The concern of parents for the education of
their children is a fundamental survival mechanism in all higher
species, and becomes stronger as human civilization becomes more
complex.

Throughout our evolution it has been possible for parents to prepare
their offspring for their environment because parents were familiar
with that environment—they grew up in it themselves. The educational aspects of the parent-child relationship are dependent upon
environmental continuity from generation to generation. Now, because
of accelerating sociocultural and technological change, a cultural gap

has formed between consecutive generations, and this gap is continuing to widen.

A problem of American society comparable in its importance to the crisis in the parent-child relationship is the problem of poverty. There is now a growing awareness of the fact that poverty is not a financial phenomenon but a behavioral one. Poverty begins in childhood; it is an attitudinal, emotional, intellectual, and cultural condition. Education can help eliminate, or at least mitigate, poverty.

We do not know in detail what the characteristics of the civilization of the future will be, or precisely what kinds of demands it will place on its members. But we can say with some assurance that the citizen of the future will have to be a more rapid learner, more flexible, more adaptable, more technologically oriented, more verbal, and more capable of abstract reasoning than the citizen of today. Unfortunately, these are traits which are mainly acquired early in life, before the age of 10. By the time a child is in the sixth grade, it is largely too late. Parents cannot develop these traits in their children because they cannot teach roles they themselves do not know, nor can they instill attitudes and personality traits which they themselves do not value highly. This problem can be seen in an accentuated form among certain immigrant groups, where parents bring their children into a completely new sociocultural environment. The severe stresses on the parent-child relationship among immigrant families are largely a consequence of parents' ineffectiveness in educating their children for life in the new culture.

Many middle-class parents sense that they have a serious problem in preparing their children for the world of tomorrow, and are becoming even more aware of it as a result of the increasing barrage of publicity about the importance of early education. The flood of publicity and the failures of the existing school systems form a basis for realistic concern of parents about the education of their children. This concern is turned into bewilderment at the variety of approaches and products which are being offered. Exhortations to take an active part in the education of children produce reactions ranging from vague uneasiness to extreme guilt and confusion. Most parents have no basis for deciding what actions to take and what products to buy. They become acutely aware that they are not doing what they should or could and are at the same time frustrated by their lack of confidence and direction. Every new sales pitch from a manufacturer of educational materials merely adds to their frustration.

The increasing concern of parents with education is an irreversible trend. It will probably increase over the foreseeable future. A different kind of education, starting earlier in the child's development, will become increasingly important if children are to be prepared for a more technological and rapidly changing world, and parents will need increasing help in providing such education. Parents are already now demanding and accepting help from diverse sources. In short, today's educational crisis, which lies at the heart of the parent-child relationship, is here to stay, because it is a corollary of the technological age in which we live.

Public education has failed to provide the children that which the parents cannot. With the financial woes of more and more American cities, the mechanism for compensating teachers becomes more and more questionable. The teachers' unions become more powerful, resulting in strikes and more classroom time lost. Teacher loads, crime, and low salaries drive many of the valuable teachers into other pursuits.

So much for the broad outlines of the problem. Among the possible formulations for a solution that the education-industry entrepreneur might begin to toss around in his mind are:

Location.   Is it necessary for the students and teachers to come gether all of the time to a certain place?

Technology.   How much classroom material may be transferred to videotape? Portable computers to take to and from school; use of satellites.

Mechanisms of attracting students.   Have performance contracts with school systems; set up after-school learning centers; operate an experimental school using cost-efficient methods; measure results using standardized tests; sell off results.

Staffing.   Kinds of management skills required; where to find qualified managers; compensation methods.

Endorsements.   Testimonials from the Lincoln's and Jefferson's of society; how to have this happen

There are numerous balls bouncing, all of which seem important. Entrepreneurs frequently wonder which step to take first. To organize the various factors into some kind of systematic approach, the Rand Corporation in the early 1960s developed a very useful tool known as the PERT chart. PERT stands for "program evaluation and review tool," and we may thank Sputnik for it, because one of our reactions to the Russian space probe was a short-lived phenomenon called operations research, or, planning. PERT charting, like the schematic design of an integrated circuit or sentence diagramming, forces us to think in interconnected steps. In a PERT chart, events are plotted against time with cost factors assigned to the events. The personal computer and several spread-sheet software packages, such as VisiCalc™ and SuperCalc™*, enable an entrepreneur to do PERT charts quite rapidly and to change the variables to see how they affect other events and factors in the PERT chart.

In the education industry examples, one might PERT chart the first six months as shown in Exhibit 3.4.

At each of these blocks there is a cost. It may only be travel, lodging or lunch, but there is a cost. The entrepreneur, or his achiever partner, must count the beans from the start or the project will be weakened throughout by its initial shoddy bookkeeping. Further, there will be a risk of raising too little capital, a frequent cause of business failures.

Once the costs for the six-month period are counted, the PERT chart should be reformulated to a six-month delay of a key variable, such as obtaining the performance contract from the board of education. Note that the salaries and overhead will have to be paid for an additional six months without any revenues. Then, assume that suitable software and hardware products cannot be located by Month 5 as shown in the original PERT chart, but take until Month 7. Again, costly delays and more airplane tickets to visit with authors, producers and manufacturers. It is frequently not in the nature of the entrepreneur to do this much planning and to exercise this much caution, but that role can be handled effectively by the achiever, the second member of the entrepreneurial team.

*VisiCalc™ a trademark of Visicorp, Inc., and SuperCalc™ a trademark of MicroPro International, Inc.

EXHIBIT 3.4. PERT Chart: Private Education Company.

	Month 1	Month 2	Month 3	Month 4	Month 5	Month 6
Products	Experiment with tapes.	Experiments continue.	Advertise for software producers.	Test software.	Select product.	Package product.
Equipment	Experiment with portable computers.	Experiment with video.	Experiment with cable, satellite.	Make equipment choices.		
Plant	Begin conversations with board of ed for performance contract at one school.	Explore alternative physical plants.	Negotiate.	Negotiate.		Award contract.
People	Interview for position of chief curriculum person.	Interviews continue.	Interviews continue.	Hire.	Plan goals.	Begin interviews for other positions.

In addition to the PERT chart, the entrepreneur must write a complete and thorough business plan, one that contains all of the data relevant to a sophisticated investor. The purposes of the business plan are to provide a map for the entrepreneur to follow and to attract financing at the appropriate time.

The entrepreneur's version of the business plan should be complete and exhaustive with every detail accounted for. It can be stored on a word processing disk and updated monthly as factors change. For purposes of raising venture capital, portions of the business plan can be pulled off the disk and printed out. A guide for a complete and thorough business plan is presented in Exhibit 3.5.

The executive summary is an overview, a one- or two-page summary that defines why the game will be played, where the game will be played, how it will be played, and why the game will be won.

Why played	boundaries of the business
Where played	international, domestic, limits of the market
How played	strategy summary
Why won	competitive advantages

A practical format for the executive summary appears in Exhibit 3.6.

The environment section of the business plan is a thorough discussion of the external conditions in which the company will grow. It defines and analyzes the factors that the company will face as it looks out its front door at its market. This section is a snapshot of the problem formulation/reformulation activity that plays such an important part in the creative process. To the entrepreneur, the view of the environment is fluid, always changing, posing new opportunities and submarkets. For example, it may become helpful for the customer to be able to telephone the company with questions about the product. The environment might show a constant and growing need for the product, but many questions as to its utility. Perhaps the customer's name and address should be kept on file to send him or her product updates. This might suggest another change: to a monthly newsletter with information on how others are using the product. Calls may then come in to the company requesting that the customers

EXHIBIT 3.5.   Outline of Business Plan.

1.0 *Executive summary*

   1.1 Boundaries of the business

      1.1.1 Product(s)

      1.1.2 Markets

      1.1.3 Customers

      1.1.4 Investment and return

   1.2 Strategy summary

      1.2.1 Overall

      1.2.2 Marketing

      1.2.3 Product and technical

      1.2.4 Manufacturing, etc.

   1.3 Competitive advantages

   1.4 Ranked uncertainties

2.0 *Environment*

   2.1 Need(s) to be or being filled

   2.2 Product(s) filling existing needs

   2.3 Markets for products

   2.4 Customers in markets

   2.5 Competitors

   2.6 Environmental change

   2.7 General information on environment

3.0 *Functional plans*

   3.1 Organization plan

      3.1.1 Chart as of now

      3.1.2 Chart six months from now

      3.1.3 Chart two years from now

      3.1.4 Function roles to be filled

      3.1.5 Key executives

      3.1.6 Financial objectives

      3.1.7 Board of directors

      3.1.8 Professional support

      3.1.9 Recruiting needs

      3.1.10 Tactics

EXHIBIT 3.5. *(Continued)*

3.2 Business plan

    3.2.1 Product definition
    3.2.2 Product opportunity
    3.2.3 Product development
    3.2.4 Product packaging
    3.2.5 Management support
    3.2.6 Tactics

3.3 Technology plan

    3.3.1 Product planning
    3.3.2 Product design
    3.3.3 Resources needed
    3.3.4 Patents
    3.3.5 Tactics

3.4 Manufacturing plan

    3.4.1 Resources needed
        3.4.1.1 Technical competencies
        3.4.1.2 Other competencies
        3.4.1.3 Facilities
        3.4.1.4 Equipment
        3.4.1.5 Processes
        3.4.1.6 Quality assurance
        3.4.1.7 Industrial relations
        3.4.1.8 Purchasing

3.5 Sales and merchandising plan

    3.5.1 Sales plan
    3.5.2 Merchandising plan

4.0 *Financial plan*

    4.1 Ranked uncertainties
    4.1 Management information and control systems
    4.3 Profit and loss statement
    4.4 Balance sheet projections
    4.5 Cash flow statement projections
    4.6 Break-even analysis
    4.7 Accounting system

EXHIBIT 3.6. Executive Summary.

1.0 Overview			
	1.1 Boundaries of the business	1.1.1.	Product(s)
		1.1.2	Markets
		1.1.3	Customers
		1.1.4	Capital requirement
	1.2 Strategy summary	1.2.1	Overall
		1.2.2	Marketing
		1.2.3	Product and technical
		1.2.4	Manufacturing
	1.3 Competitive advantages	1.3.1	Overall
		1.3.2	Marketing
		1.3.3	Product and technical
		1.3.4	Cost and performance
	1.4 Major uncertainties	1.4.1	Action necessary to reduce uncertainties

might wish to meet one another and exchange ideas. This could lead to a quarterly users' conference, with panels, speakers, and an opportunity to sell add-on products.

Because of the fluidity of the creative process, this section of the business plan may have to be updated continually. A useful beginning outline is presented in Exhibit 3.7.

The organizational plan defines the functional areas that must be staffed and the characteristics of the people who should staff those functions. Frequently an entrepreneurial team is unbalanced because friends get together at a large corporation and leave to implement the product idea that the corporation rejected. The friends might be perfectly capable engineers, but unable to manage others or persuade customers to purchase the product they have designed. There is a reluctance among entrepreneurs to delegate responsibility to others, either because no one else can do the job or because they think that is the case. The company crawls when it should be in a trot, for lack of a barn-burner marketing person or a thorough production person or financial officer.

By using an organization plan outline along the lines shown in Exhibit 3.8, the entrepreneurs can alert themselves to the functional skills that must be hired and when. This section ties in neatly to the PERT chart.

The product plan (see Exhibit 3.9) forces the entrepreneur to think about the solution that the company will be offering to the market. What should it look like and feel like? The name is important, as is the packaging. What should the price be? Should it be sold with a service contract, maintenance contract, teaching, or installation service? Should these have prices? Should there be a lease option? This section of the business plan should define the decisions made about the product, how they were arrived at, alternative plans, and opportunities for ancillary, add-on, and peripheral products.

The manufacturing plan details the technical requirements to manufacture that exist in-house and the support necessary for this operation. It describes the physical equipment requirement, the plant requirement, and the people resources. The manufacturing plan is written in stages, beginning with initial requirements, then tracking the production rate as the company enters an operating mode. An outline of this section of the business plan is given in Exhibit 3.10.

EXHIBIT 3.7. Environment Section.

2.0	Environment			
	2.1	Need to be filled	2.1.1	Basic need
			2.1.2	Need by market segment
	2.2	Products to fill need	2.2.1	Basic product
			2.2.2	Products by market segment
	2.3	Markets for products	2.3.1	Total available market (TAM in units and dollars)
			2.3.2	Segmented TAM in units and dollars
	2.4	Customers in markets	2.4.1	Customers ranked
			2.4.2	Customers ranked by segment
	2.5	Competitors	2.5.1	Description
			2.5.2	Strengths and weaknesses by competitors
			2.5.2.1	Product
			2.5.2.2	Cost and price performance
			2.5.2.3	Marketing
			2.5.2.4	Technical
			2.5.2.5	Manufacturing
			2.5.2.6	Financial
			2.5.2.7	Other
			2.5.2.8	Market share
			2.5.2.9	Net sales billed (NSB) in dollars and in units
			2.5.3.0	Strategy

EXHIBIT 3.8. Organization Plan.

3.1	Organization Plan	3.1.1	Organization Chart	3.1.1.1	Chart as of now	
						3.1.1.1.1 Name and title
						3.1.1.1.2 Age
						3.1.1.1.3 Years with company
						3.1.1.1.4 Stock owned/options
						3.1.1.1.5 Cash compensation
						3.1.1.1.6 Number of Employees Reporting
						3.1.1.1.7 Performance satisfactory or unsatisfactory
				3.1.1.2	Chart six months from now	
				3.1.1.3	Chart two years from now	
		3.1.2	Function roles to be filled	3.1.2.1	Marketing	3.1.2.1.1 Job design
				3.1.2.2	Production	3.1.2.1.2 Job design
				3.1.2.3	Engineering	3.1.2.1.3 Job design
				3.1.2.4	Finance, administration	3.1.2.1.4 Job design
		3.1.3	Key executives	3.1.3.1	Work history (Use résumé, business and	3.1.3.1.1 Description of employees
						3.1.3.1.2 Description of duties

	personal references, etc.)	3.1.3.1.3	Magnitude or scale of duties (dollars, number of people, etc.)
3.3.3.2	Past accomplishments and failings from work history	3.1.3.2.1	Description
		3.1.3.2.2	Scale
3.1.3.3	Demonstrated strengths and weaknesses (capabilities) from past accomplishments	3.1.3.3.1	Strengths
		3.1.3.3.2	Weaknesses
3.1.3.4	Rank order objectives in present assignment	3.1.3.4.1	Next six months
		3.1.3.4.2	Next two years
3.1.3.5	Appraisal (capabilities from 3.3.3 vs. objectives from 3.1.3.5)	3.1.3.5.1	Next six months
		3.1.3.5.2	Next two years
3.1.4	Financial objectives		
3.1.4.1	Present financial incentives	3.1.4.1.1	Salary
		3.1.4.1.2	Stock owned
		3.1.4.1.3	Options
		3.1.4.1.4	Employment contracts
		3.1.4.1.5	Other

EXHIBIT 3.9. (Continued)

3.1 Organization Plan				
		3.1.4.2	Proposed financial incentives based on appraisals in 3.1.2.5	3.1.4.2.1 Same as 3.1.4
				3.1.4.2.2 Potential value in two years if company meets plan
	3.1.5 Board of directors	3.1.5.1	Past board performance	3.1.5.1.1 Appraisal
				3.1.5.1.2 Style of meetings, etc.
		3.1.5.2	Individual board member's work history, etc.	
		3.1.5.3	Individual board member's anticipated performance and voting tendencies	
		3.1.5.4	Potential conflicts	
	3.1.6 Professional support	3.1.6.1	Accounting	
		3.1.6.2	Legal	
		3.1.6.3	Banking	
		3.1.6.4	Other	
	3.1.7 Recruiting needs	3.1.7.1	Management	
		3.1.7.2	Directors	
		3.1.7.3	Others	
	3.1.8 Tactics			

EXHIBIT 3.9. Product Plan.

3.2	Business plan			
	3.2.1	Definition of product as solution		
			3.2.1.1	Need to be filled
			3.2.1.2	Product to fill need
	3.2.2	Product opportunity		
			3.2.2.1	Unit forecast
			3.2.2.2	Price @ unit
			3.2.2.2.1	vs. cost
			3.2.2.2.2	vs. competition
			3.2.2.2.3	vs. market share
			3.2.2.2.4	vs. order size
			3.2.2.2.5	vs. channel
			3.2.2.2.6	vs. standard or custom
			3.2.2.2.7	vs. time
			3.2.2.2.8	vs. units manufactured
		3.2.2.3	Total available market (TAM) (units and dollars vs. time	
			3.2.2.3.1	vs. net sales entered
			3.2.2.3.2	vs. net sales billed (NSB)
			3.2.2.3.3	vs. backlog (NSE minus NSB)
			3.2.2.3.4	Percent penetration
		3.2.2.4	Product profitability	
			3.2.2.4.1	Price vs. cost
			3.2.2.4.2	Product P&L vs. product life
	3.2.3	Product development		
		3.2.3.2	Product design	

EXHIBIT 3.8. (Continued)

3.2   Business plan

    3.2.3.2   Development schedule

    3.2.3.3   Development costs (incremental)

    3.2.3.4   Development costs (by unit)

        3.2.3.4.1   vs. time

        3.2.3.4.2   vs. units manufactured

    3.2.4   Product packaging; name

    3.2.5   Management support

    3.2.5.1   Market research

    3.2.5.2   Customer service

    3.2.5.3   Applications

    3.2.5.4   Other

    3.2.6   Tactics

3.3   Technology plan

    3.3.1   Method of working with product planning to develop new products

    3.3.1.1   Description

    3.3.2   Product design

    3.3.3   Resources needed

    3.3.3.1   Technical competencies

    3.3.3.2   Equipment, supplies

    3.3.3.3   Other

    3.3.4   Patents and other proprietary items

    3.3.4.1   Patents

    3.3.4.2   Copyrights

    3.3.4.3   Trade secrets

    3.3.4.4   Other

    3.3.5   Tactics

The sales and merchandising plan (see Exhibit 3.11) enables the entrepreneur to think of the optimal means of getting the product to the customers. The marketing plans utilized by competitors and similar companies can be observed. For example, microcomputer entrepreneurs might model their marketing plans after their mini-computer predecessors. Or, they may discard traditional methods and set out on a new course, such as in-house or Tupperware-style selling.

The merchandising plan describes how the product will be presented and positioned. Notice IBM's use of Charlie Chaplin in its advertisements for the personal computer. Chaplin is considered friendly, easy to get along with. IBM wants people to come and test its personal computer, not to consider it awesome and only for programmers. A product's advertising, promotion, and positioning are as important as its technical qualities. Entrepreneurs know relatively little about advertising and promotion as witness the juvenile advertisements and common themes in most trade publications in the newer industries. Most printed circuit boards, for example, are floating in space. Most word processing systems are on top of a desk with a pretty girl in front of them. The equivalent advertisement in Vogue would be to show the lipstick and list its contents rather than the gorgeous face of Lauren Hutton. I am a proponent of turning the advertising responsibility over to professionals early in the game.

The financial plan, which is a 36-to-60 month forecast that quantifies the actual and forecast results of the business plan, begins with a listing of things that could go wrong, or major uncertainties (see Exhibit 3.12).

It bears pointing out that the business plan is important to the entrepreneurial team as the strategic plan that is to be carefully followed much as a road map for a cross-country trip. However, it is doubly important as a means of attracting venture capital. The business plan, in most instances, points out a cash flow deficit in the early months—it is known as the well of the "S-curve." This well is filled with water from the venture capital bucket. A carefully prepared business plan is essential to raising venture capital. Thoroughness counts big at this stage of development.

EXHIBIT 3.11. Sales and Merchandising Plan.

3.5	Sales and merchandising plan	3.5.1	Sales plan	3.5.1.1	Channels selected	3.5.1.1.1	Salesmen
						3.5.1.1.2	Representatives
						3.5.1.1.3	Distributors
						3.5.1.1.4	Dealers
						3.5.1.1.5	Direct mail
				3.5.1.2	Location of sales forces	3.5.1.2.1	Trained salesmen vs. untrained salesmen
						3.5.1.2.2	Training program
				3.5.1.3	Accounts and territories by sales forces		
				3.5.1.4	Incentive plans	3.5.1.4.1	Quotes
						3.5.1.4.2	Commissions
						3.5.1.4.3	Incentives
				3.5.1.5	Major customer selection	3.5.1.5.1	Rationale
						3.5.1.5.2	Strategy
				3.5.1.6	Sales forecast	3.5.1.6.1	In dollars and unit total (include assumptions)
						3.5.1.6.2	By major customer in dollars and units
						3.5.1.6.3	Major customer action plans

EXHIBIT 3.11. *(Continued)*

3.5	Sales and merchandising plan			3.5.1.6.4	Document unit and dollar histories of similar companies to support
	3.5.2	Merchandising plan	3.5.1.7		Sales contracts
			3.5.2.1		Benefits to customer
			3.5.2.2		Sales aids (written)
				3.5.2.2.1	For salesmen
				3.5.2.2.2	Distributable
			3.5.2.3		Sales aids (other)
			3.5.2.4		Other support for sales forces
				3.5.2.4.1	From technical
				3.5.2.4.2	From manufacturing
				3.5.2.4.3	Other
			3.5.2.5		Other manufacturing
				3.5.2.5.1	Advertising, trade shows
			3.5.2.6		Tactics

EXHIBIT 3.12. Financial Plan.

4.1 Major uncertainties and their effect on P&L

4.1.1 Major uncertainties

4.1.1.1 Description
4.1.1.2 Quantified by impact on P&L
4.1.1.3 Ranked by impact on P&L

4.1.1.3.1 Action to be taken to minimize uncertainty

4.2 Management information and control systems

4.2.1 Description of accounting and control practices

4.2.2 Critical measures of performance

4.2.2.1 Organization plan
4.2.2.2 Product plan
4.2.2.3 Technology plan
4.2.2.4 Manufacturing plan
4.2.2.5 Sales and merchandising plan
4.2.2.6 Financial plan

4.2.3 Management reports

4.2.3.1 Operating reports

4.2.3.1.1 Contents
4.2.3.1.2 Distribution
4.2.3.1.3 Frequency
4.2.3.1.4 Purpose
4.2.3.1.5 Effectiveness

4.2.3.2 Financial reports

4.2.3.2.1 Contents
4.2.3.2.2 Distribution
4.2.3.2.3 Frequency
4.2.3.2.4 Purpose
4.2.3.2.5 Effectiveness

EXHIBIT 3.12. (Continued)

4.2	Management information and control systems			4.2.4	Meetings	4.2.4.1	By functional area	4.2.4.1.1	Contents
						4.2.4.1.2	Attendance
						4.2.4.1.3	Frequency
						4.2.4.1.4	Purpose
						4.2.4.1.5	Effectiveness
4.3	P&L	4.3.2	Historical	4.3.2.1	1st year by month	4.3.2.1.1	Assumptions
		4.3.2	Forecast	4.3.2.2	2nd year by quarter		
				4.3.2.3	3rd, 4th, and 5th years annually		
4.4	Balance sheets	4.4.1	Historical	4.4.2.1	1st year by months	4.4.2.1.1	Assumptions
		4.4.2	Forecast	4.4.2.2	2nd year by quarter		
				4.4.2.3	3rd, 4th, and 5th years annually		
				4.4.2.4	Inventories	4.4.2.4.1	Materials
						4.4.2.4.2	Work in process
						4.4.2.4.3	Finished goods
				4.4.2.5	Receivables aged 30, 60, 90, and 120 days		
				4.4.2.6	Fixed assets schedule	4.4.2.6.1	Cost
						4.4.2.6.2	Improvements
						4.4.2.6.3	Additions
						4.4.2.6.4	Write-offs
						4.4.2.6.5	Depreciation

Selecting the Entrepreneurial Team

It is exceptionally difficult to form effective entrepreneurial teams. My research indicates an average age difference of 16 years between entrepreneurs and managers. The development stages of the entrepreneur and his achiever partner, are markedly different. The personality characteristics and social values overlap in relatively few areas. The social values of the entrepreneur, are usually more liberal. This could be a function of age and life experiences, but a 27-year-old entrepreneur and the 43-year-old former corporate manager that he or she selects are bound to have different views of life. The manager is outer-directed, and the entrepreneur is inner-directed. An entrepreneur is more likely to have few assets, live in the city, and drive a European car. His partner has a house in the suburbs and other assets, and drives an American car. They vote differently and have different opinions on marijuana, politics, pre-marital sex, taste in music and use of their leisure time.

The unifying factor is that both members of the team want to build a successful company. The manager's goals are perhaps more capital-gains-oriented, while the entrepreneur's goal is to do some one thing extremely well. But the partners need each other for several very important reasons, not least of which are: (1) the entrepreneur needs someone around to direct his talent, focus his energy, and orchestrate the increasing number of people and departments; (2) the manager needs an energetic, innovative, imaginative entrepreneur to provide him with a growing company to which he can apply his managerial talents.

The entrepreneurial team works somewhat as follows. Two people decide to go on a photographic safari to Africa. The first boards the plane in casual attire, unburdened by carry-on luggage. The second carries six cameras, filters, guidebooks, camping equipment, a tent, and other paraphernalia. The plane lands in Kenya and the two set off on foot into the jungle. The first goes out in front and the second decides to stop and put up the tent. The first is about a mile away from where the tent is being set up when a tiger jumps out from behind a tree, growls, and charges. He spins around and runs back to the tent as fast can be, with the tiger in hot pursuit. The tent is part-way up, and the tiger's would-be prey runs into the tent, swings around the pole, and heads out in the same direction, shouting back at his busy partner: "This tiger is for you. I'm going to go back for mine."

An entrepreneur can generate weeks of work in the first three hours of the day, drop it off on his partner's desk to be organized and implemented, and then change his mind by the afternoon. The manager is delighted for the opportunity to clean up after the entrepreneur. He is used to making management decisions; now, for the first time, he owns a meaningful portion of the company that he manages.

The method by which entrepreneurs select their partners is, alas, all too frequently random, uncertain, and subject to chance. As venture capitalists become more knowledgeable about the lift–off stage, they are able to step in and advise the entrepreneur that management talent is needed; indeed, that it is a criterion for the financing, and that they intend to assist in the interview process. Executive search consultants are very valuable people. Entrepreneurs and venture capitalists with increasing regularity are turning to these hiring professionals, often called "head hunters," to assist them in building the entrepreneurial team. When Sutter Hill Management Corp., the lead investor in the Qume Corp. start-up venture capital financing, decided to back David Lee, one of the engineers who developed the Diablo printer, in developing a high-speed printer for Qume, they simultaneously selected Robert Schroeder, an executive vice president from Cummins Engine Co., as the manager.

Some pairings of entrepreneurs and managers do not work out. I suspect the premise on which they get together is incorrect. The worst premise is capital: the manager has some capital and wants a business to run. In all likelihood he or she knows little or nothing about the entrepreneurial process; almost certainly the manager knows very little about the technology or innovation that is at the heart of the business. But the entrepreneur is desperately out of capital and has been living hand-to-mouth for months. The manager, with $100,000 to invest, time to help run the business, and experience in management looks like the white knight. Without thinking about all of the things that could go wrong, the entrepreneur accepts the capital and trades equity at far too low a price.

The $100,000 runs through the business like Sherman through

Georgia, and in a month's time, the company is once again out of funds, and the manager cannot bring order to the chaos. He or she tries to impose rigidity on an amoeba-like organism but cannot generate sales because of failure to learn the product. Several key engineers tell the entrepreneur that if the new manager does not leave, they will.

But the manager has a no-cut contract; that is, if fired, he or she gets to keep the stock. The entrepreneur senses that it may be better to try to work things out than sever the relationship quickly. The two of them visit the manager's bank and jointly guarantee a $100,000 loan. The entrepreneur elects the guarantee over issuing more stock to the manager. But the bank sees that the entrepreneur has no assets. It is looking to the manager for protection. Thus, the manager asks the entrepreneur to pledge some of his or her stock in the company to secure the loan partially. If the company fails to begin growing and needs another injection of capital, the manager will continue accumulating equity. This becomes an untenable position for the entrepreneur, who must use the equity to attract and keep people and for major injections of capital. To keep adding to the manager's stack of chips does not serve any purpose other than enriching the manager.

When the blowout comes, as it inevitably does, there is a legal battle, and someone ends up with the company and the other person ends up with cash. Both parties will have incurred substantial legal bills and bitter memories. They will have wasted their time.

William von Meister, inventor of the SOURCE*, a database that users of personal computers can call into for a variety of information, needed capital and a manager to do the thorough, nitty-gritty, detailed work while he improved the product technically and began the marketing effort. The company, Digital Broadcasting Corp., rented open channels on FM radio stations in several large cities in 1979 and 1980 in order to make the SOURCE available to computer users. Each rental was expensive, and nationwide hookups were important. Thus, the manager's billfold had to be rather thick. Jack Taub, a member of the Scott Publishing Co. family, publisher of books for

---

*The SOURCE is a trademark of Source Telecomputing Corp. of America.

postage stamp collectors, and an entrepreneur who was responsible in large part for reactivating the philatelic windows around the country, was the manager that von Meister selected. But Taub had no management experience; he was a salesman with demonstrated innovative marketing ideas in the postage stamp field. Digital Broadcasting Corp. arranged over $3 million in financing largely via an Economic Development Administration loan guarantee from the North Carolina National Bank. It burned capital at the average rate of $300,000 per month in its attempt to wire new cities and sell the utility to customers. Soon it was out of capital, and the two entrepreneurs began to blame one another for the predicament they were in. Taub exercised some options, took control of the company, and sold 51% to Readers Digest to raise much needed capital. Von Meister left the company to start something new, and the question of values and justice was settled in court. Readers Digest has increased its ownership in the company, now known as Source Telecomputing Corporation of America, and neither entrepreneur is particularly satisfied with his return on capital or time.

The error frequently made is to look for a manager and capital from the same source. It happens rarely that a manager has enough capital really to matter. A truly qualified manager has been extremely busy climbing the corporate ladder. Although this is not always the case, the median age of managers in start-up companies is 43, and that is relatively young to have begun accumulating liquid wealth. Even if a manager is capable of making a meaningful investment, it is his skill that is being sought by the company, not his capital. The 5 to 10% equity position that a manager is entitled to in a rapidly growing innovative or high-technology company could make him or her very wealthy; a lot depends on the management skills. Witness Frank Lautenberg's unique contribution to Automatic Data Processing, Inc. A computer-based payroll processing company doing several million dollars worth of business a year when Lautenberg joined the entrepreneur, Henry Taub, in 1964, ADP is currently one of the most successful computer service companies in the world, with annual revenues in excess of $700 million. Lautenberg diversified the company through dozens of acquisitions, hired and trained a middle management team to manage the acquired companies, and led the company from batch processing to data networks and other markets.

When Gary Stoltz of Pathfinder Venture Capital Co., Minneapolis, negotiated the venture capital financing for Central Data Corp., Champaign, Illinois, with its 22-year-old entrepreneur, Jeffrey Roloff, the venture capitalist, insisted that 10% of Central Data's common stock be set aside for a chief marketing officer. Roloff preferred to be the chief technical officer of the company, but he had been responsible for Central Data's $2.5 million in second-year revenues from computer board products. Roloff had minimal work experience and two years of post high school studies. Yet his administrative abilities were remarkable, with most minute details well documented and covered. Roloff had even written a "Welcome to Central Data" brochure for new employees before he had even 10 workers, with facts about the company, its customers, suppliers, and his high ethical standards. Despite Roloff's abilities in marketing, production, and administration, Stoltz insisted that a manager be found, interviewed, and hired within six months after the closing of the financing.

Stoltz hired an executive search firm to do the leg work. Champaign is a lovely university town, but to a fast-track executive from Silicon Valley, if you've seen one midwestern town, you've seen them all. Pathfinder did most of the initial screening of candidates, and those men it ranked the highest were interviewed by Roloff. Within eight months after the venture capital financing, the wunderkind entrepreneur had landed a manager. Earle Jacobson, 51, had been a product manager at Topaz Inc., San Diego, a power supply manufacturer, and his abilities in marketing enabled Roloff to spend more time in product design and development.

The age of the lone wolf entrepreneur has passed. Launching and managing successful growth companies are both much too complex. There are exceptions, such as direct response companies; but when they begin to succeed and develop a responsibe market, complexities multiply.

Producing and Test Marketing the Product

The computer industry is a school for entrepreneur watchers. There are many start-ups in that arena, and hundreds of venture capitalists vigorously selecting the companies and entrepreneurs that they plan to help grow into IBM's and Control Datas. There is an increased amount of planning and systematization being applied to the start-up phase, including the initial product test and evaluation done on the customer's site. This is called the beta test. The alpha test is done at the prototype stage, occasionally at a customer's location but usually on the home court.

An entrepreneur with an innovative high-technology product is able to obtain a beta test if he or she can convince the potential customer that the product has demonstrable economic justification and if he or she offers a meaningful discount on the initial order. If the product works to the customer's satisfaction, he or she can keep the beta test model for the company's manufacturing cost plus a small premium.

In other instances, the new product is a small component that can be added to a large product and does not warrant a beta test. The entrepreneur might telephone several potential customers to experiment with the component while permitting the entrepreneur to de-bug ("fix") it. The entrepreneur can meet potential customers at trade conferences. It is also very effective to present a technical paper at those trade conferences in order to set forth the attributes of the component to the interested technical people in attendance.

Entrepreneurs are not likely people to perform successful new product introductions, unless somewhere in their outer-directed lives they learned about test marketing and new product introductions. However, for the entrepreneur who has no one to turn to for guidance in this area, trial and error is the teacher. You can compare the first issues of many successful magazines with current issues and see that once cherished columns are not in the current issues. One's perception of a market need is frequently inaccurate. Entrepreneurs have as good a chance as anyone to design a successful new product marketing plan. They are wrong much of the time.

A. C. Markulla, formerly vice president of marketing for Intel Corp., joined Apple Computer as its manager at about the same time that a venture capital syndicate led by Arthur Rock, Don Valentine, and Henry Singleton began to launch the Apple. Markulla elected a marketing plan to create brand awareness. Despite the fact that personal computers are not significantly different in their attributes and qualities, Markulla and the advertising and marketing team that he put together made the market of potential personal computer purchasers aware of the Apple II. It became synonymous with the personal computer. Advertisements appeared in family magazines and on radio and television. The Apple II seemed friendly, and the ads beckoned the reader to bring one home.

Followers into the personal computer industry have found it difficult to go head to head with Apple. Radio Shack uses Isaac Asimov, the science fiction and science history writer, in its ads. Texas Instruments relies on Bill Cosby. Commodore uses William Schatner, a popular Star Trek actor. Xerox Corp., with more capital than most of the competition, has chosen the marketing method most used by companies with undifferentiated products: Sell the salesman. A recent ad for Xerox's computer stores says: "We have the best names in the business, Xerox, Apple, Osborne, Phil, and Sidney." When a company begins thinking that way, it is being run by managers and not entrepreneurs. For instance, insurance companies sell the salespeople ("You're in good hands with Allstate"); car companies sell the salespeople ("The Good Olds Boys"); oil companies sell the salespeople ("You can trust your car to the man who wears the star"); airlines sell the pilot or other responsible people ("We're American Airlines, doing what we do best"); and even Frank Perdue sells himself rather than his chicken. Xerox is being run by the people with heads but no heart. This does not bode well in a race with entrepreneurs.

It may be important to stress here that the personal computer, which as all of us know is one of many extensions of the microprocessor, or integrated circuit, will in all likelihood soon become as ubiquitous as cars, insurance, gasoline, and chicken. Every business will have one or more of them, as will every school, church, government agency, and most homes. Bookkeeping, planning, mail, communications, and entertainment will rely on the existence of the personal computer. Numerous clerical tasks will be eliminated, permitting the reorientation of people into more creative tasks. This is not more tripe and drivel about the positive aspects of that *bête noire*, "automation." It is simply a statement of the fact that the computer will change the way people work in meaningful ways. The portable computer alone means that many white-collar workers who presently commute to large cities can work for their companies on a beach in Tahiti. Workers will become more entrepreneurial as low-cost systems for telecommunications permit the decentralization of large organizations. They will live in areas that satisfy their lifestyles and "telecommute" to work.

New product introductions will be more systematized as well. Salespeople can interview early users at the user site, feed the data by voice or keyboard into a portable computer, and send it over telephone lines to a larger computer filled with market research and market analysis programs. A trained marketing person can interpret the data and fairly quickly contact the salesperson to suggest answers to customer questions, changes, modifications, and other improvements. For instance, customers may object to the shape of a product's package, its feel, the color, the texture, or the price. These could be modified rather quickly, enabling the company to be more responsive to the marketplace.

Entrepreneurial companies and those with more innovative and less risk-averse managements will likely be the first to adapt the personal computer in meaningful ways. For example, Federal Express is able to tell a shipper within three minutes the precise location of his or her package. The U.S. Postal Service, if asked about an Express Mail package, has a great deal of difficulty answering. Emery Air Freight and other small package delivery companies caught flat-footed by Federal Express cannot locate a customer's package with any degree of certainty, either. Handling large amounts of data quickly has been part of the Federal Express business plan for many years. The company is computer based and its management is computer fluent. Federal Express has the entrepreneurial management to succeed in the passenger airline business should it choose to enter that field.

With deregulation, the airlines will be able to market their services on a price basis. Up until now, they have had only the destinations and feeling of flying to sell. Now they can move prices around and fill the planes. The airlines run by entrepreneurial teams such as Continental and Midway will probably be the most innovative and eager to implement.

This will be done somewhat as follows. An airline employee with a portable computer will stand in the terminal checking the screen for available seats on its flights. If he or she notices 20 open seats from New York to Pittsburgh and 10 from Pittsburgh to Albany and an over-sold situation from New York to Albany, the employee can drop the price of a triangulated fare from New York-Pittsburgh-Albany to the New York-Albany price and flash the change on an overhead screen. It may take the passengers two extra hours to get to Albany, but (1) they will get there, and (2) the price will be fair. The airline will be more profitable and the passengers will feel that the airline is sincerely trying to please. They will appreciate the effort.

There is a period of intense, highly focused energy when an entrepreneurial team is producing and test-marketing a product for the first time. Entrepreneur-engineers, technicians, and members of management work side by side, frequently around the clock, to get a product to market. It is one of the most exciting, exhilarating times in the life of a company. It is similar in many respects to giving birth to a child. It is biological. Workers on the project make extraordinary sacrifices, and their lives become altered by the experience.

In *The Soul of a New Machine*, Tracy Kidder brings to life the efforts of a small entrepreneurial team inside Data General Corp., Cambridge, Massachusetts, to design, develop, and produce a new desktop computer in the space of one summer. The team leader was Tom West; the computer was named Eagle. Tom West and his team represent an entrepreneurial effort within a large corporation. Predictably, the team did not stick together because they did not enter a performance contract with Data General, which would have tied the new machine's marketplace successes to their personal rewards. Nonetheless, the last pages of the book are revealing:

> Adopting a remote, managerial point of view, you could say that the Eagle project was a case where a local system of management worked as it should; competition for resources creating within a team inside a company an entrepreneurial spirit, which was channelled in the right direction by constraints sent down from the top. But it seems more accurate to say that a group of engineers got excited about building a computer. Whether it arose by corporate bungling or by design, the opportunity had to be grasped. In this sense, the initiative belonged entirely to West and the members of his team. What's more, they did the work, both with uncommon spirit and for reasons that in a most frankly commercial setting seemed remarkably pure . . .
>
> Presumably, the stonemasons who raised the Gothic cathedrals worked only partly for their pay. They were building temples to God. It was the sort of work that gave meaning to life. That's what West and his team of engineers were looking for. They themselves like to say they didn't work on their machine for money. In the aftermath, some of them felt that they were receiving neither the loot nor the recognition they had earned, and some said they were a little bitter.

But when they talked about the project itself, their enthusiasm returned. It lit up their faces.

The first time a product is produced and test-marketed, the entrepreneur's original idea gets its first test. As Tom West says, it's "pinball." If the player scores, he gets to play again. If the product misses the market, the entrepreneur may have to leave the game. It's like playing a par three water hole in golf with one ball and one club, but not being absolutely sure of the distance to the green.

The degree of paranoia among entrepreneurs has a lot to do with the rules of their pinball game. For example, if the game is like the Broadway theater, and an entire investment can be lost with poor reviews on opening night, one would expect to see particularly tense entrepreneurs. Movie producers share some of those characteristics, as do direct mail entrepreneurs and magazine publishers. However, where the marketplace is more heterogeneous, with different geographical demographics, and is more forgiving in one region or at one level than in or at another, the tension level among entrepreneurs tends to deflate.

Raising Venture Capital

This stage of the entrepreneurial process is less under the direct control of the entrepreneur than any other. If he has formed an entrepreneurial team at this point in the company's development, then the manager takes charge. Managers and venture capitalists have more things in common than entrepreneurs and venture capitalists, although only roughly one-tenth of the country's approximately 700 venture capitalists are themselves proven, successful choosers and monitors of successful entrepreneurs. *Fortune* magazine complains with some justification that there are not too many venture capitalists, merely too many incompetent ones.* About 150 venture capitalists have risen to the top of their field, have been rewarded with tens of millions of dollars to manage, and have built teams to manage the investment of venture capital. In most instances, entrepreneurial teams must solicit venture capital from relatively

---

*"Are There Too Many Venture Capitalists?," *Fortune*, October 2, 1982.

inexperienced people who report to more experienced people, come back with more questions, and do more investigation prior to an investment decision. The process of raising venture capital is far less systematic than it could be, but it has improved. For instance, Christopher Columbus waited six years for King Ferdinand and Queen Isabella, tied up all day in meetings regarding the Inquisition, to grant him a meeting to answer his original request for three ships, men, and provisions to sail to India. They responded only after hearing that Columbus was about to seek backing from the brother of the King of England. We've come from six years in the early sixteenth century to six months in the late twentieth century. Money walks. Entrepreneurs run. Venture capitalists travel a great deal of the time, and are not in their offices. Thus a process that should go quickly goes slowly. A second reason that it goes slowly is that the venture capitalists are not investing their own money. They have a fiduciary responsibility to their investors, who are pension and endowment funds and insurance companies in the main, to make prudent investments. Thus, they take longer to investigate.

Andre Meyèr, senior managing partner of the investment banking firm of Lazard Freres for a quarter of a century until his death in 1980, made venture capital investment decisions within an hour. He was investing his own money and that of his partners and close friends, but Meyèr trusted his judgment completely. He told an entrepreneur once that one hour was all that he needed, because:

> I can tell within 15 minutes by listening to you if you are smart. I can tell within 30 minutes of hearing the description of the business if the product is good and the market is ready. If it is too technical, I can describe it to a technical consultant within 30 minutes and have an answer. Then, to find out if you are honest, I need to call some of your references, and that takes another 30 minutes.

Lone wolf venture capitalists have expired along with solo entrepreneur acts. Nonetheless, a venture capital firm frequently assumes the personality of its founder and leader. There are three kinds of venture capital investors: thieves, passive, and active.

Thieves are in the business to take control of the companies they invest in and increase their fortunes by aggrandizement. There are relatively few thieves in the venture capital business, but they do exist. One of the ways in which a thief operates with an entrepreneurial company is as follows. If the company is in default under the terms of the investment agreement and needs more capital, the investor provides the needed capital but takes control of the company. The next time the entrepreneur makes a mistake, the investor fires him. Several prominent venture capitalists have followed this system with great success.

A passive investor provides the entrepreneurial company with capital, but no other form of assistance. He attends board meetings primarily as a critic and assists management in arranging the bank financing and in other chores only when to do otherwise might cause it to lose the investment or suffer dilution. Although he does not adopt an adversarial stance, the passive investor receives monthly reports from the entrepreneur and telephones either to complain or compliment depending on the information received. He does not provide meaningful assistance to the entrepreneurial team.

There are a surprisingly large number of passive venture capital firms in the market. Their portfolios are relatively large, frequently over 75 companies, and their staffs are small. They claim to monitor their investees "by the numbers." For this system to work efficiently, they invest primarily in more mature companies where the entrepreneurial team is in place and works well. Passivity would not work for start-up companies of an entrepreneur, a product, and two customers.

Active venture capital investors are the newest factor in the marketplace. These firms, such as Kleiner Perkins, Pathfinder and Mayfield, frequently handpick the manager, hire the chief marketing officer, interview for the chief financial officer, arrange bank financing, call on key customers, and do other tasks for their portfolio companies. The Silicon Valley venture capitalists reach into earlier success stories to pull out their next managers and entrepreneurs. Arthur Rock pulled A. C. Markulla out of Intel, an earlier investment, to guide Apple. David Lee was plucked from Qume to launch Diablo.

Microsoft, Inc., a Bellevue, Washington developer of MICROSOFT BASIC, compiler and interpreter software that is practically a standard in the microcomputer industry, raised a million dollars from Technology Venture Associates in August 1981, for 5% of Microsoft's common stock. The private placement valued the six-year-old company at $20 million. Its 1982 sales projection was approximately $14 million per annum, up from $7.5 million in fiscal 1981, and its pre-tax earnings were in the 30% range. "We didn't need the capital," says Bill Gates, founder and president of Microsoft, "but we did need Technology Venture's advice and assistance in a number of areas. Our goal is to get to sales of $100 million in five years and the experience of David Marquardt and the others at Technology Ventures in launching companies was more important than the money."

The Consumer Products Division, then headed by Vernon Rayburn, develops new products internally, or licenses programs developed by other authors, which it sells through conventional distribution channels. "One such distribution channel is Lifeboat Associates," says Rayburn, "which is an important value-added distributor of software packages that supports 45 different formats. Since we only support six formats, Lifeboat is uniquely important to us." Lifeboat publishes a catalog of over 500 software packages.

What services could Technology Ventures perform for Microsoft that the company could do less well on its own? "We interviewed two dozen venture capital firms to determine which one would help us the most," said Gates. "We need help primarily in hiring key middle management. We need professional assistance at all levels to help a largely entrepreneurial company become well managed. Were Technology Ventures merely to deal with me, they would be tying up my time, and that's one of the company's more valuable resources at this point. I wanted a venture firm that would help make other members of management equally valuable."

Discussions with venture capital firms began in mid-1980, and serious discussions with Technology Ventures began in January 1981. For six months, the two firms met every few weeks to run a test to determine how they might work together in the future. "Their investment also placed a value on the stock, which was important in attracting and awarding key employees," said Gates.

The valuation of Microsoft's common stock, roughly three times revenues, reflects positively on Microsoft's proprietary product and perceived upside potential. It also points up the fact that with most of the venture capital firms located on the West Coast, there is more competition among investors which bids up the valuations. Lifeboat

Associates, a New York Company, with sales roughly equal to Microsoft's, although a distributor rather than a producer of software, raised venture capital privately at a valuation of less than one times sales. There are fewer venture capitalists in New York.

In some industries, the venture capital funds throw nickels at companies as if they were manhole covers. But in computer software, biotechnology, and robotics, the opposite is true. Dozens of venture capital companies tried to invest in Microsoft, and the experience at several other software companies is similar. For example, Digital Research, Inc., developer of the CP/M operating system used in many personal computers, took in $4,000,000 for 45% ownership from TA Associates and HQ Ventures in July, 1981. Its sales at the time were approximately $6 million. Peachtree Software, Inc., whose sales in fiscal 1981 were $2,200,000 was acquired by Management Science America, Inc. in late 1981 for $5,900,000.

The $1.4 billion of institutional venture capital that was invested in 1981, was distributed as shown in Exhibit 3.13.

There is no other country in the world where a person can set sail on his or her own, formulate a problem in need of a solution,

EXHIBIT 3.13. Venture Capital Investments by Industry: 1981.

Industry	Millions of Dollars	Percentage of Total	
		Investments	Millions of Dollars
Computer related	$ 480.2	30.0%	34.3%
Electronics related	183.4	14.5	13.1
Communications	156.8	11.4	11.2
Genetic engineering	156.8	6.2	11.2
Medical/health related	81.2	.0	5.8
Energy	81.2	4.9	5.8
Industrial automation	74.2	6.2	5.3
Consumer related	26.6	4.9	1.9
Industrial products	47.6	4.4	3.4
Other	112.0	10.5	8.0
Total	$1,400.00	100.0%	100.0%

Source: Venture Capital Journal, July, 1981, p. 8.

create the solution, build a company to produce and market it, and then attract a portion of $6.0 billion of helpful, professional capital. There is no other time in the history of the planet where dreamers and planners have been able to raise so much money to realize their dreams.

Kenneth Clark, a thoughtful and perceptive art historian, writes:

> I don't say much about economics in this book, chiefly because I don't understand them and perhaps for that reason believe that their importance has been overrated by post-Marxist historians. But, of course, there is no doubt that at a certain stage in social development fluid capital is one of the chief causes of civilization because it ensures three essential ingredients: leisure, movement and independence.*

He goes on to say that fluid capital permits more important uses of money such as art and architecture.

Given that $1.4 billion in professional venture capital was invested in 1981. Did it fund start-ups and lift-offs or more proven innovation and technology? The majority of the capital was invested in start-up and early-stage companies as shown in Exhibit 3.14.

EXHIBIT 3.14   Venture Capital Investments by Stage of Development: 1981

| | Percentage of | | Average Size of Investment |
	Investments	(Millions of Dollars)	
Seed	40.0%	2.0	$1,000,000
Start-up	26.0	31.0	2,200,000
Early stage	19.0	19.0	2,000,000
Total early stage	49.0	52.0	2,000,000
Expansion, other	51.0	48.0	1,750,000
Total	100.0%	100.0%	$1,900,000

Source: Venture Capital Journal, July, 1981, p. 9.

*Kenneth Clark, Civilization (New York: Harper & Row, 1969).

Of the $1.4 billion in venture capital, over half went into dining room table and garage start-ups; that is, post research and development stages of development.

Start-up and early-stage companies received over half of the professional venture capital in 1981 and the average investment in the start-ups and early stage situations was $1.9 million. The average investment in the more seasoned companies was $1.75 million. For the first nine months of 1982, $2.5 billion of private venture capital was invested. Clearly, the entrepreneur has a fluid capital market from which to attract launch capital.

It was not always this way. In 1970, there were no more than 25 venture capital funds in the United States. In 1982, there were approximately 220, with 30 more raising capital to begin operations. In 1970, the 25 funds—primarily affiliates of wealthy families such as the Rothchilds, Rockefellers, Whitneys, and Phippses plus one or two pioneers including the legendary Tommy Davis and Arthur Rock— and the Small Business Investment Company industry, which prefers more mature companies, invested approximately $350 million in start-up and expanding companies. In 1981, four times that amount was invested. In 1970, there were perhaps 20 professional venture capitalists in the country, that is, people experienced in all phases of company launching. In 1981, the number of professional venture capitalists had increased by seven times.

What is the catalyst behind this formation of capital? On the one hand, investment managers are getting better at selecting entrepreneurs. They have earned their stripes as employees of small business investment companies or corporate venture capital subsidiaries where compensation included salary plus bonus tied to the performance of the portfolio. But they were denied "a piece of the action." After many years of making entrepreneurs rich, the desire to have an equity interest in the companies they select becomes an overwhelming necessity. They calculate the rate of return that they have turned in for their employer and write an offering circular to investors that says in effect, "We have earned Bank of America or Citicorp an average return of 30% per annum for the last 10 years, and we can do the same for you." From 1978 to 1983, close to $6 billion was raised in this manner, primarily from pension funds, endowment funds, and insurance companies.

A second stimulus to the growth of private venture capital funds was the simultaneous liberalizing of several unrelated federal laws. The Labor Department reversed a temporary ruling in 1979 that prohibited pension funds from entrusting some of the funds under their management to independent third parties such as venture capital fund managers. At about the same time, the capital gains tax was lowered by Congress, which helped to make equity investments more attractive. Quite independent of those actions, but at approximately the same time, the Securities and Exchange Commission liberalized the rules governing the sale of securities, permitting this to occur in certain instances without a registration statement. Capital can be assembled more rapidly.

On the surface, these macroeconomic events may appear to have very little effect on the entrepreneur sweating out a meeting with his brother-in-law to borrow $15,000 to cover some checks that were mailed against an expected large order that failed to materialize. But the brother-in-law reads the paper, and somewhere he will notice that entrepreneurs are the "in" thing to back and that being a venture capitalist by investing in an unrelated business is part of the new "go for it" lifestyle.

Private venture capital funds are generally partnerships of 10-year lives, owned 80% by the providers of the capital and 20% by the investment managers. However, the 20% is generally distributed to the venture capitalists only after they have returned 100% of the institutions' investment. For example, if the fund begins with $70 million, and in the second year one of its investments goes public at a $15 million gain and another is written off for a $2 million loss, the investment managers do not receive a dividend of 20% of $15 million less 20% of the $2 million loss; rather, the $2 million loss is deducted from their $2 million share of the gain. The institutions receive $13 million, and the venture capitalists still owe them $57 million before they can share in the capital gains. The venture capitalists have a very strong incentive, therefore, to have all of their investments go public or be acquired in as short a period of time as possible. The emphasis on achieving capital gains in a short period of time naturally creates a focus on companies that will growth quickly when given fuel. Technology-based companies fill that need. Industries undergoing major changes also fit that requirement.

Given these requirements, it is clear that professional or institutional venture capitalists have a strong preference for early-stage investments where they can buy huge percentage ownership positions relatively cheaply, industries undergoing dramatic changes, such as electronics, computers, and biotechnology, and companies that have a strong management team in place to help the entrepreneur with the lift-off. It generally takes 60 to 75 days after a business plan has been submitted to a venture capital fund to close on the money. The financing goes quicker if there is an active new issues market into which venture capitalists can liquidify their investments; and slower if the stock market is weak and the new issues market flat. If a financing has not taken place by 90 days, there is a good chance that it never will without changes in the business plan or the management team. One would think these things should move along more quickly, but venture capitalists act slowly and carefully. They do extensive reference checking on the people, technical checking on the product, and investigation of the demand for the product. Also, they have small staffs and large portfolios to manage, new deals to read, board meetings to attend, and administrative duties to take care of. Most venture capitalists travel extensively and are physically unable to respond as quickly as one would like. Thus, an entrepreneur is well advised to allow 90 to 120 days to obtain a financing, including 30 to 45 days once a venture capital fund has shown interest.

It is prudent to send the business plan to 15 to 20 private venture capital funds. Frequently an investment banker can be helpful, as can one of the directories that categorize the funds by their areas of interest, although the directories become obsolete rather quickly. In any event, newer venture capital funds should be given top priority because they are less preoccupied with portfolio problems and board meetings. Among the nearly 220 private venture capital funds, the investment criteria differ in several key respects. The entrepreneur should ask several questions of the venture capitalists at the time of his or her initial telephone call to determine if the business plan should be submitted. These questions should include: (1) Do you have any other investment in a company such as mine? (2) Could you list the companies in your portfolio? (3) At an appropriate time, may I speak directly with them to see what you are like to work with? It is important to avoid submitting a business plan to a venture capitalist who has invested in a competitor. Although venture capitalists, for the most, part have high ethical standards, one should never offer them tempting information about a competitor's strategic plan.

Venture capital investments are categorized by stage of development, industry, area and geographical location. The four stages of development are as follows:

Start-up
First stage
Expansion
Buy-out

A start-up situation is a company without revenues. Most private venture capital funds have a strong preference for start-ups. This is true for several reasons. First, they are able to obtain more ownership in a start-up situation and frequently control. Second, they know a great deal about the risks involved in start-ups and how to manage those risks. Third, if the entrepreneur or inventor needs a manager until he has located one, the venture capital fund can fill the slot temporarily or find someone to fill it. Fourth, many venture capital funds have lift-off-experienced managers on their staffs. They are free to go in and troubleshoot a new company experiencing launch problems.

Start-ups are frequently divided into three subcategories: (1) dining room table, (2) laboratory, and (3) garage. The dining room table or "seed capital" start-up is not really a company. There is an idea or concept for a new product or service, an entrepreneurial team, and a timetable of events (or PERT chart) with dollar values assigned to those events. In a dining room table situation, the costs of the launch are known as well as the events that need to take place. The problem is being formulated and the opportunity identified. But no money has been spent on creating the solution.

It is frequently better for the entrepreneur to raise family or friendly capital to move a dining room table deal to a more advanced stage of development, because if all the capital that needs to be raised, according to the PERT chart, is raised from private venture capital funds, the entrepreneur will in all likelihood yield majority control from the outset. The entrepreneur needs to retain as much ownership as possible in order to reward key employees and attract a manager. Because many emerging companies require several rounds of financing, the entrepreneur's ownership would very likely be whittled down to less than 20% within three years if he or she goes to the venture capitalists at the outset. Laboratory start-ups are much more risky than post-R&D start-ups. But the payoffs can be larger as well. Chester Carlson sought venture capital for 12 years for his xerography invention with a bar of stainless steel, a rabbit's foot to keep it shiny, a sheet of paper with typing on it, a clean sheet of paper, and some gray powder. He might have lopped off 5 or 6 years from the search had he used a business plan instead.

Family members and friends generally are interested in investing at this stage, and they are usually willing to give their proxy to the entrepreneur to vote their shares. They frequently are able to provide a few more dollars after the first round, if necessary. Occasionally they can be persuaded to sell some of their shares to provide a sweetener to venture capitalists in future rounds of financing; and they usually understand that they will be diluted significantly in future rounds of financing. The negative is that family and friends usually remember all of the stories and promises and inferences of guarantees of success. They can be approached on only one deal.

If the PERT chart indicates that the launch will require $1,200,000 over a period of 15 months until monthly cash receipts begin to exceed monthly cash expenditures, it might be possible to have the expenses of the first six months, say, $150,000, funded by family and friends with a business plan updated for venture capitalists at that stage to raise more capital. If the PERT chart calls for $85,000 in equipment, $20,000 in parts, and the salaries of three people for a few months, say, $45,000 or $150,000 overall, it is reasonable for many entrepreneurs to raise that sum at a wedding or funeral. To improve the return to investors, the new company can form a sub-Chapter S corporation and allow the investors to take most of the loss as personal income tax deductions. Thus, to an investor in the 50% income tax bracket, the net dollars invested would be $75,000.

Congress revised sub-Chapter S in 1981 to permit 25 natural persons (no corporations or partnerships) to invest. The limit had previously been 15 persons. Further, one or more of the investors might wish to own the equipment and lease it to the company, in order to use the investment tax credit ($8500 in this example) plus accelerated depreciation to save income tax payments and to lower the net investment cost. An attorney familiar with securities laws should be consulted in regard to the sale of stock to family and friends in order to ensure proper legal housekeeping from inception.

The laboratory stage of the start-up period generally occurs when a product is in development but is not sufficiently completed to be tested. The problem has been formulated and a creative solution has been designed and developed. However, it has not been tested on a customer's site; or, in the vernacular: "beta-tested." Few of the risks of the very earliest stage have been abated. The major risks (Can it be produced? Can it be sold? Can it be sold at a profit?) still exist. What distinguishes the laboratory stage from the dining room table stage is that *a risk has been taken*. The entrepreneur has begun to spend time and money to develop a product that he or she believes solves a large problem. The entrepreneur has left his or her job, which shows faith in the product more than any other action. Venture capitalists turn thumbs down on entrepreneurs who have not left their jobs. The entrepreneur may have asked other potential team members to moonlight on the development of the product until he or she can afford to pay them cash; but they can apply their hours of work toward stock. Venture capitalists like to see an entrepreneur risk his or her time and job, because they risk their time and job with every investment they make.

Entrepreneurs cannot include as part of their cash investment the number of hours they have invested in the start-up times their current hourly rate. After all, the investors are not charging for their time. Many entrepreneurs seek funding at the laboratory stage of emergence, although it is preferable to complete product development before raising professional venture capital. The ownership level that is necessary to attract venture capital at this stage is generally too great to leave enough incentive for the entrepreneurs. It is advisable to attempt to grow to a more advanced stage before obtaining professional venture capital. Customer financing, family, friends, and the savings accounts of team members are usually relied on at this stage. Once a customer has tested the product, venture capital is considerably cheaper. Many ways to raise capital in the very early stages of a company's existence appear in Chapter 6.

Who else might invest at this stage? A local industrialist, successful entrepreneur, or wealthy doctor or other professional who has an affinity for the entrepreneur's project or area of interest. The investment may be structured in a manner that saves income taxes or otherwise reduces the investor's risk in order to make the decision-making process move along rapidly. Frequently private individuals have difficulty saying no right away and string the entrepreneurs along rather than "hurt their feelings." For the entrepreneur who legitimately cannot approach family or friends, because of an absence of contacts, it is useful to visit the local Industrial Development Authority Office and ask them for the names of local private investors who might be inclined to increase employment in the community. Of course, certain communities reach out for the entrepreneur and pull together the financing for him or her, but this occurs principally in the Deep South and in industrial areas of the Northeast and Midwest that have been losing employment. Lowell, Massachusetts, a once-booming shoe manufacturing town which fell into a postwar decline, has bounced back as a town full of microcomputer cottages. Entrepreneurs generally become good at "networking," that is, bringing together community leaders to help with the launch. The key is to make them feel they will lose something—deposits, a real estate commission, a key man insurance policy, and so on—if the company is not launched.

The garage stage is that start-up period at which most early-stage companies receive professional venture capital. The term "garage" probably originated in the early 1960s when men such as William Hewlett and David Packard asked investors out to their garage to see their electronics instrument. Some of my friends think it refers to the start-up of the automobile industry. Entrepreneurs still lift off in garages. They build prototypes of new devices or machines and they invite investors and customers to come over to the garage for a demonstration. In the garage stage, the entrepreneurs have built a prototype, tested its performance, estimated the costs of tooling and unit costs of production in volume runs, and may have run a few beta tests on customers' premises. In a non-manufacturing garage start-up, the concept would have been tested, or a "dummy" of a magazine prepared with a limited dry circulation test-run.

Garage start-ups are the most popular investment candidates raking in over $600 million in professional venture capital in 1982. The entrepreneurial team has generally taken the career risk. They have personal or family money at risk, they have worked together for awhile, and they have formulated and reformulated the problem and worked out many of the bugs that develop in highly risky, intense, tightly controlled environments. The production risk is also mitigated somewhat by actual proof that the product can be produced and that it works as advertised. What remains is the marketing risk. Can the product be sold at a profit? If the people and production risks are minimized, many private venture capital firms will tackle the marketing risk head-on. This is particularly the case where the market for the product is very large and rapidly growing. But very few venture capitalists will assume knowingly more than one risk.

First-stage investments are equally popular with private venture capital funds. In this stage, the company has generally been operating for one year after the product development period and it has made a number of sales. Venture capitalists like this stage because they can contact the customers and do "due diligence": ask the marketplace how it likes the product and the people, how they use the product, and whether they intend to reorder. The products have been de-bugged in a user environment and frequently modified at the customer's request or with his or her input. The entrepreneurs have learned something about customer service and, moreover, have been in the marketplace and gotten their hats handed to them a few times when the product was delivered late, or was missing a part, or was sold or installed incorrectly. In one or two instances, a customer is willing to place a large order if the company can demonstrate a more solid financial footing. This information reflects back on the revenue forecasts in the business plan. Once a customer told me in response to my "due diligence": "They don't know what they've got there. They should charge double what they're charging. The product is *that* good." The customer wants to know that if he or she needs additional product or parts in 24 months, or service or parts just a few months in the future, there will be a manufacturer to provide these services. If the company cannot obtain capital, it probably will lose the order.

Prior to making an investment in a first-stage company, a professional venture capitalist always makes an in-depth investigation of how the product is received and, indeed, used in the marketplace. As many as a dozen customers might be called and asked to speak candidly about the product, and the people, service, training, parts replacement, price, and possibility of expanded uses. Competent venture capitalists ask about the competition as well.

In early-stage, high-technology companies there are generally three kinds of customers: distributors, end-users, and original equipment manufacturers (OEMs). Distributors or dealers purchase the product for resale, occasionally adding value such as software, but primarily retailing the product in their geographic market for a commission. End-users buy the product in order to use it for a specific in-house function. OEMs purchase the product in order to integrate it with one of their manufacture and resell the two as a system. OEM orders can become very large, steady, and profitable. To a venture capitalist, it is a positive feature when a first-stage company stresses OEM sales, because it minimizes marketing expenses, produces long production runs, and ramps sales faster. Convergent Technology Corp., which designs and builds microcomputers for two OEMS—NCR Corp. and Burroughs Corp.—has had a meteoric lift-off in sales and market value. Of course, excessive reliance on one or two major OEM accounts is excessively risky because should they vanish for whatever reason, the emerging company would begin bleeding red ink by the buckets. A mixture of OEM, end-user, and distributor sales is the happy medium, although sales to distributors or dealers are frequently less expensive means of generating sales in the early years than is fielding a direct sales team.

Professional venture capitalists are also interested in suppliers and supplier relationships. They expect the first-stage company to have tested the components of most of the available sources of supply and have solid reasons for selecting each supplier. They expect that the first-stage company will have a procedure for testing incoming components in order to control their quality. Further, they expect that there are alternative sources of supply for each component. This is called being "second sourced," an important requirement especially for critical components because a supplier could fail, be struck, or encounter production delays. Symbiotic relationships can be dangerous. Although Denver Software Co. was pleased to receive Apple Computer's contract to develop Apple III software, when the Apple III was delayed due to production problems, Denver Software gasped for breath for several months.

The value-added aspect of a first-stage company is critical to the private venture capital fund. The fund's life cycle is usually about 10 years; thus, the investment managers seek companies whose products materially improve the users' efficiency or profitability. If the products are proprietary—that is, protected by patents, formulas, trade secrets, or know-how—all the better. What is crucial is lead time. If the value added to the end-user is 30% or better in terms of speed, efficiency, or price (or a combination of the three), the product may have a two- or three-year lead time over larger competitors. Wealth creation through the entrepreneurial process is the maintenance of a monopoly position for as long as possible. Companies such as Polaroid, Xerox, Monogram Industries, Digital Equipment, Intel, Federal Express, and others made such dramatic impacts on the lives of their customers that they created not only wealthy entrepreneurs and investors, but also new industries. Their products and sometimes their corporate names became generic means of classifying the functions they performed, as in "Let's Xerox it" and "I'll Federal Express it to you." The stock of the investor who went all three rounds in Federal Express' hair-straightening series of financings is priced at less than $1 per share while the market price is currently around $70 per share.

The valuations of first-stage companies are markedly greater than those of start-ups, other things being equal. Whereas $500,000 might purchase 40 to 50% of a start-up, it rarely gets more than 25% of a first-stage company. That is a sweeping statement, and there are a multitude of exceptions. Nonetheless, many of the risks encountered at the start-up stage have been reduced or eliminated at the first stage. Start-up investors in Apple Computer paid about thirty cents per share and first stage investors paid approximately $5 per share. The market price of Apple is currently $31 per share.

The expansion or second-stage financing occurs generally two to three years after start-up. The company is operating at a sales level around $5 million and requires another round of venture capital to boost it to an annual sales level of $20 million. The boost is usually to expand nationally from a regional base, to broaden the product line, or to systematize the marketing effort and hire and train a captive sales and installation force. Frequently, expansion financings can be provided with debt or via a public offering; but, prudent entrepreneurs realize that venture capital at this stage is relatively inexpensive. A $1 million injection might cost as little as 5 to 10% of the ownership if the growth curve has been fairly vertical, earnings are trending up, and sound management practices are in place.

Private venture capital funds like to put 10 to 20% of their capital at the expansion level to balance the general riskiness of their portfolio. If private venture capital funds invested only in start-ups, they would be too reliant on the new issues market three to five years hence. If that market were in bed with the flu, the venture capitalists would get pneumonia.

Often venture capitalists invest in later rounds to avoid having their previous investment severely diluted. To gain more equity at the mezzanine level, private venture capital funds occasionally purchase some of management's stock. They also investigate the prospects of a public offering prior to investing with the thought of going public fairly soon after their capital goes in.

Some private venture capital funds have corporate partners to whom they have promised co-investing opportunities. Thus, if a fund puts in $1 million at a first-stage level, it may offer the expansion level to one of its corporate partners. The corporation may be interested in licensing the company's product for a certain market or using it internally. Olivetti, an investor in Oak Investment Partners, Stamford, Conn., occasionally puts in first stage capital in companies where Oak has invested start-up capital. Citicorp Employees Benefit Fund co-invests with the 14 venture capital funds it has invested in.

Finally, the fourth stage at which certain private venture capital funds are active is the leveraged buy-out. This is a radically different kind of investment than the high-technology start-up, and it requires radically different kinds of expertise. There are very few leveraged buy-outs financed, for example, by San Francisco-area venture funds, because of the plethora of high technology start-ups in that marketplace. On the other hand, New York and Chicago have several active leveraged buy-out funds because there are more buy-out opportunities in these regions. Kohlberg, Kravits & Roberts is the best known of these kinds of funds, and it has the backing in most instances of several large insurance companies. The role they play in leveraged buy-outs is to fill the gap between the purchase price and the money that can be borrowed on the assets and from the sellers.

Entrepreneurs should realize that venture capital is *not permanent capital*. It is temporary. It is opportunity seeking. It is for three to five years. The venture capitalists are thinking of ways to get out just as soon as they get in. More permanent capital is provided by banks and insurance companies, who must be actively courted in much the same manner as investors, but to finance the longer-term needs of the company.

The private venture capital funds are interested in achieving a rate of return on start-up and first-stage investments, between 45 and 60% per annum compounded. This translates into ten times their investment in five years or five times in three years on the high side to seven times in ten years and three times in three years on the low side. The range between high and low depends upon the venture capitalist's assessment of the degree of risk. Exhibit 3.15 illustrates these rate of return goals by using the primary tool of the venture capitalist's trade: the hockey stick. The venture capitalist investigates the business plan and the facts that support it and makes a value judgment about the earnings projections; that is, the angle of the hockey stick. The mathematical analysis that he or she then applies to the hockey stick to price the deal is explained in Exhibit 3.15, which I prepared for an article in *Venture* magazine in August 1981.

It should be clear from Exhibit 3.15 that venture capitalists are interested primarily in new business with a high probability of success rather than new concepts that offer unusually high rates of return if they happen to succeed. Note also that the venture capitalist multiplies projected third year earnings by a P/E ratio of 10, which is relatively low for a growth company. This is his hedge against the company's earnings coming in lower than projected, a regrettable but frequent occurrence.

Exhibit 3.15. Compound Growth Rates

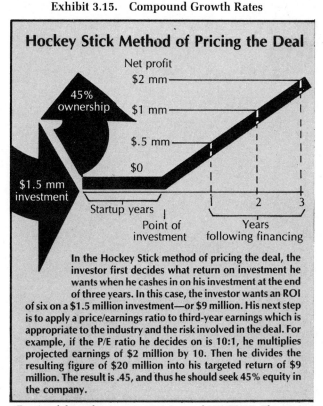

Hockey Stick Method of Pricing the Deal

Net profit

45% ownership

$1.5 mm investment

$2 mm

$1 mm

$.5 mm

$0

Startup years

Point of investment

Years following financing

1   2   3

In the Hockey Stick method of pricing the deal, the investor first decides what return on investment he wants when he cashes in on his investment at the end of three years. In this case, the investor wants an ROI of six on a $1.5 million investment—or $9 million. His next step is to apply a price/earnings ratio to third-year earnings which is appropriate to the industry and the risk involved in the deal. For example, if the P/E ratio he decides on is 10:1, he multiplies projected earnings of $2 million by 10. Then he divides the resulting figure of $20 million into his targeted return of $9 million. The result is .45, and thus he should seek 45% equity in the company.

Source: Reprinted from the August, 1981 issue of *VENTURE*, The Magazine for Entrepreneurs, by special permission. © 1981 Venture Magazine, Inc., 35 West 45th St., New York, N.Y. 10036.

153

4

ILLEGITIMATI NON CARBORUNDUM EST

No matter how carefully the plans are laid, how imaginative is the solution, or how exceptionally balanced is the entrepreneurial team, Murphy's law is infallible: If something can go wrong, it will. As Charlie Brown's friend Linus says: "There is no heavier burden than a great potential." Look at Sanders Associates, Ruben Engineering, and Jartran—all founded by entrepreneurs with previous winners behind them. Their venture capitalists were top-drawer as well: Adler & Co., Citicorp, and Walter Heller, among others. As Richard J. Dumler, a partner in Bessemer Venture Partners, says, "Companies rarely fail because of a flaw in the business plan or even poor execution of the plan. They fail because something was overlooked." One of the reasons sophisticated investors work together is to minimize the risk of overlooking something.

When a company begins to get into serious trouble, lenders and investors climb into their life jackets, lower the dinghies, and sail away from the sinking ship. Suppliers put the company on cash only, customers begin to hear rumors about the trouble and cancel shipments, and employees start to freshen up their resumés. The entrepreneur sees himself backsliding.

THE RULES OF SURVIVAL

No matter how grim the circumstances, there are certain people who cannot permit themselves to fail. Successful entrepreneurs and athletes have this unique ability. In *The Soul of a New Machine,* Tracey Kidder describes why certain engineers were selected at Data General Corp. to create a new computer:

> There was, it appeared, a mysterious rite of initiation through which, in one way or another, almost every member of the team passed. The term that the old hands used for this rite—West invented the term, not the practice—was "signing up." By signing up for the project you agreed to do whatever was necessary for success. You agreed to forsake, if necessary, family, hobbies and friends—if you had any of these left (and you might not if you signed up too many times before).

> The vice president of engineering, Carl Carman, said much later on: "Sometimes I worry that I pushed too hard. I tried not to push any harder than I would on myself. That's why you have to go through the sign up. To be sure you're not conning anybody."*

Once an entrepreneur has "signed up," failure is impossible. It is one thing to be determined not to die when you have a coronary and it is another thing to know how to stay alive. Following are the 10 rules of survival:

1. Buy something
2. Sell something.
3. Begin a development project.
4. Involve more people.
5. Change banks.
6. Put on a seminar.
7. Leverage your customers.
8. Change comptrollers.
9. Play the float.
10. Prepare new cash flow statements weekly.

*Soul of a New Machine, p. 227.

Buy Something

It may seem contradictory, but successful entrepreneurs understand that they are able to wring cash out of companies that conventional managers write off and walk away from. Generating cash from illiquid assets is one of the mystiques known to leveraged buy-out entrepreneurs. An entrepreneur *doubly* experienced in both leveraged buy-outs and turnarounds (salvaging sick companies) is able to buy a sick company using leverage and squeeze cash out of it to save another or the mother ship. Hence the axiom, "When you're broke, buy something."

Sandy Sigolof, the most successful workout entrepreneur in the country—he has been called in to turn around Ampex, Republic, Daylin, and in early 1982, Wickes, the retail lumber and home repair chain—has posted on his bathroom mirror the friendly reminder: "You are the meanest S.O.B. in the valley." That little pick-me-up is from the longer battle cry, "When you walk through the valley of the shadow of death, be the meanest S.O.B. in the valley." If you are going to be a workout or turnaround entrepreneur by choice or by chance, do not approach it timidly.

Five venture capitalists, their $200-per-hour attorneys, and the chief executive officer and chief financial officer of an emerging tire recapping company that the venture capitalists had launched sat in a boardroom 25 stories above Park Avenue in New York City one morning in late 1980, making some very hard decisions. Nearly $10 million had been pumped into the tire company and it had not been able to achieve a break-even level of operations in 24 months. As a matter of fact, it was out of money, the investors were out of patience, and the entrepreneurs were out of time.

One of the attorneys came up with a scheme that would enable the venture capitalists to come out ahead. The entrepreneurs were asked to leave the meeting and were subsequently terminated. The venture capitalists exercised their rights of creditors in a senior secured position arising from the default in payment of interest and principal on their subordinated convertible debentures. They took control of the company. The lawyers had a plan.

The venture capitalists then looked through their stack of incoming deals to find a profit-making company where an 80% ownership position could be acquired. They found one whose earnings were approximately equal to the size of the losses of the tire company. They put $2 million into the tire company which then invested it in the leveraged buy-out and took back 80% of the common stock of the latter company. The profitability of the leveraged buy-out would be protected for several years by the $10 million tax loss carry-forward of the tire company. Thus, the $2 million, leveraged with debt to finance the buy-out, earned a minimum $5 million (the tax savings), which could be invested to expand the buy-out company or to salvage the tire company. If the tire company is salvageable, the investors will have two ways to get their money back. Leave it to the lawyers to come up with temporary bandages. I say temporary, because the Internal Revenue Service could interpret a transaction of this nature as a scheme to avoid taxes. The venture capitalists, of course, see it as a way to salvage their investment.

The tax loss carry-forward is an asset if the company that owns it can find a profitable company to acquire. Then the earnings of the acquired company can be sheltered by the tax loss carry-forward of the acquiror. The IRS allows companies to carry their losses forward for five years. Thus, if in the tire company example the tax loss carry-forward was $10 million in 1981, it would expire by 1986. The acquired company would have to generate taxable income of $20 million from 1982 to 1986 to utilize effectively the full amount of the tax loss carry-forward.

Peter Kennedy, the president and largest stockholder of the old-line brokerage firm of Dominick & Dominick, Inc., New York, was presiding over the demise of the firm in 1975 when a plan dawned on him. Dominick had closed dozens of offices around the country, had broken leases and let hundreds of employees go. The red ink was spilling all over, but a small brokerage and investment banking business was maintained at 55 Water Street in New York. The investment banking activity involved arranging acquisitions for clients. Kennedy asked himself, "Why not an acquisition for Dominick?"

Month after month, he and his corporate finance department staff put on a full-court press in search of a large, profitable seller. Dominick's losses exceeded $50 million. Thus, an acceptable seller would have to have an earnings capability of $20 million per annum.

Dominick had precious little equity to invest, so the seller would have to be fully leverageable as well. Finally, they found one: Drexel Furniture. One of the finest names in home furnishings, Drexel had been put on the market because its owners were not enthusiastic about the business any longer. Kennedy and his staff, knowing next to nothing about the furniture business, were terribly enthusiastic about it. A drowning sailor will reach out for a life preserver or a rotten log, so long as it floats. The lenders knew that the Dominick crowd did not know much about the business they were buying, but their $50 million in loans was well protected. The deal closed in 1978, and the marriage has been a happy one.

These are telephone book numbers. The entrepreneurs are sophisticated deal-makers with high-priced lawyers. What about the little guy who needs $50,000 or $100,000 to survive? Can he apply the "When you're broke, buy something" axiom? If so, how?

The same rules apply; they apply proportionally. Assume an entrepreneur in the carpet distribution business has lost $150,000. Further, assume that with a downturn in housing starts and an overall slow economy, the carpet business is in a slump and recovery is not in sight. Accounts receivable average 90 days, inventories are turning fewer than three times a year, creditors have called their loans, and suppliers have put the company on COD terms.

The entrepreneur decides to salvage his company by purchasing a healthier one in an unrelated field and sheltering its taxes with the carpet company's loss carry-forward. Since he has no cash, he must find a fully leverageable seller. The search begins. Merger and acquisition brokers and investment bankers are contacted, lists of sellers are scoured, and advertisements are placed in the *Wall Street Journal*. After weeks of reviewing acquisition candidates, the entrepreneur finds a fully leverageable tent manufacturer. Its financial statements appear in Exhibit 4.1.

Assume that the seller's price is $335,000 for the entire business and that he wants all cash. Small, nonproprietary manufacturing companies are quite difficult to sell.

Frequently, other competitive manufacturing companies are not interested, would prefer to see a competitor leave the market, or are prevented by antitrust laws from making a horizontal acquisition.

EXHIBIT 4.1. Tent Manufacturer Leveraged Buy-Out Candidate.

Balance Sheet, Fiscal Year Ending 12/31/82

Assets			Liabilities and Net Worth		
Current assets:			**Current liabilities:**		
Cash	$	35,000	Accounts payable	$	90,000
Accounts receivable		245,000	Accrued expenses		25,000
Inventories		180,000	Notes payable		120,000
Total current assets:		460,000	Total current liabilities		235,000
Plant, equipment (net)		85,000	Stockholders' equity		335,000
Other assets		15,000			
Total assets	$	560,000	Total liabilities and net worth	$	560,000

Operating Statement, 12 Months Ending 12/31/82

		Percent
Sales	$1,350,000	100.0
Cost of goods sold	904,500	67.0
Gross profit	445,500	33.0
Selling expense	135,000	10.0
General and administrative expense	222,500	16.5
Net operating income	88,000	6.5
interest expense	20,000	1.5
Net profit before taxes	$ 68,000	5.0

Also, acquisitions are sometimes frightening to people, because they are stressful and upsetting. Thus, attractive little companies such as the $1.4 million (sales) tent manufacturer cannot attract a premium price. They are sold off at or below book value and usually for a package of cash and notes, rarely for all cash. Thus, the seller might accept $300,000. Let's see if that amount can be raised from the balance sheet.

Conventional loan ratios used by asset lenders such as commercial finance companies are 85% against the value of accounts receivable less than 90 days outstanding, 50% against the value of finished goods and raw material inventories, and 75% against the liquidation (auction or quick-sale) value of property, plant, machinery, and equipment. If we assume that all of the accounts receivable of the ten manufacturer are less than 90 days old, that two-thirds of the inventories are either raw material or finished goods, and that net book value of plant and equipment is equal to liquidation value, then the entrepreneur can raise the following cash from the tent manufacturer's balance sheet:

	Book Value ×	Loan Ratio =	Cash Advance
Cash	$ 35,000	—	$ 10,000*
Accounts receivable	245,000	0.85	208,250
Inventories	120,000	0.50	60,000
Net plant, equipment	85,000	0.75	63,750
Total	$485,000		$342,000

*Excess over amount needed to operate the business.

From the $342,000 cash advance, we must deduct the $120,000 note payable, which will have to be repaid. This leaves $222,000 to pay the seller. To squeeze more cash from the balance sheet, we ask the seller to guarantee the collectibility of 100% of the accounts receivable. Normally sellers will agree to this request. The negotiation is quick and simple. If the seller will not guarantee their collectibility, then the buyer surely does not want them. The seller can keep the accounts receivable as part of the purchase price in order to borrow 100% of the value of that particular asset. In any event, an additional $36,750 in cash can be squeezed out of this balance sheet, bringing total cash on hand at the closing date to approximately $260,000. Some of that is needed for closing costs. Assume then that the entrepreneur offers the seller $230,000 in cash and a $50,000 note secured by the inventory in second position to the commercial finance company, bearing interest at 9% per annum and due in five years. With the lure of his condominium nestled behind the fourteenth green in Tarpon Springs, Florida beckoning the seller, he is not likely to refuse.

Not so fast, you say. How can the entrepreneur afford the debt service on a $260,000 loan at 20% interest, of which the equipment portion amortizes in 84 equal monthly installments immediately, plus 9% on $50,000? The first year's debt service is:

$260,000	×	0.20	=	$52,000
50,000	×	0.09	=	4,500
63,750	÷	7	=	9,107
Total Annual Debt Service			=	$65,107

The company's net operating income is $88,000 per annum, so it can fairly comfortably support $65,000 in debt service. However, if sales slip by 10%, the company will be operating at break-even. Fortunately, in leveraged buy-out situations, general and administrative expenses are frequently overstated. The wife's car is occasionally a company expense, as are country club dues, lots of travel and entertainment card charges, and the ubiquitous indigent brother-in-law in the shipping department. Rather than $88,000, adjusted net operating income is more like $108,000. Further, the entrepreneur in this example has a carpet company to pay his salary, and the seller's salary is saved and becomes cash flow. The result is an extra cash flow of approximately $40,000 after-debt service ($108,000 minus $65,000) plus $40,000 in salary savings. This results in close to $7,000 per month additional cash for the combined operations. Remember, taxes will not be paid for awhile due to the buyer's tax loss carry-forward.

Furthermore, the entrepreneur received from the lenders a check for $260,000 at the closing, paid his professional fees of $10,000, and handed over $230,000 to the seller. The additional $20,000 can be used: to sprinkle among the carpet company's creditors. The additional cash flow of $80,000 brings to a total of $100,000 the amount of cash generated by the broke carpet entrepreneur by buying something.

Even if the seller had refused the package and held out for more cash, the entrepreneur could have found ways to squeeze more cash out of the balance sheet. A favorite method is to sell the equipment to a leasing company or partnership of individuals, and lease it back. Another is to let the seller keep the inventory and sell it to the buyer for cost as orders are taken. Still a third is to find a subordinated lender to add $50,000 to the inventory loan. The Small Business Administration will frequently do this. However, in instances where speed and timing are critical, it is best to sit and hammer out a deal with the seller. He wants to fee it up at Innisbrook as badly as the entrepreneur needs the cash flow.

Sell Something

I have many memories, as have all venture capitalists and investment bankers, of imaginative survival strategies. Several of these memories involve stories of assets not on the balance sheet that the entrepreneur sold to someone for cash. Better than magic tricks, they are in the same genre. Keep your eyes on their hands and you may eventually see how the trick is done.

These stories are not endorsements of fast-dealing practices intended to screw someone. Certain rags-to-riches authors have suggested schemes that were not illegal, but should have been. Promoters of pyramid schemes have recommended that their distributors use borrowing schemes, such as making several simultaneous loan applications to different banks and obtaining credit cards under false names, in order to buy their territories or initial products. Nothing of that kind is intended here. If an entrepreneur cannot do his thing honestly, he should work for someone else instead. Rather, the intent is to show the imagination of entrepreneurs when they are on their backs with one shoulder pinned to the mat. Desperation, after all, not necessity, is the mother of invention.

A corporation near Dallas, Texas owned an electronic components wholesale distribution business. It printed a catalog once each year that listed all of the inventory in its six warehouses around the country. The catalog was mailed to 250,000 customers and to some 25,000 new names—purchasing agents at manufacturers—each year. A few salesmen traveled the country to stimulate business and to determine which new components should be stocked. About 25% of the revenues were generated in that manner and 75% by catalog recipients telephoning the nearest warehouse. If the goods were in stock, they were shipped the same day.

The corporation agreed to sell the electronics wholesaler to its general manager on a leveraged buy-out basis for $8 million. The general manager had $95,000 to invest, and a lender agreed to provide $7.5 million secured by the accounts receivable and inventory. The entrepreneur was $405,000 short, and the corporation would not take back a note because all of the assets had first and second liens on them. An obvious solution to close the gap in a leveraged buy-out is to raise venture capital: sell common stock or equity-linked securities to a private investor. But that is a time-consuming process, and the corporation was giving the manager a short time period in which to respond. He had less than 15 days to deliver the certified check for $8 million.

The solution occurred quite by accident. The manager's investment banker was describing a direct response business to the general manager when the latter leaped up from his seat and said, "Let's borrow on our names." It was a brilliant idea. One of the least well understood businesses in the country is the purchase via mail business. There are three forms: direct response, direct mail, and mail order. The electronics wholesaler was in the third category. It mailed catalogs to people who ordered via the mail or by telephone and sent in a check or paid the UPS driver when the goods arrived. The better known mail order firms are the Horchow Collection, Modern Merchandising, and virtually every major department store. There are very small selling costs in this business, and so prices are better for the customer. His risk is that the goods shipped may not look or act like the goods ordered. As transportation costs increase, more and more people rely on mail order. Naturally, lenders have become acclimated to mail-order marketing as well.

Direct response is selling products via advertisements in newspapers, magazines, television or radio commercials. Direct mail is selling products via an envelope full of coupons mailed to carefully selected names and addresses. These new forms of marketing will expand and grow with the development of cable TV, particularly direct response television.

In any event, a customer who orders product through the mail is an off-balance-sheet asset. His name and address have collateral value to a strapped or pressured entrepreneur. Converting customer lists to cash works as follows. The list, which is normally in computer printout format on sticky-backed cheshire labels, ready to be pulled off and affixed to envelopes, is shown to several list brokers. These people are in the business of renting lists to direct-mail marketers, credit card companies, magazine publishers, book clubs, oil companies, and other users of direct mail.

A qualified list broker can review a mailing list to determine its number of "turns"; that is, the number of times he is likely to be able to rent the list in one year. A second criterion for determining a list's value is its freshness. Since people move at the rate of once every four or five years, one-fifth of a mailing list becomes obsolete each year. The mailing pieces are returned "Addressee Unknown." Thus, a fresh list—90 days since the names were assembled—has greater value than a one-year-old list, which is more valuable than a two-year-old list. A third measure of value is the average size of the customer's purchase. If the average order is $12.00, it is not as valuable a list as one where the typical order is $120.00.

The range of prices for customer lists is between 2 cents and 6 cents per name, depending upon the three primary measures of value. The electronics wholesaler had one other criterion in its favor: the names were corporations and institutions, much better payers, larger buyers, and easier to collect from than individuals or governments. Parenthetically, companies that sell to the federal government are not leveraged buy-out candidates because the government is a poor payer and tough to collect from.

Several list brokers reviewed the electronic wholesaler's customer list and put a valuation on it of 5 cents per name. The number of turns varied among the brokers from a low of 25 to a high of 50. That may seem like a lot of times to rent a list of names, but not when you consider how many items of third class mail you receive each day.

Assuming a mid-range of 40 turns, each name is worth $2.00 and

275,000 names are worth $550,000. The general manager's investment banker located a commercial finance company delighted to provide a 75% advance against the appraised value of the list, subject to the hiring of a list broker to begin turning the names. The general manager squeezed $412,500 out of the list and appeared at the closing, checks in hand, with a great big grin on his face.

Another form of off-balance-sheet financing that can be used to close the gap in leveraged buy-outs or to raise emergency cash is borrowing on "imputed receivables." A client in Connecticut and I discovered a lender willing to bet that the accounts receivable that we were willing to hand over to the seller as part of the purchase price would sprout up once again on the balance sheet within 90 days. The financing worked out that the lender advanced to the leveraged buy-out entrepreneur 60% of the value of the accounts receivable that the lender believed would be created over the next 90 days. The purchase price of $20 million was raised by letting the seller keep the accounts receivable and by borrowing on the inventory and equipment. However, the buyer needed an additional $2 million to give to the seller and $1 million in working capital. Accounts receivable at the time of the closing were approximately $5 million. The seller took them at the closing, leaving the entrepreneur with the need to generate $15 million. He squeezed $13 million out of the rest of the balance sheet, and the lender added another $3 million to the deal by making what amounted to a 90-day unsecured loan. The additional loan would be secured by the accounts receivable as they were generated. The entrepreneur sold an off-balance-sheet asset to the lender who knew that it would be solid collateral within 90 days. Thus, he borrowed on imputed receivables.

Another Connecticut entrepreneur in the telecommunications equipment business, doing about $6 million per annum (sales), had an accounts receivable loan with a large New York bank. The bank advanced 85% of the value of shipments to the Connecticut company against presentation of invoices. The company shipped $500,000 to a large industrial corporation, sent the invoice to the bank, and $425,000 was deposited in its account the same day.

The customer, however, found the products unsatisfactory and would not accept them at the dock. They went into a warehouse while the customer and the telecommunications company exchanged strong words. The customer claimed the products were defective. The company claimed that the customer was trying to weasel out of a purchase order. As is the case with so many disagreements, both sides engaged lawyers who began the procedure of threatening letters followed by litigation and the inevitable ruling by a judge.

The telecommunications company had a bigger problem. It was out of cash. The $500,000 order was not going to be paid inside of 90 days, and when the bank next reviewed its collateral position it would see that $425,000 of its loans were unprotected.

The entrepreneur began to move quickly to take the offensive. It visited with its attorney in order to obtain a strong letter to be handed to the bank saying that the charges made by the customer were without merit. The entrepreneur then asked his lawyer to sue the customer for a variety of things brought about by the nonpayment of the $500,000 order. The lawyer came up with some creative items such as fraud and antitrust, and the entrepreneur sued the customer for $1.5 million in damages. His lawyer said that the telecommunications company's law suit had a great deal of merit. The telecommunications entrepreneur took the second letter to his bank and obtained a $500,000 loan secured by—as I called it at the time—a "litigation receivable." It was a creative solution to turn adversity coupled with an overall need for cash into a $500,000 cash advance. If every entrepreneur were able to convert litigation into cash, the economy would be embroiled in lawsuits and very little work would get done. However, occasionally an entrepreneur's case is so strong that he is able to borrow against its eventual settlement.

There are other off-balance-sheet assets that a lender might be interested in to provide emergency cash. Restaurant chains have been able to assign their leases as collateral in order to generate cash. Computer software companies have sold their source codes on several programs in order to gin up survival cash. Magazine publishers rent their lists of subscribers more vigorously when cash is precious. Consumer electronics products manufacturers rent their lists of warranty card holders in order to generate cash.

Hollywood has brought us many wonderful things, usually visually exciting and stimulating. Among these are its financing techniques. No industry has as many ways to sell "smoke" (otherwise known as discounted cash flow) as the film industry. Raising the money to produce movies is so difficult that it is truly amazing that anyone has the energy left to produce the film once the financing is in place. My experience suggests that the means are frequently more entertaining than the ends.

Once an undercapitalized independent producer—known in other arenas as an entrepreneur, but Hollywood puffs up titles—offered Elizabeth Taylor $100,000 plus a sable coat for a cameo appearance in his film. She could keep the sable coat to be worn in her one scene. Not a bad idea, thought Ms. Taylor, until one of the film's creditors knocked on her door a few months later and claimed the sable coat was his collateral.

To provide ideas to entrepreneurs on exquisitely creative methods of selling off-balance-sheet assets, witness the Hollywood producer. Here he (let's say the producer is male) sits in New York, reading a script just presented by a writer. The producer likes it and signs an option to pay the writer $75,000 plus 5% of the distributor's gross income (the box office receipts less 50% which is the theater's cut). The producer must deliver $25,000 within 90 days and $50,000 by the first day of shooting.

The producer thinks that a semi-unknown actor who co-starred in a recent successful film would be a good male lead, and he is considered affordable, bondable, and bankable. These are important characteristics. Some stars such as Marlon Brando are simply not affordable by most independent producers. They want several million dollars plus a large percentage of the distributors' gross income, sometimes as much as $5 million plus 10%. Bondable means that the collection of actors, actresses, and directors have the reputation for hard, focused work in order to bring the film in on budget. Some stars have been known to come to the set too drunk to work, thus blowing a day of shooting at great cost to the producer. Performance bonds are not obtainable on these people. And without bonds, the producer cannot convince lenders that the budget is realistic. If overruns are not financed, the film cannot be released; thus no revenue stream.

Bankable means that the revenue projections are believable. If an actor's last few movies had box office results of $10 million, $8 million, and $6 million, in that order, then projecting that his next film will do $15 million will convince absolutely nobody. If his last film achieved box office results of $10 million, projecting $8 million for the current project is more sensible.

The producer calls the semi-unknown actor's agent to ask that he read the script. That is accomplished rapidly (sometimes the producer sits in the adjoining room and pushes telephoning to new heights of excitement in order to demonstrate the "moving train effect," (of which more later) and the actor agrees to take the role. The producer and the agent negotiate a flat $250,000 price for the actor's services, payable $25,000 on signing, $112,500 on the first day of shooting, and $112,500 on the last day of shooting. This is a rather modest contract and fee. Certain stars have the right to change the script, approve the director, receive a percentage of the gate, and select where their name will appear in the advertisements. Whenever you see a strange grouping of names of stars of relatively equal ranking, such as Michael Caine, Sean Connery, and George C. Scott, you can be sure that each wanted to appear to the left of the other two and not on a line below. The compromise is sometimes a pyramid, or a pyramid of their faces and the names on a straight line. The negotiations are so tedious and difficult that movie producers sometimes survive on antacid liquids and tension relievers.

The independent producer now has a script and a star. He needs a director. The good directors and stars are booked well into the future, in most cases, so it is up to the producer to find out who is available, what his or her track record is, and what he or she will cost. For this, the producer flies to Los Angeles and begins brain-picking, telephoning, and searching for the optimum candidate. This process is excruciatingly difficult because the director is as critical to a movie as a chief operating officer is to a business. The director is the conductor. He or she will determine the budget, the scenery, the locations, and most of the crew as well as the other actors and actresses. He or she may want a script rewrite. Budget overruns are largely a matter that rests with the director's abilities and emotions.

The difficult search for an available, bankable, bondable, and affordable director continues until director and agent sign a contract. Let us assume that in this situation the director agrees to $400,000 for 16 weeks of shooting and 16 weeks of editing, plus 5% of the distributors' gross. He receives $80,000 on signing, $120,000 on the first day of shooting, and $200,000 on the final day of shooting, protected by a letter of credit. For the $80,000 advance, the director agrees to deliver a budget and an edited, shooting script to the producer within 60 days of the date of signing the contract.

To summarize what has happened at this point, an independent producer has obtained the rights to a script and the services of an actor and a director for a certain period of time. The producer's balance sheet at this point in time is shown in Exhibit 4.2.

EXHIBIT 4.2. Independent Producer's Balance Sheet.

Assets		Liabilities and Net Worth	
Cash[a]	—	Payable to:	
		Writer	$ 50,000
		Actor	225,000
		Director	320,000
			$ 595,000
Script	$ 75,000	Net Worth	(520,000)
		Total Liabilities	
Total Assets	$ 75,000	and Net Worth	$ 75,000

[a]The independent producer has spent the following sums:

Travel, telephone, legal	$ 20,000
Writer advance	25,000
Actor advance	25,000
Director advance	80,000
Total out-of-pocket expenses	$ 150,000

The producer must deliver $520,000 by the first day of shooting, some 60 days in the future. In addition, he must raise the amount of capital that the director says it will cost to shoot the film. Let's assume those costs are $4 million, which includes a 20% cushion for overruns. Therefore, the overall costs of this film come to $4,670,000—say, $5 million after additional travel and legal costs. At this point, the revenue stream has been diluted by 10% to the director and writer and another 10% to friends of the producer who put up a $175,000 war chest. The producer has 60 days to raise $5 million, and he is working with 40% of box office receipts.

The independent producer has several off-balance-sheet assets to sell. These are as follows:

U.S. Theatrical Distribution.   The producer can sell the right to distribute the film to U.S. theaters for a fee equal to from 25% to 60% of distributor's gross income. A U.S. distributor such as 20th Century Fox or MGM might advance all or a portion of the budget. The more they advance, the greater their percentage. Independent producers would rather negotiate with more tender lambs for the money than enter the jaws of the U.S. distributor. But dealing with them is practically inevitable. Technological change will someday permit movie distribution from studio to theater via satellite and obviate the distributor; but that is two or three years away.

Foreign Theatrical Distributors.   The rights to distribute the film in 30 to 50 foreign countries are quite easily sold at the film industry's annual trade show: the Cannes Film Festival held every May on the French Riviera. A French distributor advanced Francis Coppola $100,000 for the French rights to "Apocalypse Now," and when the film was number one at the box office for most of 1980, the French distributor made over 20 times his investment. Winners like this one keep the market very active and responsive.

U.S. Network Television.   The three major U.S. television networks are forever in the market for product. They buy movies "by the pound"; that is, four hours' are worth twice as much as two hours'. The one hour of out-takes to "King Kong" were put back into the two-hour film for the television sale, which brought the price up by $2.5 million from $5 million to $7.5 million. The film "Annie" was sold to a network for $20 million to finance the shooting.

U.S. Independent Television.   After a couple of runs on one of the networks, the independent stations would like to fill some of their hours of programming time with Hollywood's finest. Because the air time will be further out in the future, the advance from the independents is less than from the networks; but the product is nonetheless salable to them.

U.S. Cable Television.   An increasingly important market for Hollywood's product is cable television. It has the audience, hence the capital to pay a fair penny for its chance to show the film. Twenty million homes are wired for cable TV. The only major city in the United States today without cable television is Chicago. Cable and pay TV frequently advance as much as 20% of the amount advanced by network television.

Home Video.   With the explosive sales of Betamax and VHS devices, the market for watching movies at home is currently estimated at one-fifth of theatrical. If a film grosses $10 million at U.S. box offices it should generate $2 million in home video cassette rentals over the subsequent three to five years. Thus, the film can be discounted at something under $2 million; perhaps $1.2 million in advance of shooting.

Military and In-Flight.   These are two small but interesting markets in which to sell the rights. For in-flight, the film must be rated G or PG and be less than 90 minutes long.

Book Rights.   Is there a paperback book possibility in this script? There may very well be that and more. Some people have sold paperback books on the making of their movie. The photographs are there, after all, and so are a few thousand words.

Product Rights.   In the film "Rocky III," when Rocky smiles at his little boy and says "Wheaties! What are Wheaties?" and the child giggles uncontrollably and says to Rocky, "The breakfast of champions," I could see the check from General Mills to the "Rocky III" producers. My estimate: $300,000. When Apollo Creed, the former heavyweight champion of the world, appeared in training camp with his Nike workout suit on, I said to myself, "$150,000." I never quite saw the name on Rocky's motorcycle, but it had a three-minute spot in front of an audience of 30 million viewers, so my estimate was "Honda: $250,000." I missed a few of the obvious advertisements that appeared during "Rocky III," but I mentally raised $600,000 to pitch into the budget.

Other Rights.   If you are Gary Kurtz or George Lucas, capable of conceiving the Federation and producing the movies that depict the wars between the stars, then you might end up with toys, games, calendars, clothing, bed linen, and robots. Lucasfilms could be one of *Fortune's* 500 largest industrial companies on its product sales alone. The $40 Darth Vader mask has sold close to 25,000 copies. The producers of "Star Wars" own a bank. They have sold only the theatrical and home video rights and own all others. I would say that the remaining rights to the "Star Wars" series are worth more than most American steel companies.

At any rate, we return to the fearless independent producer who must raise $5 million in 60 days on the strength of a script, a director, and a semi-unknown actor. There are some bicycle scenes and some running scenes in the movie, so the producer bases the U.S. box office projections on the figures generated by the recent hits, "Breaking Away" and "Chariots of Fire." He cuts these in half for conservatism and projects $10 million in box office receipts. Were this the case, the distributors' gross would be $5 million, less perhaps $2.5 million or 50% of net box office receipts, to the U.S. theatrical distributor, less perhaps $500,000 for advertising and prints, less $500,000 to the writer and director and $500,000 for the producer's friends. The producer would keep the remaining dollars, or $1 million for his efforts. This, of course, is subject to his being able to sell the other rights to raise the $5 million.

The $5 million might be raised as follows:

Foreign theatrical (20 countries sold preshooting at an average $25,000 each)	$ 500,000
U.S. network television (assume $1 million per hour, and a two-hour film)	2,000,000
U.S. independent television (not to run for three years, thus a steep discount)	400,000
U.S. cable television (20 million homes have cable, or 40% of the U.S. population, thus networks value × 40%)	800,000
Military, government, and in-flight	150,000
Products (assume bicycles, soft drinks, running clothes, one flight on United Airlines, and other advertisements)	750,000

| Book advance | 50,000 |
| Total | $5,050,000 |

The independent producer scampers around from source to source picking up contracts and checks and arrives on location to give everybody his or her advance. He banks the contracts with a film lender which provides working capital for the film, gets eight hours' sleep the night before shooting, which is his vacation for the year, and stays on the set for 16 weeks to assist the director.

No entrepreneur works harder or more intensely than the independent film producer. He or she may be forgiven for occasionally flying off the handle at a theater critic who pans a movie. A producer's profits are very hard to come by. The nature of the business demands that he or she know how to sell off assets without giving up the basic business.

Begin a Development Project

For the next example of survival, we drive the Porsche that we bought from the film's profits from the Beverly Wilshire Hotel in Beverly Hills, mandatory lodging for filmdom's entrepreneurs, to Rickey's Hyatt House in Palo Alto, headquarters of the microprocessor garden, otherwise known as Silicon Valley. The reason it is a Porsche is that entrepreneurs prefer European cars and film producers tend not to have families to drive around.

In Silicon Valley, the primary method of surviving the cash shorts is to raise professional venture capital and to discount accounts receivable to get through the cyclical troughs. However, high-technology start-up manufacturing companies are notorious consumers of cash and inevitably run out of capital just inches within sight of first revenues from a new product. Where do you turn when all of your assets are scientific people busily engaged in developing new high-technology products? You cannot sell their time, because that is fully committed.

Some high-technology companies have sold the marketing rights to the products they are developing. Notably, Genentech and Cetus have given away some of their top lines for cash advances from pharmaceutical and chemical companies. Thus, should they indeed discover new drugs, the marketing benefits will accrue to Eli Lilly stockholders rather than Genentech. Francis Coppola could have brought a good deal of wisdom to the Genentech board of directors. That is Interferon over the test tube now.

A better sale is a research and development tax shelter. Agrigenetics Corp. has the marketing rights to all of its products. David J. Padwa, the company's founder and chairman, saw to that, and acquired the seed distribution companies to be an effective marketing company. To raise capital to feed the hard-working scientists, Padwa hired Oppenheimer & Co., New York, to raise $55 million in an off-balance-sheet transaction. Oppenheimer & Co., known for extraordinarily creative financings, was also DeLorean Motor Company's investment banker.

The limited partner investors in Agrigenetics Research Co. could write off against their income tax obligation the amount of their investment. Thus, the federal government picked up half of the tab. There are ways of structuring R&D tax shelters to provide a tax savings greater than the amount of the investment. In addition to the tax savings from an R&D tax shelter, the limited partners are entitled to a royalty from the sale of the products to be developed with their dollars. If the products are indeed developed, produced, and marketed, the investors will see some attractive returns. If not, they will at least have the tax write-off without further obligations. In the case of Agrigenetics, the research that the investors sponsored is to find methods of genetically engineering new forms of plants, ones that can grow in water-poor regions, or without fertilizer. The upside is very exciting; but that is always the case with R&D tax shelters.

This form of raising capital is effective for smaller companies as well, where the need may be $250,000 or less. One of the constraints on size is the legal fees. A $25,000 fee for a tax opinion is not unusual. Thus a financing that yields only $50,000 might produce a very small amount of money after legal fees. In any event, Silicon Valley has fallen in love with the R&D tax shelter.

In 1982, I saw over $350 million in private placement memorandums for R&D tax shelters; and I do not believe that I am witness to more than 10% of the high technology offerings, and I would say closer to half that. There was probably close to $3 billion worth of such offerings made in 1982. Why are they popular?

In a service organization or a brain factory, the technical people must be fed, oiled, and kept going. It does not matter to them what they are developing, what programs they are coding, what integrated circuits they are designing. A hydraulic lift at a Midas muffler shop couldn't care what kind of car it gets under as long as it gets under a car every 30 minutes. So it is with technical people. If they have significant projects and enough money to live on, they are happy.

When a muffler shop entrepreneur puts together financing, he or she does not finance the purchase of hydraulic lifts with equity capital. There are too many lenders eager to finance muffler shop equipment. The same applies to scientific and technical talent. Why sell stock to finance their development activities when the federal government is willing to provide at least half of the money if you can find a qualified investor for the other half? Indeed, the route to finance development costs should be the R&D tax shelter.

The logic is right and it is wrong. It is right because it is relatively quick and wrong because competitive sources of capital are not enamored of having an important chunk of revenues go to a gaggle of limited partners rather than to their stockholders. Thus, if the dollars invested by limited partners in an R&D tax shelter produce a major commercial success that bleeds off significant revenues, an underwriter in the future will ask that the limited partnership be "rolled up." That is, the underwriter will raise an extra $10 million publicly in order to buy out the limited partners. That, of course, means further dilution of stockholders' equity, but at a much higher price than when the tax shelter financing was initiated.

Faced with a pressing need to keep a think tank going, the entrepreneur usually thinks R&D tax shelter. The relative costs and time considerations of raising $1 million in that manner are compared with the other conventional means of raising risk capital in Exhibit 4.3.

For the entrepreneur who begins a new development project as a survival mechanism, the project should not be kept a secret. Creditors and bankers about to go for the throat should be invited to the plant to see the preliminary plans and a copy of the private placement memorandum. It may be advisable to use the services of an investment banker to handle the R&D tax shelter financing in order to reduce the cost of search and attenuate the time period. Further, a back-up plan should be initiated at the same time in case the tax shelter financing aborts. The back-up plan should be very realistic

EXHIBIT 4.3.   Comparison of Alternative Sources of Venture Capital.

	Relative amounts of capital to be raised	What the entrepreneur must give up	Management advice and assistance	Time required to raise capital	Up-front (Prefunding) costs to the entrepreneur
Institutional Venture Capital	$1,000,000	Equity	Abundantly provided	75-120 days	$ 7,500
Tax shelter Limited Partnership	$1,000,000	Sales Royalty	Not provided	6 months	$35,000
Government Guaranteed Loans	$ 750,000	Assets as collateral; personal guarantee	Not provided	6 months	$15,000
Public Offering Common Stock	$2,000,000	Equity	Not provided	6 months	$35,000
Customer Financing	$ 500,000	Future income	Not provided	60-90 days	$10,000

and do-able, for instance, merger or sale of an important product to another company. Both plans should be pursued vigorously with a goal of succeeding at each. Random collisions will inevitably occur that will deter, impact, alter the course of, and delay the survival plan financings. Failure due to lack of capital should not be a consideration with so many options around. But in the dark of the night, when things look their gloomiest, remember country and western singer Jimmie Peters' prescription for success: "Get up one time more than you're knocked down."*

Involve More People

When directing a biblical movie, the colorful director Samuel Goldwyn was heard to say: "Why only twelve disciples? Go out and get

*Paul Dickson, *The Official Explanations* (New York: Delacorte Press, 1980).

thousands." Think big. Involve lots of people. Bring in others who will have a stake in your demise. If you sneeze, they will catch a cold. If you go down, they will suffer as well.

Many first-time entrepreneurs make the mistake of thinking small and thinking privately. They are fearful either that their ideas will be taken by others or that no one will want to take them. I endorse the notions of invisibility, discretion, and propriety, but only up to a point, and that point is when the new company is about to fail due to lack of sales or lack of capital or lack of momentum. Then it's time to get dozens of disciples.

The first group of people to involve are consultants. Known by a variety of names and titles, these are people experienced in various areas who can advise the entrepreneur, suggest changes, and assist in implementing the changes. Depending upon the nature of the company's problems, consultants are available in the fields of product evaluation, personnel, production, marketing, and finance. The entrepreneur should ask other companies to recommend consultants who have been helpful to them.

The obvious place to find assistance is the company's board of directors. It is critical to put together a strong board of directors from the beginning, right after the first financing. These people should be experienced businessmen, not lawyers, not accountants, not bankers. They should know how to scale up production, how to design and implement a marketing plan, how to locate, interview, hire, compensate, and manage middle managers. A responsive, intelligent board of directors can be attracted by getting them excited about the company's growth prospects and by selling them a small amount of the company's common stock at a cheap price.

Even in a small town, effective boards of directors can be assembled. Harris Rogers, founder of Computer Dimensions, Inc. in Florence, South Carolina, a leading developer of computer packages for churches, added a radio station entrepreneur-turned-manager to his board of directors. This led to the development of software for radio stations that removes tedious logging chores from announcers and saves personnel costs. The radio station package gave the company a second source of revenue.

I have been a proponent for many years of having at least one board member selected from a company that developed and maintained a monopoly or near-monopoly position in its industry. A retired executive of IBM is a perfect candidate. Monopolists have clear, concise thought processes. They know how to take an offensive position and maintain it. Their spirit and tenacity can invade, affect, and uplift an entire company that gets into difficulty. Former monopolists make excellent board members, but they are hard to find.

Further, monopolists know a great deal about pricing. When the board agonizes over a decline in sales and begins to think about a price reduction, the monopolist is more inclined to think about raising the price and lowering the maintenance charge, or raising prices and charges but giving more training and service. IBM's dominance was hard earned by its management. The founder of IBM, Thomas J. Watson, was not the entrepreneurial force that his son was. The father once estimated publicly that the company would be lucky if it sold five computers in total. People who spent their business careers becoming achievers at IBM have exceptional business minds. The same applies to the people of other monopolistic or near-monopolistic organizations such as Digital Equipment Corp., Caterpillar Tractor, AT&T Corp., Cummins Engine, and others.

Other excellent board candidates besides monopolists and former entrepreneurs are achievers in rapidly growing companies. They may never have crossed over to the entrepreneurial side of the human development path; they may never have "signed up" to develop a new machine in record time; but they have laid out production lines, scaled up plants, opened new manufacturing sites, read leases and contracts, implemented new marketing plans, and done the most difficult thing of all: hired competent people. If you are thinking about two outsiders for your board of directors, a retired former monopolist and a lean, mean fighting machine would be two excellent candidates. In any event, people the board with problem-solvers, not problem-finders. You are the creative force; hire others to help you implement your ideas.

A board is not Goldwyn's "thousands." Problems won't vanish because your board has good ideas which it feeds to you regularly. For solutions to difficult problems, it is best to hire consultants. Large companies do this all the time. They go to McKinsey & Co., Booz Allen & Hamilton, Cresap, McCormick & Paget, The Boston Consulting Group, and other experienced management consultants and unload their problems on them. The fees are not small and the advice is not always good, but calling the doctor for an examination is the correct thing to do when the patient is sick. The results can be staggering. The *New York Times Magazine* has always dealt with tough subjects such as disarmament, equal rights for women, civil rights, nuclear holocaust, and crises at the top levels of government. These are not subjects for light reading, and for years, very few people read the magazine because it was boring. When Max Frankel became its editor in the early 1970s, he hired a consultant to find out why so few advertisers wanted to enter the pages between equal rights and nuclear disaster. The consultant reiterated the problem and provided the solution: Make every article about a person.

Since that time, the magazine has been about people and it has tripled in size with advertisers. Rather than articles about disarmament, the magazine features articles about what the president is doing about disarmament. Instead of a story about possible CIA involvement on the side of Libyan terrorists, the magazine features a story about Luke Thompson, a former Green Beret from Fayetteville, North Carolina, and his entrapment in the Libyan terrorist episode.

J. Gordon Lippincott, co-founder of Lippincott & Margolis, the most successful corporate identification firm in the 1960s and early 1970s when smokestack America was getting new images, was personally responsible for dozens of the new logos of that period. American Brake Shoe became Abex, Cities Service became Citgo, Atlantic Richfield became ARCO, Socony Mobil became Mobil, Standard Oil of New Jersey became Exxon, and Eaton Yale & Towne became Eaton. Lippincott & Margolis also changed United Rubber Co. to Uniroyal, but the company ran two logos in parallel for a number of years—red and black and blue and white, one with a tire tread one without—in order to confuse the consumer. When management does things like that, it is easy to see why entrepreneurs take over so many new markets ahead of the larger corporations.

One learns from a discussion with Lippincott the value of a corporate identity and a logo that says what the company is. Radio Corporation of America told Lippincott that it wanted to convey tension as if it were ready to spring forth into the future. The result was the RCA logo, a set of three tense wires.

Apple Computer Inc. has a logo that conveys its image. It is multi-colored and friendly. A bite has been taken out of the apple. It will soon be an image as well known around the world as a Coke bottle. Friendliness is important in the sale of computers. Fifty years ago, the dog with his head tilted looking quizzically at the first radio helped RCA sell millions of sets.

But the rest of the personal computer industry needs to learn a great deal about corporate identity. Hundreds of manufacturers and hundreds of software companies are competing for space in what promises to be one of our largest industries, but very few of the companies understand how to set themselves apart from the crowd. A corporate identity expert knows how that is done. When an entrepreneur faces a marketing crisis, he should contact corporate identification consultants. They can help the entrepreneur decide what he wants to say about his company. These consultants are expensive, but payment to them is not all up front; by the time their suggestions are implemented, sales are probably turning upward and the fees can be handled.

Another kind of marketing crisis is when the corporate image is well known, but product sales are flat or falling. A marketing consultant can go into the marketplace and find out what the customers are saying and why they are not buying. A decline in bubble gum sales was once discovered to be attributable to a rumor that spider eggs had been found in the gum. Entenmann's Bakery, a division of Warner-Lambert, once lost sales when it was rumored that the company was owned by Reverend Moon. Market research discovered for General Motors that although the name "Monza" might sell cars in the United States, it was evoking belly laughs in Italy. "Monza" is a familiar four-letter word in Italy.

For the start-up company poised to launch its new product, what better people to counsel with than marketing consultants? I had a client in the early 1970s who owned the rights to import a German moped. A moped is a gas-saving, pedalized motor bike that is the leading form of transportation (after walking) in Jamaica, France, and certain other countries. Yet, there were no mopeds in the United States in the early 1970s.

The entrepreneur hired a marketing consultant at my behest and sent him on the road to discover how to sell mopeds in the United

States. There were many choices: bicycle shops, company-owned retail shops, franchised shops, farm equipment dealerships, tire distributors, automobile dealerships, department stores, lumber retailers, and so forth. The marketing consultant's answer was imported car dealerships. Reason (remember, the year was 1974): Their customers were the most energy-conserving of all consumers.

A competent marketing consultant is a key person to bring into a troubled small company. Marketing consultants are articulate, intelligent problem-solvers. Their thought processes are systematic yet creative. They bill out their services on a per diem basis, affordable by even the smallest company. Beware the consultant who in Carl Ally's magnificent quote "borrows your watch to tell you the time, then charges you for it." Ask the consultant his or her initial thoughts, plan of attack in finding solutions, reporting mechanism (in writing), estimate of the time required, and estimate of cost. Check references as thoroughly as possible. Hand over a tiny down payment to begin and wish him or her Godspeed.

A more interesting person whose services to engage is the communications consultant. This person's role is to interview each member of middle management and senior management to determine three things:

Are their goals and objectives clearly defined?

Have they reached their goals and objectives?

If not, why not?

Many times in an entrepreneurially run organization, communications from the top down are extremely poor. The entrepreneur has the corporate identity, product designs, marketing plan, production plans, and advertising plans in his or her head. The entrepreneur means to sit down one day and tell his or her people the roles they are expected to play, but things keep cropping up that must be attended to. The company runs off like a loose flywheel, with predictable results. Sales of certain products fall; sales of others rise; personnel come; personnel go; some customers are satisfied; others bring litigation against the company. The results are uneven and productivity is less than it could be.

These kinds of difficulties are normally part of a larger problem or series of problems. It is not unusual in instances such as this for the entrepreneur to be replaced by a more seasoned manager in the role of chief executive officer. If (1) the commercial banker is being uncooperative, (2) the investors will not put in more capital, and (3) customers are complaining about service, a communications consultant may be able to locate the problems.

With everyone's knowledge of his or her job design, the communications consultant begins interviewing substantially everyone in the organizational hierarchy in a salaried position. This takes several days, of course, because a thorough interview frequently lasts an hour.

When the interviews are analyzed, then synthesized by the consultant, they are presented to a committee of the board of directors. In many cases, more than half of the officers and managers of the company do not have goals and objectives. If they do, they lack definition, and they certainly do not know if they are doing what is expected of them. Sometimes a chain can be found in lack of communication. One division, say, engineering, may be very responsive and well organized, while another division, say, marketing, may be in disarray. This does not mean that the head of marketing should be fired. Perhaps he or she should go into sales and a senior marketing executive hired.

When Codex Corp. was an entrepreneurial manufacturer of modems and multiplexors, with sales of about $10 million per annum, its two founders died suddenly. The likely succesors were the managers of finance and marketing, but neither had any management experience above divisional responsibility. I was at Kuhn, Loeb & Co. then (1970), and we were involved in a $3 million venture capital private placement at $3 per share. The venture capitalists returned their private placement memorandums by the pound, except for Tankard G. Schiavoni, then at Becker Technical Ventures, who spent some time interviewing the two candidates. The board of directors, the investment bankers, and the new investor felt that the market for modems and multiplexors (they convert digital signals to voice and back to digital to enable computers to send data over telephone lines) was going to keep growing, that the company's products were favorably positioned, and that even if one or both of the middle managers could not do the job, there was still time to locate, interview, and hire a veteran manager from industry. The marketing vice president became the chief executive officer and the decision has never been regretted. Codex was acquired by Motorola in 1980 at $36 per share. Its sales are currently around $200 million, and it is one of Motorola's most profitable divisions.

If the company's problem is purely financial (it rarely is that, or purely anything, for that matter), a financial consultant can be hired. His or her assignment is usually to see what kind of capital can be raised, what the costs and trade-offs are, and what the timing is. Financial consultants are normally referred to as investment bankers. However, the investment banking industry has suffered over the last few years, and rare is the investment banker who is able to devote time to the start-up or early-stage company. The Yellow Pages in most cities list the names of financial consultants.

Even after these people have been engaged on retainers, we still do not have Mr. Goldwyn's thousands. The troubled company must put itself in a position where others will suffer it it fails. An entrepreneur I once worked with whose background was in public relations knew how to do this very well. He referred to it as a New York deal. In this sort of deal, you involve at least eight separate organizations, making each one responsible for a part of the company's financing or acquisition, or whatever is to be accomplished. He would bring in the accountants to prepare the financial statement projections, the lawyers to make sure everything was kosher, the local industrial development agency who wanted to see jobs created in the region, the federal government to guarantee any loans that might be made, the commercial banker who might finance part of the transaction, the commercial finance company which might take another piece, and the venture capitalist or investment banker for the equity component. He would get them in a room together and catalyze discussion to try to get a deal to happen. If he went into a meeting with the seller (if it was an acquisition), as much of his retinue as he could gather went with him. Although he was a lone wolf leveraged buyout entrepreneur, by involving others, he made things happen. All of the professionals were working on a speculative basis, so if a deal did not happen, they would not get paid. To squeeze the two government agencies, he used the press effectively to announce several hundred jobs created or saved, as the case might be. Then if the deal fell apart, their agencies would suffer the criticism, not he. When others were involved whose payment or reward depended upon something happening, something usually happened.

Change Banks

There are well over 5,000 commercial banks in the United States, but there are less than 100 competent commercial bankers. No offense intended. Competent commercial bankers either move up into bank management or move out into industry. A very good loan officer does not remain in that job long.

Industry is peopled with former commercial bankers. Banking is dull and boring. It does not pay very well. It is intensely cyclical. The loan officer is frequently turned down by his or her credit committee unfairly. Also some of his or her loans go sour for unexpected reasons, which slows career growth.

Commercial banks frequently have very conservative senior managements and boards of directors. They are slow to move, either to action or reaction. Banks are hampered by federal regulations which occasionally force them to change policies suddenly.

Who suffers? Small companies which maintain small depository relations suffer the most. Their lines of credit are capped, overdrafts not permitted, payroll checks not cashed, and other evidences of bank fright come about suddenly. Or, in some cases, the company's banker leaves and goes elsewhere. The new loan officer does not understand the company. Although the entrepreneur and his or her chief financial officer sit down with the new banker to explain their company, they are met with lack of interest.

Why fight it? With a little bit of looking, a new banker can be found who finds the company interesting and wants to participate in its growth and development.

Whenever you hear stories about the growth of Silicon Valley as an entrepreneurial high technology center, remember who made it possible. It was not the Stanford Engineering School. There is an engineering school in Brooklyn that produces more EEs than Stanford. It was not the existence of venture capitalists who threw money at anyone who left Hewlett-Packard with a good idea. There are nearly as many venture capitalists in New York, Connecticut, and Boston as there are in Northern California. IBM is less than two hours north of Wall Street, and over 40 of *Fortune's* 100 largest corporations are headquartered in New York and Connecticut. It was not the existence of entrepreneurs in Northern California in greater per capita ratios than in other parts of the country. Entrepreneurs are not location-specific.

Silicon Valley exists because of the imagination of the commercial bankers who service the high technology market in California. Wells Fargo, Bank of America, and Crocker made Silicon Valley. Proof: Over a dozen venture capitalists converged on Ms. Lore Harp in 1980, offering her $1 million of venture capital for Vector Graphic Corp., her Westlake Village, California microcomputer company. It had sales of $3 million in its third year of operations and it was projecting growth to $8 million. The business plan showed a need for $1 million in additional capital.

Ms. Harp heard all of the stories that the venture capitalists told her, smiled politely, and said she would get back to them. She mentioned all of the offers to her Wells Fargo banker one day. Knowing that venture capitalists do not regularly ingest or inhale controlled substances, the banker said, "If they are that interested in Vector Graphics, I'll loan you the million dollars for no equity."

He made the right decision. A year later, Ms. Harp needed venture capital again, this time to grow the company to $20 million. Jean DeLeage of Sofinnova, a French-owned venture capital firm, made the investment, but Sofinnova received far less equity than it would have the previous year.

I have had the same experiences with Bank of America and Crocker Bank. Their loan officers respect the investigative processes and intellectual skills of venture capitalists. They will make risky loans, permit overdrafts, and do other favors for companies that have been endorsed by sophisticated investors. Certainly this happens in places other than California; creative commercial bankers are scattered throughout the country. The job of the entrepreneur, among others, is to keep changing banks until he or she finds one that understands and wants to help.

Put on a Seminar

Let's explore an entirely different kind of problem. Assume for a moment that you have an idea for a new service that solves a significant problem for an industry or a group of people. Following the entrepreneurial pattern, your drivers will not let you remain employed where you are. The idea overcomes you and you leave your job, incorporate, describe your service in writing, send out letters to potential customers offering the service, and await the invitations. They do not come. You then get on the telephone to see if the people you sent the letters to would prefer a meeting. They would not. You have lunches with people well placed to help you, but they don't feel right making introductions because they do not understand the service you are offering.

You rewrite the description of the service, rearrange it on the paper, and ship it back out to the likely purchasers, the people with the problem you can solve. You receive a few calls, and two or three meetings are held. The service is fairly well understood, but they need to understand their problem a little better before they go out and buy your solution. After all, they may find a solution in-house. One small study contract comes out of a $5,000 investment in stationery, word processing, postage, and telephone calls. You know the service is valid, but the people with the problem are not ready to buy it. You may be too far ahead and you will go broke waiting for the market to catch up with you.

The solution: Put on a seminar. Whenever a problem is not well understood by the people who have the problem, it is not only difficult but also impractical to try to sell a solution to it. People who are not concerned with the immediacy of their problem will not pay for its solution. They will, however, pay for more information about the problem.

Over the last several years, the customary means of enlightening people about their problems is via seminars. People seem to enjoy paying $150 to $750 to join with others in the same situation in a conference room at a hotel, motel, or resort and hear speakers describe some new developments that the people should begin to worry about. If the seminar attendees are sufficiently pleased with the seminar and if they feel comfortable with the level of awareness of the problem to which they were elevated, they might begin to seek a solution. The seminar company would be pleased to offer the solution, but at a higher price.

In the back of each seminar room is the ubiquitous table full of tapes and books, including an order form for a tape of the present seminar. The attendees can buy the tape and play it back at their homes or offices to pick up on some things that they missed at the live performance.

Personal computer seminars are very popular at the moment. People are paying $100 to $150 to attend seminars to learn how the personal computer may be used in their business or profession. Self-actualization seminars have been popular for years, under a variety of titles: est, transactional analysis, Psi, Scientology, and many more. The prices are very high, as much as $500 for a session.

Let's look at areas where the entrepreneur would be wise to sell seminars about a service rather than the service itself. One that rushes to the front is software for cable TV. We know that more and more channels will soon be available to us on cable TV, affording opportunities to independent producers to generate programs. John Coleman, the "Good Morning, America" weatherman, recently completed venture capital financing to produce a weather program to be sold to cable TV. How did he do it? Who did he see? What is important to the cable TV broadcasters? How much is a program worth in that market? A seminar entitled "How to Sell Programs to Cable TV" would do well at $300 per head. If the seminar were held in New York, Chicago, and Los Angeles 12 times per annum for an average audience of 30 per seminar, the seminar entrepreneur would achieve gross revenues of $108,000. Assuming conference room rental and food and beverage costs of $300 per session, or $3,600, and advertising costs of $3,000 per session, or $36,000, the entrepreneur would earn slightly over $60,000 for his efforts. The seminars would very likely lead to other revenue sources.

Other seminar ideas include stress relocation for corporate human resource officers, corporate alcoholism, addressed to the same group, corporate physical fitness, addressed to the same market, and ideas for businesses to launch, addressed to potential entrepreneurs.

Candidates for seminars are most easily located via direct mail, but it is possible to reach them, although not as effectively, with space advertisements. For the cost of one insert in the local newspaper, perhaps as low as $300, one can see if the seminar business might bail one out of a cash flow problem. The mechanisms for reaching the market are not difficult to learn. The point to remember, however, is this: If you can't sell the solution, sell the problem.

Leverage Your Customers

Who wants you to survive almost as much as you do? Your customers. More appropriately, your clients. Customers are sometimes one-shot, almost always impersonal purchasers of your goods or services. Clients are repeat, personalized purchasers of your services. Commercial banks have customers, whereas investment banks have clients. Clients would pine over your demise longer than customers because they got to know you better. Both would miss you and both need you to stay in business. They can be leveraged to squeeze out cash.

A large, well-known dinner house restaurant chain, which was small and rapidly-growing when I worked on its venture capital needs in the early 1970s, had outstanding top-line figures, but could not bring profits down to the bottom line. Furthermore, it was unable to generate cash for expansion. A consultant was hired to investigate the problem. The principal problem with the company's operations was that the customers were being given more than was necessary to retain their loyalty.

The restaurant chain offered soup and salad on a complimentary basis with each meal. The salad plate and soup bowl were very large. The consultant recommended reducing the size of each on the theory that people like to "decorate" their plates with salad. The colors are bright and pleasant to arrange: green, red, orange, lime, and so forth. They are just as happy to fill up and decorate salad-size plates. They were not eating all that they were taking, and if the small plate was inadequate, they could always return for seconds.

The soup bowl was also filled to the brim. Our mothers have told us not to be wasteful of food in the house, but at a restaurant, the message is "pig out." People were not finishing all of their soup, either. The bowl was cut in half.

As to the main course, primarily steak, chicken, or lobster, customers were brought baked potatoes whether or not they asked for them. The new policy, communicated immediately to the wait-resses and waiters: "Ask each customer if he or she wants a potato with dinner."

The menu was rearranged as well. The items with the highest profit margins were moved to the upper right-hand portion of each page. The reader's eye tends to go there first and return there after scanning the page. All prices were raised 10% since new menus were being printed, why waste the opportunity?

A system of automatic price increases was instituted. There are three days during the year when people are unmistakably happier than any other days. They are less eager to complain about price increases, because they are laughing and talking with friends. Thus on April 1, July 4, and December 25, price rises of 5% went into effect automatically. New menus came out on those days reflecting the changes.

Finally, the consultant pointed out, the customers were staying at the restaurant too long. The restaurant played 1940s music from 6:00 P.M. to 8:30 P.M., Benny Goodman being better for the digestive system than Little Richard. However, the restaurant chain was getting only one table turn in that period, and it should have been getting closer to two. So Benny Goodman played until 7:00 P.M., and the older people started to leave sooner, because from 7:00 to 8:00 P.M., the beat got faster and the entertainers much younger. A younger crowd began eating from 7:00 P.M. on to the Beach Boys and Simon & Garfunkel. At 9:00 P.M., the beat began to get faster, and by 11:00 P.M. it was a noisy din. The increase in volume and pace of the music sped up turnover, reduced the average age of the customer, and increased beverage sales. If you cannot hear yourself talk in a restaurant, you drink more.

All of these changes hit the customer in his pocketbook. They were introduced in such a way that he was pleased to see them happen; at least, revenues did not decline. Within six months, the restaurant chain had doubled the bottom line and was sitting on cash balances sufficient to open a new store.

Entrepreneurs are frequently reluctant to raise prices to their customers. Their attitude is "They put me in business, and they keep me in business, so I intend to protect them with the best price." But price is not everything. Shipment terms, customer service, an 800 number to assist with problems, these and many other things are more important to a customer than price.

What businesses leverage the customers most? Excluding commercial banks which house your idle funds and then charge you for performing routine services and make you wait in long lines to get to your money, the best customer leveragers are those companies which take payment today for goods to be shipped or services to be rendered much later. The best example is the insurance industry. Customers pay a monthly toll which is invested for them at very low rates. When they die, their heirs are paid a premium equal to what the deceased could have earned had he invested the insurance premiums on his own. Should the policyholders wish to borrow some of this money during the lives of the policies, the insurance company is delighted to charge them for the privilege of using their own funds. In the meantime, the insurance company uses the monthly payments to invest in a variety of businesses.

Other outstanding customer leverage businesses are monthly subscription businesses, such as clubs, magazines, and newsletters, direct response marketing, and party-plan selling. JS&A Marketing Corp., Northbrook, Illinois, which offers us the latest electronic gadgets in the pages of in-flight and other magazines, is one of the most successful direct response marketing organizations. The technique of direct response marketing is to offer a product with a magazine or newspaper advertisement. When the checks roll in, pay the manufacturer of the product his price and ship the goods. You have six weeks to deliver before committing mail fraud. JS&A got into trouble in 1980 when severe snowstorms delayed its deliveries to customers. The Federal Trade Commission forced JS&A to return its customers' cash and pay damages. Joe Sugarman, JS&A's founder and president, fought furiously and at great expense, but lost the case. The FTC is a stern watchdog of mail fraud situations.

Party-plan selling takes customer leverage to new highs. Mary Kay Cosmetics, Tupperware, and Transart Industries have armies of salespeople neatly stacked into distribution pyramids who call on their friends and their friends' friends to have parties in their homes. The salespeople will bring the entertainment.

Ellen Crolley designed Transart's business plan and marketing methods. Transart sells decorative wall accessories via the party-plan method. The glass, mat, and frame cost five to twenty times more than the print that is framed, so it cannot truly be called art. Whatever you call it, Kennesaw, Georgia's most successful company, is a bank. The salespeople bring catalogs of "art" and a sample of mats and frames to the parties. They get on their hands and knees on the floor—customers truly love the salesperson to genuflect for the order—and rearrange the objects until the sale is made. The salesperson collects several hundred dollars in checks and sends them in to Kennesaw where the money sits for awhile. On about the third week, the orders are processed and shipped. So vast is the gross profit margin that the salesperson and host or hostess can share a 40% commission and Transart can bring close to 20% to the bottom line.

It is an overwhelming fact that most entrepreneurs ignore customer leveraging. For example, consumer electronics, personal computers, and personal computer software have many of the characteristics that would make them natural products for in-home selling. Yet, the electronics and computer entrepreneurs seem bent on using conventional retailing methods. In-home and party plan selling works for Tupperware, Mary Kay, and Transart primarily because the problems that their products solve are best discussed privately rather than in a retail store environment. Mary Kay deals primarily with making women more attractive. This is best done privately. Transart's success lies in dealing with the tricky issue of home decorating in a private way. When most people are confronted with art in a gallery environment, they are confused, overwhelmed, and not sure if the salesperson's advice can be trusted. But in one's friend's living room, one is able to ask foolish questions.

Personal computers and personal computer software packages could be sold that way. The 30% to 40% profit margins permitted the retailer could be usefully applied to the salesperson's commission. The problem solved by the personal computer is frequently quite personal, and best discussed privately. The armies of American laborers being displaced by the microprocessor revolution can make more money than they ever dreamed possible by selling the little devil that displaced them. This augurs well for the future of the portable computer. Even greater demand exists for programmers of microcomputers.

It's fine, you say, to discuss the philosophy of customer leverage and using the customer's money for awhile prior to shipping; but you have a payroll to meet in five days and nothing to pay it with. The easiest solution is the customer. Explain to certain customers that you have been using all available capital for product upgrades and improvements, and you have temporarily depleted your bank account. Would the customer mind paying today rather than in 30 days? If so, you would be pleased to offer a 5% discount.

The entrepreneur of a computer software company in Woodland Hills, California who had purchased a division from his employer that produced software packages for truck dealers had agreed to a down payment of $120,000 and eight quarterly payments of $60,000 plus interest at 10%. Although the first $120,000 was paid in a timely manner, and the first $60,000 was paid out of cash flow as well, the second $60,000 payment came due without any hope in sight of paying it. The product's terms of sale were 10% of the purchase price on order, 70% of the purchase price when the system was up and running, and 20% after 30 days of operation. The price of a truck dealer system, hardware and software, was approximately $110,000.

The entrepreneur telephoned a large truck dealer who had just recently placed an order and explained that in order for him to be shipped, installed, and serviced, he would have to pay in advance. Since he had recently been sold on the idea, he was on a high anticipating what the product was going to do for him. He willingly paid the balance of nearly $90,000 and the entrepreneur made his payment in a timely fashion.

A nonfinancial form of customer leverage is the testimonial or positive reference. If your customers are satisfied, why not ask them to put it in writing, or agree to take calls from other potential customers? People change jobs, and the satisfied customer's replacement may not be willing to be as supportive as the original customer. Thus, it is better to collect the testimonials early rather than late.

Change Comptrollers

In the center of a cash flow crisis, the person in direct contact with the irate creditors is the comptroller. Sometimes called the bookkeeper or accounts payable clerk, this person handles between 20 and 100 calls per day from anguished creditors who want a simple answer to a simple question: "When are you going to pay me?"

They have heard in the course of their business careers every conceivable stall tactic. "Your check is in the mail" is a dodge as old to them as Aesop's fables, and about as believable. They understand cash. They are persistent. They are unpleasant. They keep accurate records and notes of prior conversations and promises made and either kept or broken. They know all the clever answers to clever remarks. And they don't believe anything that a comptroller of a troubled company tells them. They believe cash. They invented "Get the cash before they crash."

Naturally, a comptroller of a troubled company can stand up to the army of credit managers, collection agencies, and commercial lawyers just so long until he or she snaps. The comptroller did not create the cash-flow bind. He or she will do everything possible to hold off the wolves, but will run out of stretch-out plans, amusing stories, and most important, credibility, if the problem is not resolved in 90 days or so.

If the problem has not been resolved in 90 days, and if the creditors have received very little of the amounts they have been telephoning daily to raise, it is time to change comptrollers.

This change should not be made quietly, but in fact, rather dramatically. The credit managers should be made to feel that they killed Robert or Roberta, the original comptroller, and that he or she has been dragged from the field and given a simple burial in a cemetery for recalcitrant and double-talking comptrollers. Let the credit managers be gleeful that they killed off the first comptroller. That will delay their vicious assault for a few days. The replacement of the comptroller should be as dramatic and ceremonial as the situation will permit.

The new comptroller must be told to approach the task with three strategies: (the last will only work if the new comptroller is male):

The first comptroller was a liar and did not know what was happening.

I am honest, straight, and do know what is happening.

My wife is in her ninth month and I may be out a day or two.

It is obviously the ritual of killing the evil-doer and replacing him or her with Mr. or Ms. Clean. But why the baby on the way? Because credit managers are human beings, too, and they are reluctant to create stress for a new comptroller who is about to become a father. They will give him a short breathing spell before the bills have to be paid in full.

Play the Float

Exxon Corp., up until a few years ago, paid its East Coast bills with checks drawn on a Western bank and its West Coast bills with checks drawn on an Eastern bank. As any entrepreneur knows, Exxon was trying to gain one or two days' use of the money until the checks finally hit the bank on which they were drawn. The balance in the checking account at the bank and the balance shown in the checkbook are rarely the same for an active company. There is always float. In Exxon's case, with about a billion dollars of checks in the mail, two days' extra use of the money at an interest rate of 15% per annum is $821,000. Four days' extra use is $1.6 million. Why, in no time, with these kinds of savings, Exxon could do something frivolous with its money like buy Reliance Electric. However, a disgruntled supplier to Exxon sued for his loss of float, and Exxon has had to pay suppliers with banks located closer to the suppliers.

Hard-pressed small companies learn to stretch their dollars by paying toward the end of the week, mailing from remote places, and asking the bank to telephone the company before bouncing a check. Small companies usually keep two bank accounts. One is the major account, used to pay suppliers, and it is floated continually. The checkbook always shows an overdraft, while the balances at the bank are generally positive. When they are negative, the bank calls to say, "Wire money in or we have to send back some checks." This account is stretched to the limit and then some.

The second account is never overdrawn. It is used to pay certain bills promptly, to pay certain payroll items and critical accounts that cannot be late and cannot bounce. The second account has a small but stable balance in it, and it is replenished as needed. It is maintained at a second bank.

Entrepreneurs normally meet with their bankers in the early stages of a company's growth and development to win their favor and support. The entrepreneur needs the bank to allow the company to be overdrawn occasionally, and, just as important, to write checks on uncollected funds. If the entrepreneur treats the banker fairly and does not misuse the privileges and accommodations granted, the bank is willing to be even more generous in the future and perhaps loan the company some serious money.

Prepare New Cash Flow Statements Weekly

During a serious cash crunch, the chief financial officer, or comptroller, should prepare a new set of cash flow statements at the end of each week for the forthcoming week. The entrepreneur and the chief financial officer should meet Monday morning and make their decisions as to who gets paid during that week, how much, and when. The comptroller can then tell the creditors which ones are being paid, how much, and when. If there is a shortfall, or if some of the accounts receivable or other sources of cash look doubtful, the entrepreneur has five days to round up the money.

During these crises, the entrepreneur's primary job is to keep the ship afloat. That is done with cash. You can float the bank, stretch the trade, hurry the customers, and sell wealthy investors on the idea of investing in new product development; but, eventually—sooner rather than later—you have to get the cash to make good on the promises.

There are many sneaky, tricky things that businesspeople are capable of doing when their backs are on the mat, for example, mailing out unsigned checks, sending invoices back and forgetting to put in the check, stapling the check to the invoice and then pulling it off at the staple to make it look torn off by someone at the receiver's end, and saying the check is in the mail when it is not. These devices are temporary and ineffective. They postpone for a few days a serious problem and make the creditor even more upset than before.

A successful entrepreneur does not need to resort to chicanery at that level. For him or her, money is a means, not an end. The successful entrepreneur does not take it that seriously, believing totally in his or her goals and objectives and being absolutely sure the money will come in to pay the bills. Or he or she may have a manager partner to take care of the bills.

But the entrepreneur has some tense moments. Several creditors slip through the comptroller and get to the entrepreneur. He or she hears their rage, their threats, the meanness in their voices. They threaten to close the place down. Bankruptcy. Chapter X. These are anxious moments. The entrepreneur sees $50,000 in immediate obligations, with projected one week's cash flow of $20,000 and an overdraft of $4,500. The options seem to be running out. A top-flight salesperson may quit if the commission check is late. The pressure builds. Just when others might crack, the entrepreneur pulls out of his pocket or purse a piece of paper the size of a fortune from a fortune cookie. To the entrepreneur, it's worth a fortune. He or she reads it and smiles. It is the war cry of the entrepreneur, *Illegitimati non carborundum est:* Don't let the bastards wear you down.

5

FITTING ENTREPRENEURS INTO THE RIGHT BUSINESSES

Each of us knows one way to make money. We frequently think and are encouraged to believe that we can multiply ourselves and make money in several ways, for instance, by laboring by day and investing our profits in the stock market, or by selling real estate by night. But it is the rare individual who consistently can make money in more than one pursuit. More than likely, when we stray from the one money-making method that we know best, we lose our capital. Thus, for most of us there is one and only one thing that we can do profitably, and though we may depart from what we do well from time to time out of boredom or frustration, we usually return to it out of need.

Although there appears to be some correlation between a person's bag of social, psychological, and emotional characteristics and the probability of his or her becoming an entrepreneur, it is not as easy to predict the kind of business that an entrepreneur will succeed at. Predictions are difficult to make, someone once said. Particularly about the future.

One thing is certain. When people have the freedom to choose their occupation, and entrepreneurs have that freedom, the choice is frequently based on which group of people they want to solve problems for. In other words, *entrepreneurs pick their business area by first selecting their audience.*

A question that turns a fast-track, whirling-dervish, loquacious entrepreneur into a shy puppy is "Who is your audience?" In other words, who are you doing this for? It is a gut-level question. For every entrepreneur, there is a progression of events and forces that creates the "drivers" that turn a corporate manager or professional into an entrepreneur. They *know* who they are playing for, and they will give the answer to someone else who has signed up.

Who is your audience? Every entrepreneur internalizes this question. "I have done this for myself," is a common response. When one probes more deeply, the answers come out as follows:

> My father left home when I was 4 years old. My two older brothers and I had to work to help out. My mother worked hard, but there was never enough. Whenever I went to the grocery store for some milk, the grocer would say in front of everyone, "Be sure to remind your mother about the bill she has here."
>
> COMPUTER ENTREPRENEUR

> I have had three wives and all the women I will ever want. I live modestly and drive an old BMW. I have raised over $50 million from some of the most sophisticated investors in the world. We're going to do some things in teleconferencing that will make the 1980s and 1990s the most glorious period of creativity in the history of civilization."
>
> TELECOMMUNICATIONS ENTREPRENEUR

> I gave that company my 15 best years. I hired every key member of management and designed every new product. I did all the work for the public offering and delivered the earnings that drove the stock to $17 per share. And then they screwed me. That's the last time I will work for anyone else.
>
> COMPUTER ENTREPRENEUR

> I grew up an only child essentially without friends. My father drove a truck and was away practically all the time. My mother taught school. I read comic books and fantasized. I believe that

I am Superman. Although I cannot fly or see through buildings,
I am certain that I have those powers.
                                        COMPUTER ENTREPRENEUR

My mom had to support us since I was 8. She was little and
frail but there wasn't anything she couldn't do. When I was 12,
it occurred to me that I could make money by solving problems
for people. I haven't stopped since.
                                        LODGING ENTREPRENEUR

The drivers are set in place very early and then thrust the person
into entrepreneurship as a function either of need or of desire. The
need is basic: survival. The desire is creative: to do some one thing
extremely well. The confusion about entrepreneurs has to do with
wealth and power. Neither are important to the entrepreneur. Most
economists and journalists show their ignorance of the entrepreneurial process by thinking that entrepreneurs want to control the *means
of production*. Nothing could be further from the truth. Very few
post-World War II entrepreneurial fortunes have anything to do with
building factories to control the means of production.

Many entrepreneurial fortunes are the result of taking markets
away from those companies that control the means of production.
Clearly, the failure of transportation to move people about inexpen-
sively has catalyzed the birth of telecommunications. The same applies
to the failure of the information and entertainment industries and
the birth of data processing and cable television. Printing and delivering newspapers is inefficient. Flying salesmen to a conference in
Chicago from 35 U.S. cities is inefficient. The post office is inefficient, Detroit is inefficient, and smokestack America is inefficient.
These are portrayed as problems by the hierarchies that index the
world's problems—economics departments of major universities,
commercial bank economists, and newspapers. But they are merely
entrepreneurial opportunities.

You may rest assured that the automobile, airline, and capital
equipment industries will be dramatically downsized, that their
divisions worth saving will be purchased by leveraged buy-out entrepreneurs, and that the primary entities will rise once again, *sans*
unions and middle managers (the word processor will have put a
stake in the heart of middle management by 1990). The leveraged

buy-out process is a discipline, and hundreds of entrepreneurs are learning how to do it. Entrepreneurs are coming out of the woodwork, pulled by the magnet of $10 billion of venture capital. And billions of dollars of capital equipment—the means of production—can be leveraged to put entrepreneurs into the driver's seat, the pilot's seat, and the tractor's seat. Prediction: Entrepreneurs will run parts of Chrysler Corp., Ford Motor Co., International Harvester, Massey Ferguson and various large transportation companies by 1985.

The process of fitting entrepreneurs into these opportunities, requires stepping back a little to see what has been happening to industry for the last 25 years.

SPUTNIK

The grocer who told the four-year-old would-be entrepreneur that his mother owed the store money was to that young man what Sputnik was to America. The Russians humiliated the United States in front of 105 other countries in 1957. The Russians showed the literate part of the world that the United States had warts, flaws, and overdrafts in its technology account. As Dudley Moore said to the one-legged applicant auditioning for the role of Superman in the skit "Good Morning": "You have a deficiency in the leg department." Sputnik showed Western Europe, the Far East, the Middle East, and Latin America that the United States had a deficiency in the technology department. It was no joke.

The federal government was humiliated and began printing money to produce engineers. In the electronics industry, this translated into cost-plus contracts; the kind you can be inefficient at and still get paid. The goal: Get something into space that flies, and get it up there quick.

1957, beginning of the Age of Entrepreneurship—the year of Sputnik—was also the year Robert Noyce left Shockley Transistor Corp. to start Fairchild Semiconductor Corp. Noyce is the father of the microprocessor. He was on the road to entrepreneurship in 1957. Who was Shockley?

William B. Shockley, born in 1910, while working for Bell Labs discovered that certain germanium crystals could act as rectifiers;

that is, they would allow current to pass in one direction but not the opposite. Alternating current, passing through such crystals, was rectified, and only the surges in one direction were transmitted. What emerged then was a varying direct current. Shockley went further. He discovered in 1948 how to combine "solid-state" rectifiers in order not only to rectify but also to amplify a current. Shockley called this a *transistor*, because it transferred a current across a resistor. Naturally, Shockley left Bell Labs to form the Shockley Transistor Corp. in Mountain View, California in 1951. The company survived on government contracts, and when Sputnik was launched in 1957, the transistor was the key to the U.S. response.

Giant computers and electronic instrumentation had to be lifted into space via satellites. The mass of these satellites had to be reduced to a minimum if they were to be lifted into space without prohibitively expensive fuel and energy costs. The solution: Transistorize the computer and shrink its size. Shockley's inventions made this possible. Noyce had other things on his mind: the semiconductor and beyond.

Noyce and his team at Fairchild would take the miniaturization process beyond the transistor, to the semiconductor—a collection of transistors stuck into printed circuit boards with wires leading to the devices they controlled. The computer was becoming smaller and cheaper, but was not yet commercially successful. The federal government had established equilibrium in space with the Russians and was swaggering into Vietnam to prove itself invincible. Noyce, grown "weary of a job that had become increasingly administrative, resigned [Fairchild] in June, 1968 . . . and with Arthur Rock, a San Francisco financier, . . . came up with Integrated Electronics, later shortened to Intel."* The goal of Intel was to shrink the size of the computer's memory. The development process created the microprocessor, the "chip": a thumbnail-sized computer with hundreds of thousands of transistors crammed onto it. The price of a microprocessor is just a few hundred dollars.

From Sputnik to Shockley to Noyce to Rensselaer Polytechnic Institute, Troy, New York, and the year 1979.

---

*Electronic News, January 25, 1982.

A small group of computer scientists led by Allen Baisuck, the entrepreneur, and Alvin L. Ring, the achiever with a twenty-five year record of management experience, began work on computer-aided design (CAD) of chips in their start-up, Phoenix Data Systems, Inc., a spin-out of RPI. Why is CAD necessary? Because electronic engineers are discovering means of cramming hundreds of thousands of transistors onto a chip mathematically, but there are not enough people or hours in the day to produce these chips, known as VLSI (very large scale integration). When we have VLSI chips in 1990 developed with computer-aided design techniques, the cost of virtually every electric and electronic device we now use will plummet. X-ray machines will be hand-held and cost the radiologist less than $1,000. Implants containing insulin, kidney pumps, and heart pumps will cost less than $1,000. Education will be via satellite through CATV lines to television sets, reduced in price to $100, but containing in memory the Encyclopedia Britannica, the Great Books, an entire 12-year education, and the daily news. Without CAD, the miniaturization process cannot continue. The development costs per chip are becoming too expensive. The microprocessor evolution will slow down precipitously without CAD (see Exhibit 5.1).

The world is changing fast, because entrepreneurs are at the throttle. By 1990, entrepreneurs will be in charge of most of the significant companies in the United States. As long as there are enemies, there will be entrepreneurs. As long as there are grocers who embarrass four-year-olds, there will be entrepreneurs. The entrepreneurial Israelis can thank the Arabs for being their grocer. The United States can thank the Russians for being their grocer. You and I can thank big business and big government for being our grocers. They kept our fathers out of ownership of the means of production and keep prices so high that we are forced to miniaturize.

The "one way" that each of us knows to make money depends in the first instance on enjoying, or at least having an affinity for, the problem that we are solving. We have to like the audience that we are playing for. I like entrepreneurs, so I am perfectly content solving problems for entrepreneurs. There may have been more wealth potential in real estate or oil, but I enjoy people, direct interface with people, and problem solving. I admire real estate entrepreneurs, because buildings don't act irrationally or require late night hand holding and telephone conversations. Oil rigs don't talk back, either. Like other entrepreneurs, I selected the marketplace that I wanted to

EXHIBIT 5.1.   Development Costs per Chip (in Thousands of Dollars).

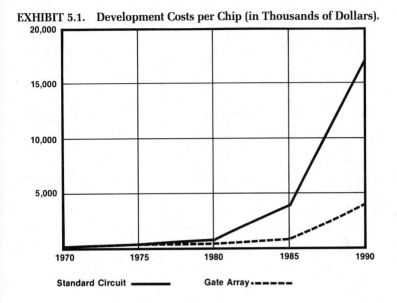

provide solutions for; *then,* I began to problem-formulate and identify opportunities for creative solutions.

There are thousands of things I could not have been, not because I lacked the skill to develop the solution—that skill is hirable—but because I did not like the audience. For example, being a mortician has no appeal to me, nor does being a doctor, teacher, veterinarian, or politician.

There are an abundance of entrepreneurs in the computer industry, because many people enjoy developing solutions for computerniks. There is an openness, friendliness, and sense of kinship in the early stages of any industry, and the personal computer field is no exception. The next great wave of entrepreneurial fortunes, however, will be in developing software that makes personal computers *addictive* to large numbers of people. In the fall of 1981, one small business in 61 owned a personal computer. This resulted in a penetration of 1.4 million personal computers by late 1982. Reaching half of the small businesses by 1990, with appropriate software, will make the personal computer industry the largest and fastest growing in the United States.

A potential entrepreneur should select that group of people (market) for whom he would most enjoy solving problems and then listen very carefully to two things: what makes them cry and what makes them laugh.

Example: You like to make movies. Your favorite audience is movie-goers. The impersonal market of tens of millions of movie-goers applauding helps you pay the grocer back. You are an entrepreneur, and so you listen to what your audience tells you. You pick up on the following words: big budgets, long lines, high ticket prices, union control of Hollywood, distributor control of theaters, low returns to producers, investor disenchantment, stars making all the money, special effects. You are problem-formulating; opportunity-identifying; free-falling through a sky full of interesting problems.

As we saw in the chapter on the creative process, you should put these words on a piece of paper and stare at them. Move them around. Paste them on the mirror in the bathroom. Say them into a tape recorder and play them back while driving. Eventually, the business plan will come to you.

The method of producing and distributing movies is obsolete and the victim of corporate bigness. Entrepreneurs are changing that. George Lucas and Gary Kurtz, the creator and producer of "Star Wars," figured out that special effects devices and robots were a lot cheaper than stars. To move the sets around, the workers at EMI in London were cheaper than the union workers in Hollywood. But they have not changed the means of distribution. Now they are too wealthy: The grocer has been paid.

Francis Coppola is still hungry, but not because he makes bad movies that do not return their budgets. Rather, Coppola bets his golf bag every time he steps up to swing a club. He self-finances, self-produces, self-directs, and now has plans for self-distributing. Because his method flies in the face of the entrepreneurial team, Coppola, the lone wolf, may not succeed. But should he, and movie buffs the world over hope he will, he will force a change in movie distribution.

Coppola believes that the distributors should not make 30 to 45% of the gross receipts for merely delivering the film in the can from the producer to the theater. Coppola's solution: satellite transmission from the producer to the theater. Here's how it works.

The theater buys an inexpensive antenna and points it to a satellite on which Coppola and others rent transponders. The theater owner signs up for a film in 24 theaters for a few weeks, and dials a particular satellite on the TRS80 personal computer at his home in Connecticut. Via telephone lines, the $2,000 computer turns on 24 antennas which begin pulling in movie-house-quality films from the satellite. The box office has no attendant; tickets are sold by a theft-resistant robot which can count or read credit cards. Popcorn and refreshments are dispensed similarly. The price of the ticket comes back to $3.50, but with 30 to 45% of the profit saved, investors are lured back into the movie game.

If the distribution method does not change soon, $5.00 tickets at theaters will drive customers to cable and home video. Neighborhoods will darken and stay dark while home video, home computer, and physical fitness stores open up several miles away.

You are not a movie maker, and technology frightens you. But the entrepreneurial drivers are falling into place. Let us say you have a grocer to pay back, a divorced wife to prove something to, and two parents who suffered so that you could become a psychiatrist. But treating patients eight hours a day, five days a week and tilling soil on weekends leaves you dissatisfied. All the signals point to entrepreneurship. What kind of business should you start?

The same creative process as previously discussed should be used. If emotionally disturbed people are your audience, then listen to what they are saying as a group. Is there a central theme? Alcoholism? Diet? Self-actualization? Stress? Job dissatisfaction? There is an entrepreneurial opportunity in any problem—emotional disorders are no different. I will save the solution for a later chapter, while you think about it.

I have found that entrepreneurs in search of problems to solve are as well served by humor as they are by tragedy. Johnny Carson's opening monologue from time to time makes humorous the same five or ten items in the news that the New York Times calls tragedies. Listen to Carson and write down the subjects he covers. He indexes problems. The New York Times and other newspapers do the same.

Finding entrepreneurial opportunities requires listening and indexing. Finding the one that suits you best has to do primarily with understanding which audience you want to perform for in your one time on stage.

6

LEVERAGE, MULTIPLIERS, COOKIE CUTTERS, PYRAMIDS, AND OTHER TOOLS FOR THE ENTREPRENEUR

There are certain operating strategies developed by entrepreneurs that enable them to succeed in the face of unusually great odds. Many of these "great odds" are created by the entrepreneur, who tilts at windmills, puts up dikes with holes, and runs off in many directions very quickly and without communicating his or her intentions to anyone. The rest of the great odds are in place before the entrepreneur begins attacking them, and they are merely defending their positions. One rarely sees these techniques employed by large corporations to introduce new products or capture market share, because they have material assets and people to throw at a situation to buy market share. But frequently large corporations cannot shoulder their way into a market, particularly a rapidly growing one which *prima facie* means entrepreneur-driven. For example, Texas Instruments' 991 microcomputer fell on its face in 1981. Burroughs, NCR, and

Honeywell have hardly been heard from in that market. The old Addressograph-Multigraph Corp., even with a former entrepreneur at the helm, went bankrupt in 1982. In the CAD/CAM field, all of the players are entrepreneur-driven companies: Daisy, Applicon, Calma, Phoenix Data, and NCA, among others; yet *Fortune* (October, 1981) calls it the most important new industry of this century.

It is the nature of entrepreneurs to develop techniques and strategies for success against overwhelming odds. These strategies are the result of desperation. As one entrepreneur once said, "Once you have stood in front of your open grave, all other problems become trivial." Each time an entrepreneur faces a payroll with less money in the bank and receivables in the mail than the payroll checks he or she is writing out, the entrepreneur is thinking how to prevent this kind of agony in the future, and thinking hard.

Here's a story Fred Smith tells. On an island in the Pacific there are three marooned sailors, a girl and a fifth of whiskey. Suddenly there is a flash of light and a booming voice which says, "You have 30 seconds to abandon the island prior to a nuclear test." One man takes off with the girl to spend his last 30 seconds with her. The second man takes the fifth of whiskey and sits under a tree. The third man, an entrepreneur, dives into the water. The others run to see what he is doing. The entrepreneur surfaces briefly and says, "I'm going to learn how to breathe under water."

Fred Smith, who raised $96 million to launch Federal Express before he was 30 years old, has employed virtually every survival strategy that entrepreneurs have conjured up over the last 35 years. He has stacked debt on top of a small equity base, gotten his employees to pawn their watches to raise capital, and convinced federal bureaucrats to rewrite the law for freight-carrying airplanes. Smith reduces most problems to the people level. He fervently believes that he is able to solve any problem by talking to people. He understands more than most entrepreneurs the principal of leverage.

LEVERAGE

Leverage is borrowing. It is acquiring an asset or time in the present, while deferring payment until a later date. When a carpenter adds a room onto your house, he is providing time and assets for payment at the end of the job. That is not leverage. When an executive puts in two hard weeks on 18-hour-per-day labor negotiations and receives the regular paycheck, he or she is not leveraging his or her time or skills, either. So very few people understand leverage that when an entrepreneur unveils a leverage strategy, it appears clever and unique, when in fact it is a crucial survival mechanism that the entrepreneur thought up in desperation.

Minor, trivial and practically inconsequential leverage tactics of entrepreneurs—ones that go all but unnoticed—include the following:

To gain or save time:

Sleep less.

Drive fast.

Eat little.

Never get sick.

Own cars that do not break down.

Own cars that maneuver well in traffic.

Wear the minimum number of articles of clothing (no vest, jewelry, cuff links etc.).

Wear short hair or uncombed long hair.

Speak quickly.

When flying

Do not check baggage.

Elbow your way in front of certain people going through the metal detectors.*

---

*There are certain people in airports who must be avoided because they have lots of time. Entrepreneurs must never permit themselves to get behind these people. How can they be identified? Very simply: by their shoes. People who lead stable, sensible, unruffled, conservative lives wear sensible, conservative shoes. The first tip-off is the thickness of the sole. The thicker the sole, the more time the person has to lollygag through the metal detector. Most of them actually like to set off the buzzers so they can go through it more than once. For the entrepreneur who is loaded with carry-on baggage and has to buy a ticket at the gate and make three telephone calls critical to the company's cash flow, all within five minutes, a 45-second delay behind a fellow traveler and his stable family enjoying the metal detector can be a nerve-wracking experience.

Sit in an aisle seat.

Sit near front door for speedy exit.

Do not smile at passenger in next seat because she or he may strike up a conversation.

Take the earliest flight to and the latest flight from the appointment in order to avoid ground and air traffic delays.

Bring lots of work to do, because there are no telephones.

Walk quickly to car rental counter in order to beat people who care to understand what all the rates, circles, checks, numbers, and letters mean.

Do not talk to rental car bus driver; he or she may slow down in order to extend the conversation.

Entrepreneurs place an inordinately high value on time. They flock to locations where time is in their favor, such as the more western time zones, industrial parks near major airports, and areas that employes are able to reach conveniently. Entrepreneurs drive quickly, take early flights, avoid maintenance breakdowns or other time-eaters, speak rapidly, and walk at a quick pace. Entrepreneurs are rarely significantly overweight, because they do not overeat. Entrepreneurs practically never get sick.

These tactics may involve merely a few minutes of each day, but they add up to hours. If an 80-hour work week is a typical entrepreneur's schedule, adding 10 more hours here and there is a 12.5% increase in assets. This optimal use of time is a fundamentally Marxian principle for it was Karl Marx who was the first to define labor properly as a form of capital. For the cash-poor entrepreneur, the substitute for capital is labor; or, as some call it, "sweat equity."

The difference is the same as that between Mozart and Beethoven. The latter was reasonably well paid for his efforts, very highly regarded by his contemporaries, and thus able to write his music at a leisurely, comfortable pace.

Mozart, on the other hand, was very poorly paid and lived in poverty, his contemporaries were critical of his work, and he wrote his symphonies under hardship conditions. The Emperor Concerto, for instance, was said to have been written in one night. Mozart sat down at the piano at midnight and began composing the piece that had to be presented the next evening. He began falling asleep two hours later, but his wife sat alongside him, pouring cold water on him and feeding him. He drowsed and wrote, briefly napped, wrote some more, drowsed some more and wrote some more and turned in a finished piece of music that was presented the next evening without rehearsal, and with the ink still wet on all the copies. Expert musicians are supposedly able to detect in the "Emperor" places where Mozart was mostly awake and places where he was mostly asleep.

Where others seek prestige, power, and wealth, the entrepreneur seeks time to build a problem-solving machine. He or she appreciates the complexity of the work and realizes that if he or she has time, then less capital and fewer people and other resources will be needed. Time is the single most important asset for the entrepreneur. Much of what he or she does is related to optimizing the use of time.

Entrepreneurs leverage people almost as well as they leverage time. They are able to persuade people to do things for them that the people had no intention of doing. Entrepreneurs have favorite stories about their persuasive powers, occasionally exaggerated, but always humorous.

There's the one about the entrepreneur caught speeding in his rental car by the Louisiana Highway Patrolman, who saunters up to the entrepreneur and says, "Do you know you were going 30 miles per hour over the speed limit, boy?"

The entrepreneur says, "I did not know that. This is a rented car. Back home, I drive an old Jeep. I haven't been in a car that can go over 60 in years. This one just took off from under me and I never felt like I was speeding. I'm terribly sorry." The ticket book went back into the pocket with a mild warning and an admonition to drive carefully in Louisiana.

An entrepreneur does not have the 20 minutes that it takes to write out a ticket or the $20 that it costs. But he does have the sensitivity to know that a highway patrolman would be interested in a full explanation of why someone speeds. Most trapped speeders probably try to give a sneaky or otherwise bullet-ridden explanation. Being in a hurry will not usually satisfy, nor will following a faster car. The highway patrolman has heard every story in the book. But give him an earnest, informative, new story and he will award it the respect for imaginativeness that it so richly deserves.

Entrepreneurs are able to talk their way onto sold-out airplanes and talk their way into restaurants without a reservation and with 20 people with reservations waiting at the bar for a free table. The airplane tactic is done by placing the responsibility elsewhere, usually between the entrepreneur's secretary and the ticket agent. The negotiation should take place at the gate, where the entrepreneur's intransigence can affect the most people and give the airline a reputation for slow boarding procedures. By tying up the line and being extremely polite to the ticket agent, asking him or her to check the screen once again, please, changing the spelling, the initials, the first name, and so forth, the entrepreneur can create a need on the part of the ticket agent to let this desperate individual on board. If the ticket agent is not falling for the "I'm sure my secretary made the reservation" routine, the entrepreneur must resort to innuendo, such as frequent flyer and executive club cards. ("Perhaps the reservation was made through the Admirals Club. Could you check there, please.") There is no fail-safe routine, except to step aside while all the people with reservations board the airplane. A telephone call to make a reservation five minutes prior to takeoff frequently has positive results, because the seats held by multiple-seat bookers and no-shows free up at this point. The entrepreneur can then run back to the ticket counter, ask the ticket agent to verify the reservation just one more time because he just checked with his office and they confirmed it. Then, when the name appears on the screen, the entrepreneur is issued a ticket and bounds down the ramp to the dismay of the slack-jawed, thick-soled people holding wait-list tickets.

How does an entrepreneur get a table at a crowded restaurant without a reservation? Simply by gliding up to the maitre d' and saying in his or her most supercilious voice, "Reservation for Dr. Silver." This technique is foolproof. No restaurant has ever refused to serve a doctor. The maitre d' assumes that if the name is not on his sheet, it is his error and not the doctor's. God forbid a doctor should ever make an error!

The persuasive skills of entrepreneurs reach into many areas other than highways, airports, and restaurants. Entrepreneurs are able to persuade customers to pay sooner, suppliers to ship faster and wait longer for payment, banks to extend credit. They can persuade employees to hold their paychecks an extra day or two, work overtime and on weekends, and perform extra tasks for the company that they never before considered. To accomplish this, the entrepreneur "packages the dream." He or she creates a vision of what the company can become in the future. To an employee, this might translate into stock options. The employee believes that the entrepreneur will realize his or her dream, and that the employee's own dream—for a new boat, a fur coat, or whatever—can be realized if he or she and all the other employees put out a little more for the company.

Entrepreneurs are quick to terminate the disloyal employee. An employee who scorns the dream and moans and groans over the extra work or longer hours reduces the credibility of the entrepreneur's vision. The employees of an entrepreneurial company either buy the dream wholeheartedly, for what it means to them, or they leave and join a less demanding company.

A microcomputer software company entrepreneur in Atlanta pulled together an initial team of 12 programmers, a marketing director, and a secretary to develop, acquire, and market software. Each programmer had either contributed a package to the company that he or she had written or was responsible for acquiring one or more packages from authors outside the firm. As the company began making sales, one or two of the packages were initially quite popular in the marketplace, most of them had a mixed reception, and one or two got no takers. The programmer responsible for the two packages that were slow to move became petulant and critical in a picky way of some of the marketing director's ideas and practices.

The entrepreneur quickly spotted a bad team player and asked him to leave. The sour grapes programmer would have impeded the company's lift-off. The launch phase requires that everyone pull together with as much force as he or she can muster. It is up to the entrepreneur to leverage his or her employees. "Man would rather work than be free," Eric Hoffer tells us. I think people would rather work in an entrepreneurial environment than otherwise. Entrepreneurs recognize this and take advantage of it. As Tom West said in *The Soul of a New Machine,* if you aren't willing to "sign up" you have no business on a lift-off team.

The reward for signing up is equity. The reward is based on the value of the company's common stock at some future date in consideration for hard work and smart work in the present. There are numerous means of issuing stock to key employees, ranging from the outright sale of common stock for a nominal price when the company's book value is negative to qualified stock option plans which require the employee to remain employed for a specified period of time. The former has the benefit of instant reward, and it is useful to lure a top-flight person from a good job to a start-up. The attitude is expressed as follows: "Barbara, I'm asking you to take a pay cut from $75,000 to $50,000, but you're going from a zero ownership situation to 5% of our company just for signing up. If you are as good as we both think you are, you can help make that 5% blossom into millions of dollars of value."

The other popular form of equity incentive is the key employee stock option plan, qualified to the extent the employee remains employed by the company. He is granted a block of stock in the beginning at a set price, or stair-stepped price, and for every year that he remains with the company, he may exercise (i.e., purchase) a portion of the stock.

Assume that a company has 3,500,000 shares outstanding among its three founders. It begins to grow and needs to attract talented people and venture capital. It estimates that it will need to set aside 1,000,000 shares for the venture capital financing, which it hopes to place privately at $3.00 per share.

The stock option plan should be done prior to the private placement of common stock at $3.00, in order to avoid creating a taxable event for the employees. The founders might agree to grant 10,000 shares to each of the key employees at $1.00 per share. It would be reasonable to permit them to exercise 2,000 shares per annum, a payment of $2,000 by each person, over a five-year period. If they leave the company within five years, they have to sell the stock back to the company at the price they paid.

Leveraging one's employees is not a one-way street. They will not work day after day for intangible rewards. Many entrepreneurs, as soon as the company is able, set up a bonus plan, buy cars for their key people, and for employees who have to travel extensively, purchase a ticket for the husband or wife. James Treybig, the founding entrepreneur of Tandem Computer Corp., built a plant with a swimming pool in the center quadrant and has an open-door policy that encourages employees to talk with him whenever they feel like it.

MULTIPLIERS

Even with the plethora of new fast-food restaurants that sprang up in the 1970s like daffodils in May, there has been no significant net addition to the universe of restaurants in America. What is new is the replacement of the mom-and-pop, one-of-a-kind restaurants by chains. The modern restaurant entrepreneur thinks chains, multiples, and cookie cutters. His predecessor one generation or more before him thought in terms of units.

When Leslie Wexner's father, the founder of The Limited, a Columbus, Ohio women's apparel store, went on vacation about 15 years ago, he asked Wexner to look after the store for him. When the father returned, the son told him in effect, "I can build this store into a chain, but you have to give me control." The Limited Stores are over 250 strong and the company recently acquired Lane Bryant, a chain made up of 150 women's apparel stores in downtown locations.

Marty, Jack, and Scott Weiner's father owned a men's apparel store on Adams Street in Chicago that did well enough to send the sons through college. Now they run a chain of Polo Shops, licensed by the designer Ralph Lauren, a chain of Robert Vance men's wear stores, and a chain of Korshak women's stores throughout the country. They have another corporation that operates going-out-of-business sales for apparel stores owned by others.

The idea of multiplying retail businesses comes from the fact that the concentration of small retail businesses or localized services (e.g., Taylor Rental, Community Psychiatric Centers) has enormous economies of scale and capital gains potential. When several restaurants sell the same food, dress their employees alike, and decorate their stores the same way, they can advertise locally and save money, make larger food and supplier purchases and get volume discounts. Thus, the profits and the rate of return on invested capital can be greater than the rate of return on capital invested in one store. For instance, Church's Fried Chicken has been ranked by *Forbes* magazine as one of the most profitable companies in the country. Over the last five years, it has earned close to 20% on invested capital. Its growth rate has been in excess of 24% per annum over the same period.

What is being multiplied? Revenue-generating locations that follow an operating formula established by the founding entrepreneurs. The Thursday edition of the *Wall Street Journal* advertises dozens of new multiple-location franchises. The ads are unrealistically hard-selling, such as "If I had a brother," for a chain of executive search consultants. The latest offering is to sell air machines to filling stations, so that they can charge customers for air. From the ridiculous to the sublime, there are dental clinics, legal clinics, Kron candy shops, cookie stores, videotape stores, and candle shops.

Knowledgeable friends tell me that the most profitable chain in the country is Arthur Murray Dance Studios. The franchisors ask a substantial price for the name plus a royalty and provide practically nothing. The franchisee merely needs a large room and a sign out front. The franchisor does not particularly care what kind of dancing the franchisee teaches. No formula for chicken or hamburgers, no instructions on how to dip candles. Dancing lessons: the premier multipliable service. For the entrepreneur interested in launching a chain, Arthur Murray is the model for a simple, profitable formula. Other ideas that come to mind using this model:

Arthur Schwartzenegger Physical Fitness Centers
Nathan Pritikin Wellness Clinics
Jane Fonda Exercise and Aerobic Dancing Centers

Coming up with names like this could replace charades as a leading parlor game.

There are several opportunities that should be concentrated under one management structure. The franchisees could gain valuable assistance in managing their stores and the franchisors could achieve greater profits through economies of scale, plus an eventual capital gain when the business is sold.

Consumer products companies have an affinity for chains. They think they can operate them more efficiently than can the entrepreneurs who built them. Pillsbury was so certain of its ability to build Steak 'n Ale from a small chain of 20 to a behemoth steak house chain that it paid 24 times earnings for the privilege. Pepsico paid even more for Taco Bell, and Royal Crown, not as well off as either Pillsbury or Pepsico, paid 24 times earnings for Arby's.

The diet has not been terribly good for any of these marriages of consumer products companies and fast-food chains. General Foods would rather forget Burger Chef, WR Grace has kicked Del Taco out the door, Quaker Oats would like to get rid of Magic Pan, and Pillsburgy has brought the Steak 'n Ale founder out of his vault (they made him one of Pillsbury's largest stockholders) to run their Burger King division. Notwithstanding the present digestion problem, chains are salable commodities, while mom-and-pop stores go away after liquidation sales.

America is in a transition from old to new, where old is comfortable and new is frightening. Thus, we walk into brand new, antiseptic, refrigerated shopping malls and half of the merchandise looks like cleaned-up items from Grandma's attic and the other half is electronic, video, and computerized. There are as many opportunities in nostalgia products as in contemporary products. For example, when Abercrombie & Fitch went out of business in the late 1970s, entrepreneurs bid to purchase the name. But the proud controlling stockholder asked $18 million for this single unpledged asset. There were no takers. Had the downstroke been less and perhaps a royalty added, a fine clothing and camping equipment entrepreneur perhaps could have taken Abercrombie & Fitch to new heights of fame and fortune. Alas, it was not be be.

There are other Abercrombie & Fitches lying dormant that could be used to give interesting and entertaining brand recognition to chain businesses. The Ham Fisher estate, for instance, is managed by the Chase Manhattan Bank trust department. Its most valuable asset, the name and the character of Joe Palooka, the boxer, could be dusted off and repackaged with perhaps as much punch as Annie, Rocky, or Pizza Time Theaters. Entrepreneurs have found the retail industry very lucrative and creative.

One of the best examples is the cookie store. Chocolate chip cookies for $3.00 per pound would have made my grandmother stop sewing and start baking. These stores are located in enclosed malls because the odor of vanilla is intoxicating. The salespeople at Thom McAn, Radio Shack, and the other shops inside the mall, even though not "cookie monsters", seem suddenly unable to get through the day without five or six cookies.

The cookie store chain is an example of a mom-and-pop business that thrives when concentrated in a larger organization. Beauty shops represent another kind of business that does well in a concentrated format. Along with performance contracts and cookie cutters, concentration of small retail businesses will be one of the growth industries of the 1980s and 1990s.

COOKIE CUTTERS

A cookie cutter business is one where a product is made cheaply and sold as a standard, off-the-shelf item at a very high price. IBM Corp. has for many years produced cookie cutters: high-priced computers sold with high-priced maintenance contracts and expensive peripheral equipment. If you needed software, before the Justice Department stepped in and ended its natural monopoly, IBM would sell you that as well. IBM's computers were, and in many respects still are, addictive. The world's largest corporations had to have computers, and the name they trusted was IBM. Large-volume orders for its computers helped IBM keep its costs low, but the price remained high, in fact, so high that it acted like an umbrella, permitting new computer manufacturers to enter the market with less expensive equipment.

This plethora of equipment gave rise to the computer services industry: thousands of programmers writing code so that the IBM and other computers could perform some useful functions. These contract service firms merely rented bodies and marked up their cost to the customer. The service business is self-limiting. More bodies must be added to accommodate additional customers. The profit margin does not increase with increased sales. No cookie cutter here.

In the late 1970s, some entrepreneurs in the computer services industry conceived the idea of vertical market software packages. They concentrated on one or two markets, selling, installing, and maintaining the same software to the same kinds of customers over and over again. The most successful vertical market software company thus far has been Triad Systems Corp., Sunnyvale, California, which sells computer systems to auto parts distributors. Triad's software is sold to customers on tape, disk, and pages of documentation, Xeroxed, and put into notebooks. The cost of the product is perhaps $100, but it sells for $5,000 to $10,000 plus the hardware on which Triad makes a small profit. Triad's sales exceed $100 million per annum.

The personal computer has created hundreds of opportunities for cookie cutters. Personal computer software can be reproduced for less than $20 and sold for upwards of $200 to personal computer users. The number of vertical markets is staggering. In the space of three years, Visicorp has sold $62 million worth of VisiCalc, a $250 (retail) package for doing spread sheets and financial statement projections. Programmers turned entrepreneurs are busily conceiving new cookie cutters and building the teams to develop and market them. No industry will be left un-cookie-cuttered. The first to be tackled will be the number-crunching industries, because the computer does this so well. These include accountants, brokers, securities analysts, financial planners, small loan companies, and income tax centers. Architects represent a large market, print shops twice as large. There are 43,000 archaeologists in the United States who deal in numbers and words continually. Lawyers, doctors, and dentists need to keep track of their practices more efficiently. Radio stations can turn their logs over to personal computers.

If the entrepreneur was not ready to emerge in this decade, the personal computer would have brought him out. Frost & Sullivan and other industrial research organizations project that there will be over 33 million personal computers installed in the United States by 1990. Further, they estimate that each installation will purchase three software packages at a price of $150. If these projections are even close, the personal computer software market will exceed $15 billion per annum in seven years. If it remains a cookie cutter business, with profit margins of 80% or better, entrepreneurs will enjoy a period of sustained achievement and perhaps long overdue recognition and investigation.

PYRAMIDS

A final lesson we have learned from entrepreneurs is how to create a problem after you have invented a solution. There are all kinds of warnings about not inventing solutions to nonexistent problems. But entrepreneurs are occasionally driven to start businesses before anyone can get to them with this warning. Listerine was invented before we were concerned about mouth odor. So Warner-Lambert's marketing gurus thought up the word "halitosis," the problem that Listerine was created to solve. We may not be aware of mouth odor, but halitosis is a serious national problem.

The entrepreneurial process rather clearly instructs one to do exhaustive problem-finding before formulating a solution. But occasionally an entrepreneur is ahead of his or her time and develops the solution first. He or she is then in a position of having to educate a demand curve, that is, having to create the sense of a problem in the minds of his or her market. After all, an entrepreneur is certainly not about to be stopped by so trivial a circumstance as lacking a market to sell to.

When this situation occurs, the solution is the pyramid. The entrepreneur determines that a lot of people would be interested in the solution that is offered to them, but he or she must make them more aware of the problem. They will pay a little bit to learn more about the problem, and when they are finally convinced that the problem is running around loose in their shop, they will pay handsomely for its solution.

Assume that we have an entrepreneur who is seeking to solve the problem of stress relocation. Assume also that the entrepreneur was until quite recently a human resources officer of a large corporation and that she became aware of the stress that her corporation could cause male middle managers with families who were relocated often. Some wives and children complained that they could not sustain meaningful friendships. Some children's schoolwork slipped badly. The middle manager or his wife might try to find solace in drink or drugs. Wrenched by the notion of corporate America being torn apart emotionally by relocation stress, the human resources officer suggested to her employer that families receive counseling before they were relocated. The corporation permitted her to do counseling with male employees with families who were asked to relocate and to learn some antidotes for relocation stress. She became experienced in the field and began to make progress within the corporation, making senior management more sensitive to this issue. The human resources officer was generally satisfied, until one day her boss left the corporation and her activity was expunged by the new boss. The new boss' attitude was simply that if an employee refuses to be relocated, he isn't a team player and should be canned.

The human resources officer went through the dissatisfaction-insight-energy stage that turns mild-mannered Clark Kent into Superman. She walked into the boss' office one day and resigned in order to start a relocation stress consulting business.

The relocation stress entrepreneur sketched a pyramid of the market which appears in Exhibit 6.1. The object is to convert as many of the 2,000 human resources officers as possible into clients. In graphic terms, the goal is to widen the pyramid at the top. This is done by making the market aware of the problem.

The entrepreneur begins business with a newsletter. The mark of any new industry is the existence of a newsletter. The newsletter is the problem-finding and problem-formulating tool. It is a unique device to heighten awareness. Want to start a business in antique eyewash cups? You are too late. The eyewash cup collectors' newsletter has been around for years. The blue cups go for $20 to $35 each, or so the newsletter says.

The stress relocation newsletter is offered to the 2,000 U.S. human resources officers on a subscription basis, 10 issues for $120.00. If 400 subscribe, the entrepreneur has $48,000 in launch capital. It is possible to attract advertisers for a newsletter, but this particular newsletter does not immediately suggest any good ideas for ads.

EXHIBIT 6.1   Human Resources Officers in 2000 Large U.S. Corporations.

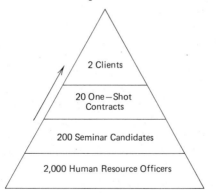

Two or three months of publishing go by. The entrepreneur reports on the subject from every vantage point imaginable: the human angle, the legal angle, the moral angle, and so forth. In the fourth month, believing that some of her subscribers are ready to meet to discuss the issues, she announces a seminar. For $500, the human resources officers can meet in Chicago for two days of panel discussions and lectures by psychologists and psychiatrists. Checks are received from 75 human resources officers, or $37,500 in revenues. The entrepreneur spends $10,000 on a first-class seminar—good lunches, good speakers, and a comfortable hotel (the guests pay for lodging). She makes that back by selling tapes of the seminar to non-attendees for $75 each.

From the seminar, the entrepreneur gets 75 leads from corporations who are beginning to understand the extent of their problems. She offers each of them a small consulting assignment: one day's analysis for $1000. Twenty corporations sign up over the next three months, for further revenues of $20,000.

From these 20 consulting assignments, the entrepreneur is awarded two performance contracts. She will counsel with all families that have been asked to relocate and recommend to the corporation whether they can handle the stress or whether they should not be moved. The contracts are worth $25,000 each plus expenses for one year. Thus, after the first 12 months of operation, the entrepreneur has generated the following revenues:

Performance contracts	$ 50,000
Consulting assignments	20,000
Seminars, tapes	47,500
Newsletter	48,000
Total revenues	$165,500

In the second year, the newsletter could double its revenues. There-could be two seminars, one on each coast, another 20 consulting assignments, and four new performance contracts. As revenues approach $300,000, the entrepreneur hires someone to publish the newsletter, assist with the seminars, and keep the books.

Entering the third year, the entrepreneur hires one of the human resources officers she has befriended and brings him into the company as a co-worker. Growth continues and the entrepreneur begins to find ways to multiply herself in order to permit growth of revenues without sacrificing quality.

The pyramid method of tackling a new market that needs to be more problem-aware is an entrepreneurial creation. For entrepreneurs in search of new markets to attack, the *Newsletter of Newsletters*, available in most large city libraries, suggests pyramids in search of entrepreneurs.

If you ever thought about becoming an entrepreneur, pick your audience and pick your problem because the opportunities will never be greater. Wherever there is a big business or government attempting to provide a solution, dozens of entrepreneurial solutions exist. Wherever there are hundreds of mom-and-pop operations doing their thing inefficiently, entrepreneur-managers are needed to bring them together to concentrate their energy and talent. Now if we could fit entrepreneurs into the right problems, capital and time could be conserved. Back to the premise: Each of us knows only one way to make money, and when we stray from that, we fail.

Need proof? Name 10 successful entrepreneurs who succeeded with their second ventures. Name 10 managers who succeeded as lift-off entrepreneurs. I do not think you can. Entrepreneurs frequently fail with their second venture. Ross Perot lost hundreds of millions of dollars that he made on EDS stock when he acquired two Wall Street brokerage firms.

Entrepreneurship is *doing some one thing* extremely well. Not two things. Thus, each potential entrepreneur must find that one thing that he or she can do very well and do it. If the wrong problem is picked, the result will be failure. The right problem means the right audience. Who is your audience, Mr. or Ms. Potential Entrepreneur?

I have some very preliminary thoughts in this area. They are primitively simple, which makes me worry about their accuracy. But in this Age of Entrepreneurship, the simple seems to offer more solutions than the complex.

7

FINAL THOUGHTS

If you have come this far, you are unquestionably an entrepreneur candidate or entrepreneur-watcher. As you know, entrepreneurs have no time for reading. A true entrepreneur has already gone back to the office to implement a new idea.

As I said at the outset, the intent of this book is to describe the characteristics of successful entrepreneurs and to describe the entrepreneurial process. It is not to explain why entrepreneurs have tended to be young men from the middle class who grew up without fathers, got professional degrees but did not use them, and had strong mothers. The "why" is for someone else to discover. If you are considering becoming an entrepreneur, the book provides you with a mirror of success factors to measure yourself against, an entrepreneurial process to follow, techniques for survival when the marketplace is trying to rub you out, and novel business strategies that entrepreneurs have created and made part of the economy. If you want to stay in your corporation, but be innovative, the performance contract that entrepreneurs have taught us can be of great help to you.

As I've already mentioned, it is difficult to make predictions, especially about the future. But, that minor problem will not prevent me from taking a stab or two at the prediction game.

LEVERAGED BUY-OUTS

Painfully difficult and complicated to achieve when first developed less than a decade ago, the leveraged buy-out will become simpler to accomplish. Whereas the entrepreneur used to bear all of the risk in a leveraged buy-out, specialist organizations such as Carl Marks & Co., Kohlberg, Kravitz and Roberts, and Gibbons, Green and Amirogen have shown that leveraged buy-outs can be accomplished systematically and profitably. More of these firms will spring out of venture capital funds that regularly fund leveraged buy-out entrepreneurs. Their track record will attract capital and sources of leverage in much the same way that lenders like Prudential Insurance support Kohlberg, Kravitz & Roberts when they assist *Fortune's* 500 in deconglomerating.

Thus, ownership will be transferred from the dead and dying managers of smokestack America to the energetic entrepreneurs of the leveraged buy-out firms. American industry is downsizing and deconglomerating, and this process is aided and abetted by the leveraged buy-out entrepreneurs. When the large industrial corporations call on the entrepreneurs directly to purchase their spin-offs, then the sellers will begin to bear more of the risk and costs of the transaction. For example, the sellers may take part of the purchase price in the form of a junior debt instrument or equity in the entrepreneur's company. The greater ease of effecting ownership transfers will reduce liquidations and bankruptcies. Before deep-sixing a company, the board might call in buy-out entrepreneurs to see if they can sell off all or parts of it and save some jobs. If the federal government suspects that this transfer is positive, they will likely dream up a loan guarantee program for helping leveraged buy-out entrepreneurs purchase companies where there is a jobs-saving feature. I believe that leveraged buy-out and venture capital funds will do more to create jobs in industrial America in the 1980s than any other single factor, legislation or "reindustrialization" program.

THE FUTURE OF ENTREPRENEURSHIP

As others begin to share the cost and risks of the lift-off, the entrepreneurs' lives will become less frenzied and more harmonious. He or she might be able to have dinner at home with husband or wife and kids. Travel requirements will be reduced, because those jobs will be delegated earlier in the launch phase.

In the year 1995, photographs of entrepreneurs of the 1960s to
1980s will seem as peculiar as Honus Wagner's tiny glove and hat
in terms of today's baseball equipment. Remember, an automobile
was launched in 1905 with a sail affixed to its hood, and it attracted
investor and customer interest. And early computers required air-
conditioned rooms to operate in.

The level of financial risk that entrepreneurs currently take will
be reduced through better-quality business plans and stronger entrepreneurial teams. The launch will be more systematized. Each team
member will have an equity interest and will see that his or her
operating module is well managed. The business plan of the future
will be so thorough that more venture capital will be available. And
the availability of more venture capital will encourage more entrepreneurs to try their wings.

INDIVIDUALISM

Small, entrepreneurial corporations are beginning to define jobs in
terms of work modules and asking employees to bid on them. This
method of working will rapidly spread to large corporations and
become standard in the 1990s. In companies that develop applications for the microcomputer, employee's frequently select their work
style. Microcomputer software companies ask an employee to develop
a new application. The manager and the employee agree on the time
required to produce the product, say, 120 days.

The company then gives the employee the opportunity to choose
one of three work methods to produce the product:

1. *Employment.* He or she can remain an employee and receive
   the usual salary and benefits, and remain employed when
   the job is completed.
2. *Consultant.* He or she can propose to the company a fee to
   develop the product, which would be more than he or she
   could make as an employee. The fee might have a bonus
   feature for speed or quality. There would be no assurance of
   a follow-on consulting assignment.
3. *Author.* He or she can propose to perform the work without

salary or fee, rather as an independent contractor who will be paid an author's royalty when the company begins selling the product. The upside would be greater and the employee would have a royalty income in the near future, rolling in every month, enabling him or her to undertake increasingly challenging assignments.

When employees are given the opportunity to choose their work methods, they have the best of both worlds: freedom to work where and how they choose and the opportunity to return to a full employee status. As telecommunications equipment becomes more mobile and less expensive, the worker can move to the woods or the desert, or wherever he or she chooses. Freedom is contagious. The employee will soon cut the umbilical cord and become an entrepreneur or a member of an entrepreneurial team. Large corporations will find it necessary to model the performance contract work method, and by the turn of the century, the country will have begun a return to pre-Industrial Revolution individualism. This radical change in industrial practices will spawn other changes, political and social, to be sure.

I recommend that all entrepreneurs and those about to sign up visit Israel. People visit this 25-year-old country for many reasons—biblical, archaeological, historical—but I believe one of the most interesting things about Israel is that most of its people are entrepreneurs. Whatever business exists in Israel, it is new, innovative, and entrepreneurial. There are very few large corporations peopled by heartless organization types. Practically every company is in an entrepreneurial phase, and practically every person has heart. This kind of society is not without its flaws, but they are different flaws than we have in America. If a group of people loses its manager class through genocide and is then forced to create new industries entrepreneurially, there are bound to be flaws and rough edges. However, the energy and intellectual level of the people compensate.

I would like to see a study of the entrepreneur away from his or her work and world. Perhaps someone will be encouraged to take on the task. The measure of what people do in life is not the money they make, but whether they can have people they love around them to share the "getting there" as well as the "got." Do entrepreneurs bring their loving, caring, sensitive natures home with them? Are they creative lovers? Perhaps they are creative at the office and dull in the bedroom. Are they fun parents who do interesting things with their children, or do the children get in the way? Are entrepreneurs as understanding at home as they are at a strategic planning session at work? Do they help solve plumbing problems and look for their wives' contact lenses on the bathroom floor with as much zeal as they attack a company marketing problem?

If they are not all of these things, then why sign up at all?

SOCIAL UTILITY OF ENTREPRENEURSHIP?

Does entrepreneurship have social utility? It has considerable social utility to the extent that the company once lifted off delivers a solution to a social problem. But the promoters who obtain financing for non-socially useful companies give entrepreneurship a bad name. Promotions are short-lived, wealth-oriented, temporarily euphoric and disruptive. Who needed a $30,000 stainless steel sports car? Some tax shelters, such as sports cars, toy molds and magazines waste investors' money and disrupt the marketplace. Most of the new issues in the Denver market in 1980 to 1981 will never see stock prices above their ten-cent offering prices. These are promotions. They are lacking in social utility. I would hope that there are enough characteristics of successful entrepreneurs in this book to assist investors in determining which entrepreneurial teams should be considered for investment or for other forms of support and which entrepreneurs are either not sufficiently driven or too promotional. If the drive of the entrepreneur or the management ability of the achiever is too opaque for a decision to be made, the investor or potential employee should investigate the entrepreneurial process that the team has undertaken. How extensive was the problem-formulation period? What were the steps, the process, the variables, the discarded ideas? How was the solution arrived at? Are there alternatives? If the company was put together without pain, discomfort or serious intellectual disagreements between the founders, it may lack the foundation necessary for sustained growth. Polaroid and Apple Computer were not built in the same 30 days that it took

Electronic Data Systems to get going. Although Polaroid ramped in 14 years and Apple and EDS in 14 months, the three of them maintained monopoly positions for sustained time periods.

Find the pain in the entrepreneur's past and you will find the company's hydraulics. Therefore, if we understand entrepreneurs and the entrepreneurial process more completely, fewer dollars will be wasted on promoters and poorly equipped entrepreneurial teams with unformulated ideas. There will be a savings in the costs of starting companies, human costs and capital as well. With improved filters, the fittest entrepreneurial teams will receive capital and thus survive, while the less deserving go back to problem formulate or to another step they overlooked in the entrepreneurial process.

THE ENTREPRENEUR'S HEART

It is virtually impossible to be a successful entrepreneur without heart. If a person remains in a corporation overly long, he or she will lose heart, because the qualities that the corporation requires—competence, coolness under stress, self-confidence—are not qualities of the heart—compassion, generosity, idealism. In *The Gamesman,* Michael Maccoby asked 250 corporate executives, managers, and engineers to list the character traits "important for your work" and those that were "stimulated or reinforced by your work."* In general, the traits considered most useful were the ones most strengthened. The trend shown in Exhibit 7.1 is that work in engineering-oriented corporations stimulates attitudes essential for intellectual innovation and teamwork, qualities of the head. Those traits are required for work. The qualities of compassion, generosity, and idealism are unneeded and remain underdeveloped.

"The traits stimulated in the corporation," Maccoby reminds us, "will in many cases have a decisive effect on the kind of people they become, not only as managers, but as citizens, husbands, wives, fathers, and mothers."† Maccoby rated the managers interviewed on their productiveness in both work and love.

EXHIBIT 7.1. Character Traits Very Important to Work and Stimulated by Work.

	Very Important for Work (Percent)	Stimulated by Work (Percent)
Qualities of the Head		
Ability to take the initiative	91	58
Satisfaction in creating something new	74	51
Self-confidence	86	50
Coolness under stress	71	40
Cooperativeness	74	37
Pleasure in learning something new	68	35
Pride in performance	88	35
Flexibility	76	33
Open-mindedness	81	30
Qualities of the Heart		
Independence	45	21
Loyalty to fellow workers	47	18
Critical attitude to authority	21	17
Friendliness	35	16
Sense of humor	53	14
Openness, spontaneity	46	14
Honesty	72	12
Compassion	18	4
Generosity	13	2
Idealism	9	1

Source: Michael Maccoby, *The Gamesman* (New York: Simon & Schuster, 1975).

"In terms of work," Maccoby writes, "none expressed the deep interest of a scientist passionately searching for the truth. . . . In terms of love, none were deeply loving, expressing the kind of interest and creative support of another person that implies profound knowledge and care. . . ." Whereas 80% expressed at least moderate interest in their work, roughly half that percentage expressed moderate interest in another person. Maccoby found that the most loving moved up the ladder the least rapidly. The most compassionate and giving, those with more heart and less head, moved up the hierarchy more slowly.

The entrepreneur makes a choice between head and heart and chooses heart. The head can distinguish right from wrong, but the heart will not permit a wrongful act. The head can perceive incompetencies and inaccuracies in corporate positions and advertisements, but it takes the heart to reject them. When the person goes through the dissatisfaction stage just prior to leaving the corporation, he or she is getting his or her heart back. It is a beautiful moment. I remember several evenings at Bob Schwartz's School for Entrepreneurs in Tarrytown, New York, where I cried openly as one entrepreneur after another stood up and told his or her story of dissatisfaction-insight-energy. A room of 200 entrepreneurs, all of us crying real tears as we listened to stories about the drivers, the pain, the energies that cause people to leave the safe and the sure for the unknown and the unsure. Could 200 corporate managers produce those kinds of emotional experiences?

When we discussed the characteristics of entrepreneurial success earlier, you will recall that none was related to the head. All were synonyms for heart: courage, guilt, childhood deprivation (the pain; the grocer), the idealized mother, happiness, intensity of focus, and confidence. These are all sensitive areas. You must have heart to feel them.

So hang the social utility, the improved capital gains, the return to individualism, the entrepreneurial revolution. If you want to get your heart back, run instead of walk, burst into song, and smile even when there is no camera around, there is only one way. Entrepreneurship.

═══ APPENDIX I ═══

ENTREPRENEURIAL CHARACTERISTICS

1. At what age did you become an entrepreneur? _____
2. How many years did it take to launch your company? _____
3. How many years after launching did it take to create wealth?
   _____
   _____
4. Where did you spend your early childhood? (Midwest, South, etc.) _____
   _____
5. What was your placement in the family? (oldest, middle, only child etc.) _____
6. Did your father live at home? _____
7. Was your family economically deprived? _____
8. Were you handicapped or deprived in any other way as a child? (physical, language) _____
9. In your opinion, are your major personality traits derived from your mother or from your father (or someone else)? _____
10. Did you complete high school? _____ 11. College? _____
12. Graduate school? _____
13. What was your degree or area of specialization? _____
    _____
14. At what period in your life did you first realize you could make money solving problems for others? _____

15. Why did you choose to go into business rather than government, etc.? _____

_____

16. Have you launched more than one company in your life? ____
17. How many? _____ 18. At what ages? _____
19. Have your energies and drives been fueled by a particular desire other than wealth or solving problems? (Can you elaborate?) _____

_____

_____

_____

_____

20. When launching your company, did you try to leverage out completely with debt? _____

21. Number the following four abilities (1 is strongest, 4 is weakest) in order of your excellence in each: (a) competing _____ , (b) attention to details _____ , (c) creative thought _____ , (d) raising money _____ .

22. In your opinion, are these the four most important entrepreneurial characteristics? _____

23. I think the most important entrepreneurial characteristics are

_____

_____

_____

24. Are there any problems to which you would apply entrepreneurial solutions right now, if you had time?

INDEX